NATURE, CULTURE AND GENDER

Breaking new ground, Indian folktales are re-read and examined in this book in the light of the Mother Earth Discourse as it manifests in the lifeworlds of women, nature and language. The book introduces ecofeminist criticism and situates it within an innovative folktale typology to connect women and environment through folklore. It proposes an innovative paradigm inspired by the beehive to analyse motifs, relationships, concerns, worldviews and consciousness of indigenous women and men who live close to nature as well as other socially marginalized groups.

In the current global context fraught with challenges for ecology and hopes for sustainable development, this book with its interdisciplinary approach will interest scholars and researchers of literature, environmental studies, gender studies and cultural anthropology.

P. Mary Vidya Porselvi is Assistant Professor of English, Loyola College, Chennai, India, and was previously Lecturer in the Department of English at Stella Maris College (2000–03), Chennai. She obtained her BA, MA and PhD degrees from Stella Maris College, and recently completed the University Grants Commission project 'Translation of Folktales with Ecofeminist Concerns from Tamil to English'. She has authored two English workbooks: *Affirmative Words and Radiant Expressions* (2012) and *Cornucopia: English Language Learning through World Folklore* (2013).

'The selection of Indian folktales is very interesting and shows what a rich vein of knowledge is stored by ordinary (and some very extraordinary) people. Highly original is the classification of tales as: *Isis Panthea, Amma-I-Appan, Her-Meta, Athena's Wit, Annamangai, Sis-Tie, Woody-Woman, Vana-Devi, Tellus-Ma, Aqua-Stree, Aves-Eve* and *Fauna-Fem*. Each of these classificatory names shows a sense of humour embedded in deep poetic and symbolic understanding of the mythic oral tradition. The author combines linguistic knowledge along with an understanding of the hidden mother lode of the story seam'.

Susan Hawthorne, Adjunct Professor,
James Cook University, Queensland, Australia

NATURE, CULTURE AND GENDER

Re-reading the folktale

P. Mary Vidya Porselvi

LONDON AND NEW YORK

First published 2016
by Routledge
2 Park Square, Milton Park, Abingdon, Oxon OX14 4RN

and by Routledge
711 Third Avenue, New York, NY 10017

Routledge is an imprint of the Taylor & Francis Group, an informa business

© 2016 P. Mary Vidya Porselvi

The right of P. Mary Vidya Porselvi to be identified as author of this work has been asserted by her in accordance with sections 77 and 78 of the Copyright, Designs and Patents Act 1988.

All rights reserved. No part of this book may be reprinted or reproduced or utilised in any form or by any electronic, mechanical, or other means, now known or hereafter invented, including photocopying and recording, or in any information storage or retrieval system, without permission in writing from the publishers.

Trademark notice: Product or corporate names may be trademarks or registered trademarks, and are used only for identification and explanation without intent to infringe.

British Library Cataloguing in Publication Data
A catalogue record for this book is available from the British Library

Library of Congress Cataloging-in-Publication Data
A catalog record has been requested for this book

ISBN: 978-1-138-67674-9 (hbk)
ISBN: 978-1-315-55990-2 (ebk)

Typeset in Goudy
by Apex CoVantage, LLC

TO
MY GRANDMOTHERS
NESAM AND VARAPRASADAM
FOR THEIR
WORLDVIEW OF ABUNDANCE

CONTENTS

Foreword   viii
Preface   xi
Acknowledgements   xiii

Introduction   1

1. Mother Earth Discourse   23
2. The Creator and the created   57
3. Silences and speech   72
4. Food, household and sisterhood   87
5. Trees and forests   105
6. Land and water   124
7. Birds and animals   144

Conclusion   169

Glossary   179
Bibliography   182
Index   193

FOREWORD

We live in times when our multiple imaginations and stories and the voices of women and Mother Earth are being silenced for a short-term myopic and violent project called 'development', which I have referred to as mal(e) development in *Staying Alive*, both because they are shaped by the worldview of capitalist patriarchy and because it is leading to irreparable and irreversible ecological and social damage. We need to move beyond the discourse of 'development' and GDP to reclaim our true humanity as members of the Earth Family. And through folktales, especially women's stories, Mary Vidya Porselvi creates another discourse – richer, nonviolent, more diverse and more inclusive. It reclaims the sacred in our daily lives.

Separation is the characteristic of paradigms emerging from the convergence of patriarchy and capitalism – first nature is separated from humans, then humans are separated on the basis of gender, religion, caste and class. This separation is at the root of violence – first in the mind, then in our lives. It is not an accident that the inequalities of the past have taken on inhuman form with the rise of the project of corporate globalisation, which has allowed few of the richest men of the world to amass as much wealth as in the hands of 50 per cent of humanity. And this process has been made possible by destroying the stories that allow us to live through a sacred relationship with and in nature, and through the sacred, put limits on greed, exploitation and appropriation. Re-reading women's life-affirming discourses of interconnectedness interrogates separation and disconnections in the world.

Capitalist patriarchy denies the creativity of nature, and hence the rights of Mother Earth. It is therefore anthropocentric. Over the last four decades having served the Earth and grassroots ecological movements, beginning with the historic Chipko (Hug the Tree) Movement in my region of Central Himalaya and in every movement I have participated in, I observe that it was women who led the actions and women who sustained actions to protect the earth and the sources of their sustenance and livelihoods.

FOREWORD

The women of Chipko were protecting their forests because deforestation and logging were leading to floods and droughts, landslides, disasters and scarcity of fuel and fodder, which led to the disappearance of springs and streams, forcing women to walk longer and further for water. The women of Chipko taught me and the world that timber, revenue and profits were not the real products of the forest. The real products were soil, water and pure air. Today, science refers to these as ecological functions of ecosystems. Illiterate women of the Garhwal Himalayas were four decades ahead of the scientists of the world.

Why do women lead ecological movements against deforestation and pollution of water, against toxic and nuclear hazards? On Earth Day, 22 April 2002, I was invited by women from a small hamlet Plachimada in Palghat, Kerala, to join their struggle against a soft drink company which was mining 1.5 million litres of water a day and polluting the water that remained in their wells. Women were forced to walk 10 km in search of clean drinking water. Mylamma, a tribal woman leading the movement, said they would not walk further for water. Likewise, the women of Bhopal, who were themselves victims of a disaster in 1984, like Rashidabi and Champadevi Shukla, continue the struggle for justice and provide rehabilitation to the children born with disabilities. I believe it is in part because in the sexual division of labour, women have been left to look after sustenance – providing food, water, health and care. Hence, it is necessary to identify these unheard voices that care for Mother Earth.

When it comes to the sustenance economy, women are both the experts and the providers. Even though women's work in providing sustenance is the most vital human activity, a patriarchal economy, which defines the economy only as the economy of the marketplace, treats it as nonwork. The patriarchal model of the economy is dominated by one figure, the GDP, which is measured on the basis of an artificially created production boundary (if you produce what you consume, you do not produce). When the ecological crisis created by an ecologically blind economic paradigm leads to the disappearance of forests and water, the spread of diseases because of the spread of toxics and poisons, and the consequent threat to life and survival, it is women who rise to wake up society to the crisis and defend the Earth and their lives, through their lives. Women are leading the paradigm shift to align the economy with ecology. After all, both are rooted in the word 'oikos' – our home.

The most violent display of mechanistic science is in the promotion of industrial agriculture, including GMOs, as a solution to hunger and malnutrition. As I have learnt over thirty years of building the movement Navdanya (*www.navdanya.org*), biodiversity produces more than monocultures; small family farms based on women's participation provide 75 per cent

FOREWORD

of the food eaten in the world. Industrial agriculture only produces 25 per cent, while using and destroying 75 per cent of the Earth's resources. Not only are women experts in the sustenance economy, but they are also experts in ecological science through their daily participation in processes that provide sustenance. Their expertise is rooted in lived experience, not in abstract and fragmented knowledge systems that are not connected to life and overlook the connectedness of the web of life.

When it comes to real solutions to real problems faced by the planet and people, it is the subjugated knowledge and invisible work of women based on cocreation and coproduction with nature, which will show the way to human survival and well-being in the future. This includes all indigenous knowledge systems and women's native wisdom. *Nature, Culture and Gender* by Mary Vidya Porselvi is an important and timely book. It recommends the study of folktales as alternative forms of discourse that offers solutions to the problems of nature-culture disparity and bridge the gap among nature, culture and gender.

Dr Vandana Shiva
February 2016

PREFACE

In an era of ecological chaos and economic crisis, ecofeminism envisions a holistic approach to life, shaped by theories and practice of feminism, environmentalism and peace movements. Though the initial impetus was a subjective one, an objective framework was later adopted in the quest, to be validated in future. And that resulted in the sowing of a seed called the ecofeminist–linguistic interface. The word 'ecofeminism' ignited a 'thought spark' in my mind. When did the first tryst with 'ecofeminism' happen? Born in Kodaikanal, a hill station in Tamilnadu, I had the opportunity to visit my grandparents every year, during the summer vacation. My grandmother cultivated vegetables and fruits in the backyard of her house. In the hilly town where my grandparents lived, I also had a glimpse of tribal life. The tribal women and children who came to the town to sell firewood, fruits and honey had plentiful stories to narrate.

The book has motivated me to go 'in search of' what Alice Walker calls the 'mother's gardens'. One fine morning, I happened to see a large honeycomb in *Mullu Murungai*, the flowering Flame of the Forest tree in my grandmother's house, which inspired me to visualise the paradigm in the shape of a beehive. Ecofeminism believes in respecting the knowledge systems of each and every individual. At the same time, human knowledge or understanding is only a speck in the knowledge systems that exist in the whole universe, and hence, the proposed paradigm is conceived as a small portion of the knowledge systems in nature. I strongly believe that the beehive model represents an open-ended, all-encompassing paradigm that promotes the integration of identical thought processes in future. Mother Earth inspires us with her simplicity, fascinates us with her diversity and enchants us with her grandeur.

The book promises the scope of folktales as life-affirming discourse that cares for Mother Earth. Ecofeminist scholars and theorists have discussed woman–nature relationships using phrases such as 'ecofeminist discourse' and 'women's environmental discourse'. When the need

PREFACE

to integrate ecofeminism with sociolinguistics/feminist linguistics arose, I decided to coin a novel expression, called the 'Mother Earth Discourse'. The ecofeminist–linguistic interface and the evolution of the Mother Earth Discourse are conceived as seeds of reflection which might, in a viable environment, sprout into life-affirming forms of positive actions. Nature has inspired me to classify the folktales with innovative names, *Isis Panthea, Amma-I-Appan, Her-Meta, Athena's Wit, Woody-Woman, Vana-Devi, Tellus-Ma, Aqua-Stree, Aves-Eve and Fauna-Fem*. The first six motifs deal with women's association with their immediate environment, *akam* or the home. The other six motifs deal with women's proximity with nature, *puram*, also known as *oikos* in Greek, our planet Earth.

In this book, the thought processes are diagrammatically represented through mind-mapping technique. As a device that communicates holism and interconnectedness, a mind map provides space for multifaceted aspects of life and augurs an appropriate method of developing the thought processes in this study. 'Every time we look at the veins of a leaf or the branches of a tree, we see nature's "Mind Maps"' (Buzan and Buzan 2010: 34). A mind map makes use of words and images that indicate a holistic discourse with equal importance given to each and every component represented in the diagram. Mind-mapping has been incorporated as a significant eco-critical instrument in this book, as it adheres to systems of folklore, nature-culture, ecofeminist thought and the idea of discourse.

Folktales enhance the simplicity of life. Mother Earth is identified as a personification of simplicity, which indigenous women emulate in all her likeness. Simplicity of thought and simplicity in action contribute to peaceful coexistence. The indigenous men and women, the narrators and the narrated, in the folktales embody simple living and promote earth-centred values in day-to-day life. By identifying the complicated net of ecological, sociological, economic and cultural chaos created by the existing dominant systems that suffocate nature and human beings alike, Mother Earth Discourse recognises the scope of indigenous women's simple stories that offer hope to mend the systems and knit a web of harmony and peace.

ACKNOWLEDGEMENTS

At this moment, I wish to acknowledge my heartfelt thanks to people who have helped me to complete this book. I profoundly thank Dr Vandana Shiva for her inspiring and erudite Foreword. I sincerely thank my PhD guide, Dr Thilagavathi G. Joseph, who has always inspired me with her meticulous work, clear-cut observations, proactive thinking and indefatigable strength. I thank her for her valuable suggestions during the regular meetings we had at different stages of my research. I specially thank her for instilling in me an interest to always aim higher and work better. I am deeply grateful to Dr Sr Jasintha Quadras, Franciscan Missionaries of Mary, the principal of Stella Maris College, for admitting me as a research student and encouraging me with her goodwill. With gratitude, I acknowledge the scholarly interventions and suggestions of experts Dr Susan Oommen, former head of the Department of English, Stella Maris College, and Dr Padma, Mangai, Stella Maris College. I profoundly thank the management of Loyola College for their consent, encouragement and blessings. I wish to thank all my colleagues and friends in the Department of English, Loyola College who encouraged me to carry out this research. Special thanks to Dr David Jeyabalan for his precise observations and critical comments on this book.

I specially thank the staff in Folklore Resources and Research Centre, Palayamkottai, National Folklore Support Centre, Chennai, and The Study Centre for Indian Literature in English and Translation (SCILET) library, American College, Madurai, who helped me to collect data in the first phase of my research. I sincerely thank Prof. Dr S. Vincent, Dean of Research, Loyola College, Chennai, for his guidance and support. I specially thank Ms Shoma Choudhury and Ms Antara Ray Chaudhury, Routledge India, for their meticulous effort, guidance and cooperation in the preparation of the book. I would like to thank the editorial team at Taylor and Francis for their professional help and support in the preparation of this book. During this study, besides the analysis of folktales from India, I had an opportunity to

ACKNOWLEDGEMENTS

meet rural women and listen to them about their knowledge of farming and agriculture. Thanks to Mrs Saalai Selvam who initiated this process. I am grateful to Azhagu Pillai from Karupaaioorani, Madurai, Innasiamma from A. Vellodu, Dindigul, and Jayanthi from Peria Obulapuram, Gummidipoondi, for sharing their wisdom and knowledge with me, which were moments of enlightenment on indigenous ecofeminist experiences. I specially thank my father, Prof. Dr S.J.A. Packiaraj, former head of the Department of English, Loyola College, Chennai, for nurturing me with affection and wisdom and encouraging me to become a conscious thinker and listener. I fondly thank my mother, Nirmala Rani, for her enormous support to my family and care for my children, which has made this book possible. I warmly thank my sister, Priya Prem, and my brother, Jaikumar, for their words of encouragement and support. I am ever grateful to my husband, Roy Arun, for his motivation and constant support during difficult times, when I tried to balance my roles at home and the workplace, besides carrying out my research. I thank my sons, Amal and Iniyan, for their prayers, smiles and enthusiasm, which gave me the confidence and strength to pursue and complete this book.

INTRODUCTION

Seeds of silence: words of consciousness

Mother Earth is at the core of ecofeminist thought. The book explores representations of woman–nature proximity in select folktales from India characterised by care for Mother Earth, respect for inherent worth and realisation of interconnectedness and interdependence of all living beings. Mother Earth Discourse is the woman–nature lingua franca that results from an ecofeminist-linguistic analysis of folktales from India. The promulgation and understanding of Mother Earth Discourse is considered as a process of conscientisation or *conscientizacao*. From time to time, many branches of ecofeminist thought have emerged from the spreading trees rooted in indigenous philosophies across the world. The scope of the book is to identify women's tales as 'seeds of silence', which have the potent 'words of consciousness' inherently embedded in them.

The object and purpose of this book are as follows: it enables a scientific study of woman's language of the environment, where one becomes conscious of the environment of the 'silent' and the 'silenced' people – more specifically, indigenous voices in relation to 'nature-culture'. It recognises woman's discourse 'of' the environment and her vocalisations 'for' the environment to bring about social change through a dynamic process of *conscientizacao*. It unravels the knowledge systems represented in folktales from India and proposes ways to 'promote and participate in learning, analysis, interpretation and communication about how to live in harmony with Mother Earth' (2009) as envisaged in the Declaration of the Rights of Mother Earth in the World People's Conference on Climate Change and the Rights of Mother Earth Cochabamba, Bolivia (http://therightsof nature.org/universal-declaration/). Apart from the broad scope of inquiry, the specific objectives envisaged by the author are: identification of motifs that represent woman–nature proximity; understanding of woman–nature concerns in the select folktales; comprehension of alternative worldviews that determine woman–nature relationships; realisation of the consciousness of nature and women who live close to nature; and appreciation of the language of women who live in oneness with nature. It initiates the ecofeminist quest to celebrate Mother Earth as a life-affirming principle and the linguistic quest to acknowledge women's voices in 'nature-culture', a culture integrated with nature.

Mother Earth: the nucleus

What is ecofeminism? What is the relevance of ecofeminism to the contemporary world? Ecofeminism can be defined as a holistic belief system that emphasises care and concern for Mother Earth, reverence for the intrinsic value of all life forms and recognition of the interdependence of living and nonliving beings on this earth. Some of the characteristics of ecofeminist ideology are as follows: (a) It deems the worth of woman–nature relationships on one hand and 'nature-culture' connection on the other. (b) It recognises interconnectedness between women, nature and other marginalised groups. (c) It asserts the rights of Mother Earth and all her oppressed children and guides human beings to understand the benefits of establishing gender equity and sustainable development. (d) It inspires human minds to realise the 'spiritual' element in all living creatures. (e) It interrogates the problems that women and nature face in an age of exploitation, destruction and indifference and motivates human beings to integrate their collective strength.

Ecofeminism is understood as the philosophy of Mother Earth. Hence, Mother Earth and the feminine principles that govern living beings are identified in folktales from India. Vandana Shiva elucidates, 'Nature, both animate and inanimate is thus an expression of *Shakthi*, the feminine and creative principle of the cosmos; in conjunction with the masculine principle (Purusha), *Prakriti* creates the world' (Shiva 2010: 38). *Prakriti* is the holistic, all-pervading and life-affirming principle that unites all living creatures together to form a unified web of life. The concept of *Prakriti* vibrates positive energy and motivates people into constructive action for the well-being of nature, women, children and men. These words are life-affirming seeds which have the power to change society. Hence, recognition of the Mother Earth Discourse promotes constructive thinking, leading onto beneficial action for the welfare of Mother Earth and all her children.

Women who live close to nature celebrate the human dependence on Mother Earth. Care for Mother Earth is central to ecofeminist praxis, according to Vandana Shiva. Mother Earth is considered as a living being, an epitome of power or *Shakthi*. Folktales abound with multifarious expressions that celebrate Mother Earth and communicate indigenous beliefs

INTRODUCTION

that promote sustainable living. Mother Earth is an important symbol in the oral tradition in many cultures across the world. A Chhattisgarhi song reads, 'Mother Earth was born first/Then men were born/They drive nails in every boundary' (Devy 2002: 158). The song is addressed to a girl as a source of comfort by an elder. The song reiterates the fact that Mother Earth, the feminine planet, 'was born first' (Devy 2002: 158) and men, who represent the dominant exploitative patriarchal culture, only harm 'Her' through their violent ways.

According to the ecofeminist school of thought, Earth no longer represents a meagre resource for utilisation. Instead, Earth Mother is seen as a living being, an origin of all life, sustenance and learning. Each and every being is related to another and forms an integral part of Mother Earth. The Universal Declaration of the Rights of Mother Earth, presented by the Bolivian Republic, advocates that human education must cater to the following principles, that 'Every human being has the right to be educated about Mother Earth' and 'human education must develop the full potential of human beings in a way that promotes a love of Mother Earth, compassion, understanding, tolerance and affection among all humans and between humans and other beings, and the observance of the fundamental freedoms, rights and duties in this Declaration' (2009). For this reason, it is essential to integrate alternative worldviews into the mainstream education. Re-reading the folktales from an ecofeminist standpoint offers new avenues towards a better society and environment. Mother Earth is an essential metaphor of life in this school of thought, which informs ecofeminist pedagogy.

The ecofeminist tree of thought

'Ecofeminism asserts the special strength and integrity of every living thing', states Ynestra King (Mies and Shiva 2010: 4). Ecofeminism attempts to raise the level of human consciousness for understanding the benefits of gender equity and sustainable growth. As Rosemary Ruether explains in *New Woman/New Earth*, women must 'unite the demands of the women's movement with those of the ecological movement to envision a radical reshaping of the basic socioeconomic relations and the underlying values of this [modern industrial] society' (Ruether 1975: 204). The ecofeminist tree of thought branches out into: environmental movements with feminist concerns that contribute to ecofeminist praxis; seminal ecofeminist literary theories, eco-critical theories, folklore theories and sociolinguistic/feminist linguistic/discourse theories relevant to this study; indigenous ecofeminist experiences of rural women in India; and ecofeminist pedagogies that are akin to Paulo Freire's idea of *conscientizacao*.

INTRODUCTION

In an era of insensitivity to life, the recognition of nature's voices and women's voices are pertinent. According to ecofeminist thinkers such as Karen J. Warren and Jim Cheney, 'As a methodological and epistemological stance, all ecofeminists centralize, in one way or another, the "voices" and experiences of women (and others) with regard to an understanding of the nonhuman world' (Gaard and Murphy 1998: 53). The analysis of folktales results in the finding of Mother Earth Discourse, the lingua franca of women and nature. Through the 'voices' of nature and women, motifs, relationships, concerns, worldviews, consciousness and expressions are comprehended. Ecofeminism revisits the practices, rites and rituals of nature-culture that empower women to live with dignity, honour and strength, which contribute to cultural ecofeminism. The identification of folktales as representations of nature promotes cultural ecofeminist praxis. The nonhuman living beings, such as trees, birds, animals and so on, are believed to be integral subjects in an environment which promotes alternative worldviews in harmony with ecofeminist thought.

Achieving an in-depth understanding of the world is an indispensable attribute of ecofeminist thought. Ecofeminism believes in research as a form of conscientisation, according to Maria Mies. Conscientisation or *conscienticazao* is a term proposed by the Brazilian educational theorist and activist Paulo Freire in his work *Pedagogy of the Oppressed*, published in 1970, which accentuates an in-depth understanding of the world. As Freire elaborates on the need to maintain a critical consciousness of the human mind, he also invites human beings to fulfil the responsibility of recording their experiences and their understanding of the world. According to Freire, a human being's creativity is shaped by conscious thinking, linguistic ability and perception of reality. Hence, the voices of indigenous people and nature promise a way out of woman–nature issues in our society. As Paulo Freire confirms, 'The more we experience the dynamics of such movement, the more we become critical subjects concerning the process of knowing, teaching, learning, reading, writing and studying' (Freire 2006: 2). Through the folktales from India, this research evolves an understanding of the epistemology of indigenous women and men who contribute to environmental sustainability and gender balance in their day-to-day lives.

This ecofeminist study intends to promote sustainable living that gets fortified by life-affirming values of women and men who live close to nature. It is enriched by worldviews that offer solutions to the problems existing in our society and environment. By challenging the systems that reduce nature and women as mere commodities, ecofeminist considerations offer an alternative trend to value the worth of all living creatures on this planet. The identification of the folk discourse as an alternative form of expression reverses the idea of women's speech and storytelling as meaningless

INTRODUCTION

and ineffective. The simple folktales, narrated by indigenous women, are deep narratives that require a conscious rethinking. They reveal women's deep understanding of their environment, culture, society and the world at large – the relationship among the parts of the whole. The women's creativity, linguistic ability and the critical consciousness are represented in their discourse.

The green crusaders

Simple and strong women and men fight for the rights of nature when Mother Earth is in distress. They are the green crusaders who strive to protect nature as their own children. Ecological movements such as the Chipko Movement, Appiko Movement, Silent Valley Movement, Narmada Bachao Andolan and Green Belt Movement are some of the movements that assert the welfare of Mother Earth. Nature and women are at the centre of these movements. Apart from spokespersons such as Vandana Shiva, Sugathakumari, Medha Patkar and Wangari Maathai, a great number of active women and men – 'nameless' and 'voiceless' – have contributed to the dynamics of such earth-centred movements.

The Chipko Movement is discussed by ecofeminist thinkers and activists such as Vandana Shiva and Sturgeon in their books *Ecofeminism* and *Ecofeminist Natures*, respectively. Subhash Sharma, in his book *Why People Protest: An Analysis of Ecological Movements* (2009), gives an account of the Save Silent Valley Protest and Narmada Valley Movement. Wangari Maathai's memoir, *Unbowed* (2006), provides ample information on the origin and growth of the Green Belt Movement. The inherent worth of trees and their role in maintaining the ecological balance of the planet are reinforced by the Chipko Movement. Chipko (literally meaning 'cling to') is a movement, born in the 1970s, mainly comprising women, children and some men against deforestation in the state of Uttar Pradesh in India. The Chipko women, who are considered as 'ultimate ecofeminists' and 'natural environmentalists' (Sturgeon 1997: 127), sing the song, 'Embrace our trees/ Save them from being felled/ The property of our hills/Save it from being looted' (James 1999: 90). Environmentalists believe that Chipko women 'embraced' the trees not only because of their love and sympathy towards nature, but also primarily because the trees were their very 'life'.

The concern for Mother Earth as a living entity is of great relevance to Vandana Shiva. Vandana Shiva is an ecofeminist philosopher and an environmental activist who participated in the Chipko Movement during the 1970s in Uttar Pradesh, India. Her outstanding contribution to the environment and women is the founding of 'Navdanya' in 1991, an organisation that promotes organic farming, conserves native seeds and encourages the

INTRODUCTION

indigenous knowledge of farmers, especially of women and girls. Dr Vandana Shiva has also started an international college for sustainable living in Doon Valley in collaboration with Schumacher College, UK. *Staying Alive* (1988) is her first book on the lives of third-world women. Her other significant works are *Ecofeminism* with Maria Mies in 1993, *Stolen Harvest: The Hijacking of the Global Food Supply* in 1999, *Earth Democracy; Justice, Sustainability and Peace* in 2005, *Soil Not Oil* in 2008 and *Staying Alive* in 2010. An excerpt from the interview to Wilma Massucco (WM) illustrates Vandana Shiva's (VS) perception of Mother Earth.

WM: 'What do you mean when you say that Earth is female'?
VS: 'It basically means that she is the Mother, life for all beings, all species, including human beings'.
WM: 'Is it important to see the Earth as Mother'?
VS: 'Yes, it is, as it is the only way we will recognize how much we received from her . . . most of the time, when we think of the Earth as dead and inert and just as a source of raw materials, we create illusions that money and welfare come from Wall Street and factories. We forget that for every factory the first material is contributed by the earth'.

(Massucco 2010: 3)

In the patriarchal consumerist society, Mother Earth is considered as a mere resource that produces material commodities. Ecofeminists defy this reductionist worldview by highlighting the power of nature. The worldviews of women and men in the folktales selected for this study reveal alternative worldviews that challenge consumerism and reductionism.

The Appiko Movement started in Gubbi Gadde, a small village near Sirsi in the (north) Uttara Kannada district. This green initiative was inspired by the 'tree-hugging' Chipko Movement. On 8 September 1983, about 30 women gathered in Salkani village with 70 men and walked eight kilometres to reach Kalase forest. Pandurang Hegde, the fiery activist, led the Appiko ('to hug') Movement. He derived inspiration from Sunderlal Bahugana and his team of men and women of the Chipko Movement in Uttar Pradesh. According to Pandurang Hegde, 'This movement, started to protest against felling of trees, monoculture, forest policy and deforestation, has succeeded in changing the forest policy. This first ever people's green movement in south India to save our natural resources has become a model of sustainable development' (Nagpal 2008). This 25-year-old movement has become a culture integrated with nature. Unlike the Chipko Movement, which had the background of Sarvodaya workers, the Appiko Movement did not have such a base. The activists revived the cultural practices that venerated nature. They celebrated the 'Forest Goddesses' of those areas. The three major objectives of Appiko were preservation, restoration and rational use. The role of women in the Appiko Movement is highlighted by the letter quoted by Panduranga Hegde in his article 'A Handful of Grain for the Cause'. When there was an alarming situation of tree felling and deforestation, women joined together to launch the Appiko Movement.

> This was the first time that women had come out to halt tree felling. At the gathering, local leaders and politicians spoke disparagingly about women. We, the members of the Mahila Mandal, reminded these dominating male leaders about the objectives of Appiko. They were not prepared to hear our questions, so they left the place. However, the members of the Mahila Mandal went ahead with hugging the trees, and stopped the tree felling.
>
> (Manushi 1984: 38)

Quite interestingly, the activists reached out to their people by using local folklore, the Yakshagana, which is performed from dusk to dawn. The word literally means the *gana* (song) of *yaksha* (nature spirits). It is an art form that incorporates dance, music, theatre, costume and makeup. This traditional folk theatre has been integrated with the idea of sustainable development and the plays have attracted wide public attention throughout the state and several parts of the country for their environmental messages. The Appiko Movement people have also launched numerous *padayatras* (a nonviolent form of protest) in the villages in the Western Ghats. Men and women of Kodagu district have also adopted the objectives of the Appiko Movement.

In the northern parts of India, when women were hugging trees to show their respect and concern towards nonhuman living beings, in the southern parts of India, another group of people silently, yet powerfully, found ways to protect rare animal species such as the lion-tailed macaque through the Save Silent Valley Movement. The interconnectedness and interdependence of human and nonhuman living beings are reiterated by this movement. The Silent Valley Movement was initiated only 'on direct ecological grounds' (Sharma 2009: 153) by people against the building of the hydro-electric multipurpose dam across the Kunthipuzha River that caused a threat to the environment. The tropical evergreen forests in Kerala – quite specifically in the Silent Valley, home for rare species of plants and animals such as the lion-tailed macaque – faced danger when industrialists decided to build a dam across the Kunthipuzha River. The Silent Valley Movement had activists at different levels. At the local level, school and college teachers joined together to form the Kerala Sastra Sahitya Parishad (Kerala Science and

INTRODUCTION

Literature Society – KSSP) and fought against the construction of the dam. At the national level, the intervention of the then prime minister Indira Gandhi and her concern for the environmental issues resulted in the conservation of wildlife. At the international level, the World Wide Fund for Nature (WWF) joined hands with the local movements in the Silent Valley and promised protection to fauna and flora in that region. The concern for endangered species and the respect for fauna and flora motivated this movement (Sharma 2009: 153). This nature-centred movement provides insights into the indigenous people's reverence for Mother Earth. Sugathakumari is a renowned Malayalam poet who fought for the rights of nature and women in conjunction with the Silent Valley Movement in the late 1970s. She is the founder of the *Prakrithi Samrakshana Samithi*, an organisation for the protection of nature, and Abhaya, a home for the protection of destitute women. In an interview, when Mary Nirmala, a researcher, asked Sugathakumari, 'Do you think you have succeeded in your ceaseless fight against deforestation and exploitation of women?' the poet-activist replied, 'It's my cause. I keep on striving. Whether I succeed or fail is immaterial. Stopping half way through . . . I call it ultimate failure. Only rarely have I succeeded. But I toil upward . . . As long as I am plunged in Karma, I derive strength from it' (Nirmala 2009).

The Narmada Bachao Andolan (NBA) originated as a movement in the year 1987 against the Sardar Sarovar Project (SSP). In 1985, when the World Bank sanctioned a loan of $450 million to construct the Sardar Sarovar dam across the River Narmada, thousands of tribal communities were destined to be homeless and survive inhuman conditions, but for the efforts of women and men who used their collective power under the leadership of a woman with a vision, Medha Patkar. Besides upholding the rights of people living in the villages of Narmada Valley, this ecological movement also inspired the understanding of the intrinsic value of rivers in India, which have been revered as nature goddesses since ancient times. Baba Amte, a spokesperson of Narmada Bachao Andolan, is a social activist and a philosopher who stayed and worked with the people of Narmada Valley for more than twelve years. He is a powerful symbol of *Ahimsa* philosophy, who led the struggle with his visionary ideals for India. His respect for the intrinsic value of life is very much evident in the incident that became a turning point in his life, when he picked up a leper from the streets and created Anandwan, a rehabilitation centre that later became a home for thousands of lepers and disabled people. His close proximity and understanding of nature is found in his words and action. Baba Amte remarks, 'The honeybee's treasure of nectar is not obtained at the cost of the flower. In fact its act of extracting honey delivers fulfillment to the flowers. You need learn not from Gibran, Gorbachev or even Gandhiji.

INTRODUCTION

Choose instead to learn from the honey bee – as your silent partners they will show you how to develop without destroying' (http://www.anandwan. in/). These words sum up the ecofeminist belief in the sacredness of life. The nonviolent protests to protect the water bodies have been discussed by many eco-sensitive writers to create awareness among people. As Arundhati Roy put it, the construction of the dam 'would alter the ecology of an entire river basin, affect the lives of 25 million people who live in the valley, displace 160 villages, (and) submerge 4000 sq. km of old-growth deciduous forest . . . The war for the Narmada valley is not just some exotic tribal war, or a remote rural war or even an exclusively Indian war. It's a war for the rivers and the mountains and the forests' (Roy 1999). The systems that dominate nature and women go hand in hand to oppress many marginalised groups in this world. The fundamental belief in the sacredness of life reverses the hierarchical structures and promises change. Ecofeminism promotes alternative thinking that values the needs and rights of nature and other oppressed entities in this planet. Therefore, it is imperative to acknowledge the voices of the silenced and the marginalised.

The Green Belt Movement is a movement of life-affirmation for nature, women, children and other marginalised groups. It offers hope and promise to future generations. Wangari Maathai, the founder of the Green Belt Movement, in her memoir, *Unbowed*, explains that she learnt patience, determination and commitment from planting trees.

> When we are planting trees sometimes people will say to me, 'I don't want to plant this tree, because it will not grow fast enough.' I have to keep reminding them that the trees, they are cutting today, were not planted by them, but by those who came before. So they must plant the trees that will benefit communities in the future.
> (Maathai 2006: 289)

Planting a tree not only creates the possibility of a healthy planet, but also contributes to the well-being of people by providing them social, cultural and economic empowerment. In her Nobel Peace Prize talk in 2004, Maathai asserts, 'Tree planting became a natural choice to address some of the initial basic needs identified by women. Also, tree planting is simple, attainable and guarantees quick, successful results within a reasonable amount of time. This sustains interest and commitment' (Maathai 2004). Wangari Maathai explains that tree-planting empowers women economically, socially and collectively. It helps them to fulfil their basic needs and support their families. She asserts the fact that, as a group, they have planted over thirty million trees, which fulfil the basic needs of people, such as fuel, shelter, food and income. Above all, the women who plant trees are also able to support their children's education. At a different level, they gain power and strength from the environment and they are also empowered in terms of economic and social position. Besides, they also contribute to the well-being of the planet and the health of soil and water bodies in their environment. By planting trees, on the one hand, and protecting trees from not being felled down, on the other, women have a major role in conserving the biodiversity of the planet, with millions of species living at the edge of peril. Biodiversity can be defined as a collection of living organisms in a particular ecosystem. The climate changes in a specific environment affect the biodiversity of that place. When climate changes affect a particular ecosystem, in turn, it affects the different kinds of species living there. In an interview, Wangari Maathai explained that the environmental problem arises when people do not understand science. She states, 'What is needed is to have the science translated into a language that people can comprehend, so that we can create a movement of citizens who understand that the planet is under threat and who are willing to take action' (Maathai 2006: 18). She also provided an action plan to plant a million trees before the next climate conference.

Wordsmiths as 'worldsmiths'

Literary authors and critics, the wordsmiths who promote ecofeminist ideology in their works, contribute to reshaping the world as 'Worldsmiths'. At this juncture, we need to identify ecofeminist literary theories that form the second branch of the ecofeminist tree of thought that shaped the proposed research framework. Some of the prominent ecofeminist thinkers in the West include Ynestra King, Karen Warren, Noel Sturgeon, Starhawk, Josephine Donovan, Carol Adams, Greta Gaard and Maria Mies. The woman–nature proximity is reiterated by Western ecofeminist thinkers in the following ways. The fundamental beliefs of ecofeminist thought have been stated by Ynestra King. According to her, the four important principles of ecofeminism are determined by the identification of the relationship between the subjugation of woman and the conquest of nature, the interrogation of all kinds of domination at various levels in society, the prominence of holistic thinking over dualistic thinking and the importance of acknowledging diversity. By uniting the concerns of women, children and the other marginalised groups with the concerns of nature, ecofeminists identify ways to challenge the dominant systems. In the words of Greta Gaard, 'ecofeminism calls for an end to all oppressions, arguing that no attempt to liberate women (or any other oppressed group) will be successful without an equal attempt to liberate nature. Its theoretical base is a sense of

INTRODUCTION

self most commonly expressed by women and various other non-dominant groups – a self that is interconnected with all life' (Gaard 2010: 1). This ecofeminist study promulgates care and concern for Mother Earth and Her silenced children. Mother Earth signifies the personification of our planet as a Woman. On the contrary, ecofeminism realises the worth of women who live close to nature and exemplify the qualities of their Earth Mother. Any form of discourse that speaks for the welfare of humankind, shows respect for forms of life and suggests sensitivity and inter-dependence among living beings on this earth is nourished by ecofeminist ideology. In the book *Ecofeminist Natures*, Noel Sturgeon systematically discusses five different ways of understanding woman–nature relationships. According to Sturgeon, ecofeminism 'makes connections between environmentalisms and feminisms; more precisely, it articulates the theory that the ideologies that authorize injustices based on gender, race and class are related to the ideologies that sanction the exploitation and degradation of the environment' (Sturgeon 1997: 23). As a predominant concern, ecofeminism recognises woman–nature relationship in different ways. They are characterised by various positions: first, nature–nurture proposition; second, binary opposition of man/culture versus woman/nature; third, women in the household and their environmental problems; fourth, women's proximity with natural cycles; and finally, women personified as goddesses of nature.

Women share common traits with Mother Earth under the nature–nurture theory. The patriarchal systems have oppressed women and nature without partiality and this has led to ecological and economic crisis in the present-day world. Gender discrimination and environmental squalor are understood as consequences of patriarchal domination and authority at various levels, such as the family, community, society, nation and world. The Western concept of binary opposition defines man as culture and woman as nature while 'culture is in many ways anti nature' (Sturgeon 1997: 28), and this form of hierarchy is understood in the second position. The Eurocentric belief in dualism is challenged by Eastern philosophies such as Ying-Yang (Zen) and concept of *Purusha–Prakriti* in the Hindu belief system. Sturgeon explains that yet another way of looking at the woman–environment relationship is to consider women's preoccupation with household work. In this position, one is also aware of women's sensitivity towards environmental problems and their proactive nature in bringing about solutions. This position also focuses on indigenous knowledge of women in agriculture. Women are the first ones to recognise water scarcity, food crisis and pollution in the neighbourhood. The patriarchal society equates women with nature as nurturers, which is the root cause of all the environmental problems existing in the planet. 'In other words, where women are degraded, nature will be degraded, and where women

INTRODUCTION

are thought to be eternally giving and nurturing, nature will be thought of as endlessly fertile and exploitable' (Sturgeon 1997: 28). According to Sturgeon, the woman–nature relationship is also strengthened by the belief that, biologically, women are close to nature with 'reproductive characteristics . . . natural rhythms, seasonal and cyclical, life and death giving' (Sturgeon 1997: 29). She also confirms that 'ecofeminists who are comfortable with this position feel that women potentially have greater access than men do to sympathy with nature, and will benefit themselves and the environment by identifying with nature' (Sturgeon 1997: 29). In the fifth position, 'feminist spirituality', 'strong images of female power' in 'nature-based religions' (Sturgeon 1997: 29) are considered as major ecofeminist concerns.

Karren Warren explores the connection between women, culture and nature in her ecofeminist works. She also distinguishes eight different ways of observing the woman–nature connection. The first type is the historical connection, which studies the patriarchal domination of woman and nature as early as in 4500 BC. The second connection is a conceptual link, reinforced by the dichotomies of man as culture and woman as nature. The third type studies the sex–gender differences and the effects of masculinisation of culture on nature and woman. The fourth type is the empirical connection that identifies the 'rape' of nature and woman as patriarchal notion of power. The symbolic connection of woman–nature relationships has been studied by Warren. It accentuates the need to identify 'liberating, life-affirming and post-patriarchal worldviews and earth-based spiritualities and theologies' (Warren 1997: 255). There is yet another way of recognising woman–nature relationships – which is the epistemological connection that unites the concerns of ecology with the concerns of women. Grassroots activism forms the sixth connection, which is termed the political (praxis) connection. The ethical connection provides space for branches of ecofeminist thought, such as ecofeminist environmental ethics, ecofeminist ethic of care, ecofeminist animal rights position and ecofeminist social ecology. The eighth connection is a theoretical connection employed by academicians to study woman–nature relationships on philosophical grounds.

Apart from the literary theories, woman–nature concerns are discussed by a number of women writers across the world. Hence, it is imperative to throw light on writers such as Alice Walker in the Afro-American literary tradition and Mahasweta Devi in the Indian literary arena, who have integrated activism with writing to provide voices to the woman–nature subaltern. Besides, writers such as Rokeya Hossain, Anees Jung, Ambai and Bama are identified as writers who uphold woman–environment concerns in their works. Alice Walker's philosophy of life is characterised by love, care, woman power, contentment, nonviolence and peace. *Anything*

INTRODUCTION

We Love Can Be Saved is the ecophilosophy of Alice Walker, as represented in her collection of works under the subtitle *A Writer's Activism*, first published in 1997. Alice Walker celebrates earth-based spirituality and strength of womanhood as she utters, 'In day-to-day life, I worship the earth as God- representing everything- and Nature as its spirit' (Walker 2005: 11). As an activist writer, Mahasweta Devi has supported the cause of tribal people of the North-Eastern parts of India through her writings. Her works include *Hajar Churasir Ma – Mother of 1084* (1975), *Aranyar Adhikar: The Occupation of the Forest* (1977), Bitter Soil, translated by Ipsita Chandra (1998) and *Chotti Munda and His Arrow* (2003), translated by Gayatri Chakravorty Spivak (2002). Mahasweta Devi has also participated in various human rights protests in West Bengal. Mahasweta Devi, a former lecturer in English literature, is a champion of denotified tribes. Her fiction reflects the concern for tribal communities such as the Shabars, who are often exploited by the powerful in the state. In an interview, she records that the tribe with which she works are landless people.

Rajam Krishnan's novel, called *Kurinjithen*, has been translated into English as *When the Kurinji Blooms* by Uma Narayanan and Prema Seetharaman. In this novel, Rajam Krishnan documents the nature-culture of tribal people in the Nilgiri Hills from Tamilnadu. *When the Kurinji Blooms* is a novel that spans fifty years of three generations of the Badaga people living in the Nilgiri Mountains. Jogi is a nine-year-old Badaga boy who lives close to nature. His family believes in the conventional ways of life whereas Kariamalla's family moves with the times. In this novel, Rajam Krishnan celebrates the traditional practices on the one hand, and welcomes progress, on the other. The word *Kurinji* in the title of the novel refers to the bright blue flowers that blossom in the shrubs once in twelve years in the Nilgiri Hills. In contrast, the Badagas very often use the *Thumbay Hoo* – the Thumbay flower, which is pure white in colour – in their customs and rituals. The Badagas use the term *kurinji* 'to denote a twelve-year period' (Krishnan 2002: viii). In Tamil, the novel is titled *Kurinjithen*, which means honey from kurinji. During the flowering season, honey bees are found in abundance in the hillside.

In the novel *When the Kurinji Blooms*, Rajam Krishnan makes ample references to Mother Nature as a living being, which is a fundamental belief of ecofeminist thought. In Part I, Chapter one, the author describes that Mother Nature has two faces, 'the awesome and the compassionate' (Krishnan 2002: 4). In Part II, Chapter one, Rajam Krishnan exquisitely documents the flowering season of Kurinji in the Nilgiri Hills. She compares the hills to a young bride 'resplendent in blue shyly averting her eyes from her beloved, the sky' (Krishnan 2002: 59). She adds, 'Mother Nature too awaits the bridegroom, having spent twelve years weaving a garment of blue flowers for her dear daughter' (Krishnan 2002: 59). Jogi upholds the ecological values of interconnectedness and interdependence in the novel. He is a dutiful son who cares for Mother Earth. As Rajam Krishnan puts it, 'Mother Earth, considering him her beloved son, gave proof of her vitality and delighted him' (Krishnan 2002: 70). Jogi considers the plants as his children. In the epilogue, the readers witness the old man Jogi, 'who had seen five kurinji-spans . . . had led a full life' (Krishnan 2002: 292).

There are several theories of eco-critical thought that nurture ecofeminist philosophy. Cheryll Glotfelty is one of the early theoreticians of ecocriticism who understood the importance of integrating literature with environment. In her introduction to *The Ecocriticism Reader*, she defines 'simply put, ecocriticism is the study of the relationship between literature and the physical environment. Just as feminist criticism examines language and literature from a gender-conscious perspective . . . ecocriticism takes an earth-centred approach to literary studies' (Glotfelty 1996: xviii). She believes that

> in philosophy, various subfields like environmental ethics, deep ecology, ecofeminism and social ecology have emerged in an effort to understand and critique the root causes of environmental degradation and to formulate an alternative view of existence that will provide an ethical and conceptual foundation for the right relations with the earth.
>
> (Glotfelty 1996: xxi)

She reiterates the importance of literary studies in the age of environmental crisis. Hence, an earth-centred approach to folk literature is considered the need of the hour. Folk texts with alternative worldviews initiate a process of understanding the benefits of sustainable living and gender equity. The eco-critical principles reinforce the interconnections of nature and culture, which form a fundamental premise in this study. Folktales bridge the gap between nature and culture. The interconnectedness of life and the interdependence of life on this earth are reinforced by the study of folktales.

Deep Ecology challenges anthropocentric or human-centred worldviews and confirms the inherent worth of life on earth. It is an environmental movement initiated by Arne Naess, a Norwegian philosopher, in 1972. Stephen Harding states, 'through deep experience, deep questioning and deep commitment emerges deep ecology' (Sessions 1995: 68). While Deep Ecology questions anthropocentrism that oppresses nature, ecofeminism interrogates androcentricism that subjugates woman and nature. Arne Naess' Deep Ecology claims that

1. The well-being and the flourishing of human and nonhuman life on Earth have value in themselves (synonyms: intrinsic value, inherent value). These values are independent of the usefulness of the nonhuman world for human purposes.
2. Richness and diversity of life forms contribute to the realization of these values and are also values in themselves.
3. Humans have no right to reduce this richness and diversity except to satisfy vital needs.

(Sessions 1995: 68)

These considerations are adopted as guiding principles in this study for the following reasons. The folktales provide a significant space for the nonhuman life. They emphasise the intrinsic value of nonhuman living organisms. A deep understanding of the intrinsic value of each and every living organism is essential to transform the existing paradigms in science, economics and commerce. In many instances, animals, birds, trees, water and mountains represent their inherent worth, free from the utility purposes of human beings in folktales from India.

Gaia is the Greek equivalent of *Bhoomi*. James Lovelock proposed the Gaia hypothesis in the 1960s–70s. James Lovelock first published his *Gaia* theory in 1965. This article is extracted from the July/August 1988 issue of *Resurgence*, no. 129.

> To see the Earth as a living organism makes tangible the concept of stewardship and focuses our hearts and minds on what should be our prime environmental concern: the care and protection of the Earth itself and especially of the forests of the humid tropics. So let's stay selfish, but be guided in our selfishness to keep a world that is healthy and beautiful, and that will remain fit for our grandchildren as well as those of our partners in Gaia.
>
> (Lovelock 2006)

In his latest book, *The Vanishing Face of Gaia: A Final Warning*, Lovelock explains, 'Until we all feel intuitively that the Earth is a living system, and know that we are a part of it, we will fail to react automatically for its and ultimately our own protection' (Lovelock 2009: 128). Predominant Western scientists considered the earth as only matter. In Lovelock's theory, he calls Earth *Gaia*, but states that 'it is alive'. Ecofeminists believe in the feminine principle of Gaia and identify 'Her' as the source of all living. The personification of Mother Earth as Gaia offers a unique standpoint that amalgamates science with spirituality. The concept of Mother Earth is scientifically described by Lovelock's theory of Gaia. The personification of nature as Mother Earth is most often considered on spiritual grounds whereas Lovelock's description of Gaia is much more scientific in outlook.

> Forty-four years ago when I was working at the then centre of space research, the Jet Propulsion Laboratory (JPL) in California and saw with my mind's eye our planet as something alive. Since then I have thought of the word Earth as inadequate to describe the living planet that we inhabit and are a part of. I am grateful to the author William Golding for his suggestion that the name Gaia was more appropriate.
> (Lovelock 2009: I)

The first and foremost responsibility of every individual is to consider Mother Earth or Gaia as a living being. Human beings are part of this self-regulating living system. The perception of Gaia, as a single organism with organic unity, reinforces the interdependence of life. Hence, Gaia motifs are identified in folktales from India.

In order to grasp the ecofeminist principles, it is important to understand ecofeminist motifs and concerns in the experience narratives of rural women who live close to nature. This research attempts to identify the unsung heroines who contribute to the well-being of Mother Nature and her children in their day-to-day lives. Ecofeminism deems the indigenous knowledge of women as specialist knowledge. Their knowledge emerges out of their experience.

Nature's natural philosophers

Thimakka, known as a natural environmentalist, is an 103-year-old woman who has planted 384 banyan trees in her village, 'Hulikal', about 70 km from Bangalore. She has received titles such as Nisargaratna, Vrikshasri and Vrikshapremi, an award by Karnataka government. 'For 25 years I could not conceive so we thought why not grow and nurture trees like our own children instead and thus started our campaign to grow trees . . . Now they are all well grown', says Thimakka in an interview to *The Hindu* newspaper. She worked as a daily wage labourer and used the money to grow these trees. The couple would work in the morning and plant trees in the afternoon. She never missed kids and she is proud of those trees. They are like her children. Women such as Thimakka rewrite their destiny by

INTRODUCTION

adopting nature as their children. Quite specifically, trees are adopted as children by childless couples and nurtured with care, and in turn, those trees become a blessing to not just one child, but an entire generation. In this section, we can assess the role of nature's natural philosophers who contribute to the well-being of the planet. The ecofeminist experiences can be recorded through personal interviews, case studies and fieldwork. The author interviewed three women involved in organic farming during the course of study. They are Azhagu Pillai, Innasiamma and Jayanthi.

Azhagu Pillai is a subsistence farmer who lives in Karuppaaioorani, a village near Madurai, Tamilnadu. She started working as an agricultural labourer from the age of seven. At present, she is an 80-year-old woman who retains her passion for cultivating vegetables and food crops in her neighbourhood using organic methods. She makes use of natural manure, such as goat droppings and cow dung. Her day-to-day routine confirms her worldviews and consciousness drawn from nature. She considers plants as 'her very own children' – the same emotion shared by Thimakka. According to Azhagu Pillai, when a person talks to plants, both of them (the human and the plant) feel happy. The old woman's belief in the intrinsic value of nonhuman living beings is reflected in her words, 'the plants certainly have a life like us'. She recalls a painful incident that happened in her life. Once, she was bitten by a snake while working in the farm. She had suggested some herbal remedy. But her children did not want to take a risk; instead, they took her to a neighbouring hospital a few miles away. She was treated in the hospital for snakebite and was cured, but quite unfortunately, when she was carried in the motorbike quite hastily, people around her did not notice that she had lost one of her toes. This episode reveals the ambivalent nature of development and modernisation and their impact on people who live close to nature.

Nature-lover Azhagu Pillai is fond of cows and goats, and especially, a little lamb that sits next to her all the time. With a gentle smile, she feeds the lamb with greens. Her neighbours say, 'She never understands the value of money; she does all the work in our neighbourhood but feels offended if we give her money. She prefers a cup of coffee instead'. The television and other technological inventions in her son's house do not distract her. When other women in the neighbourhood, young and old, watch mega serials, this nature-lover takes a stroll along the path where she has planted champak and hibiscus, smiling at those flowers in satisfaction. Azhagu Pillai's father died of jaundice at an early age. As the eldest daughter of her family, she had the major responsibility of bringing up her sisters and brothers. She did know the value of money. But she puts in plain words, 'money will never bring us happiness. It is people around us who bring us joy'. There is a sense of contentment in whatever she says. She ends each

INTRODUCTION

and every sentence with a smile. Ecofeminism believes in creating awareness of alternative systems with dominant existing systems and attempts to synchronise worldviews that complement each other. To understand the proximity in the woman–nature relationship, the researcher observed Azhagu Pillai's environment. As a result, one can infer from the case study that Azhagu Pillai's worldview is a worldview characterised by abundance, simplicity and contentment.

Innasiamma is 85 years old. She hails from a village called A. Vellodu, near Dindugal. At present, she lives in the Home for the Aged, run by The Little Sisters of the Poor. She is a mother of ten children – six sons and four daughters. However, only four sons and one daughter survive. She came to the aged home to look after her unmarried handicapped elder sister. Her sister died a few years back and she decided to stay on in the home. Her day begins at 4.30 a.m. She takes care of the garden near the chapel in the Home for the Aged. Back home in A. Vellodu, she worked as an agricultural labourer right from her childhood days and continues her green tryst with plants even at this age. Innasiamma recollects the days when she was into cultivation of *kambu, cholam*, grapes and betel leaves. She explains, 'Gone are those days when they used manure made of *kadalai punnaaku* and *ellu punnaaku*. The fruits and vegetables had a rich taste'. Innasiamma did not have a formal education. But she gained a wealth of knowledge from Mother Nature. When her brother went to school, she preferred to go up the Sirumalai hills with cattle. 'Every day I would go up the hill taking the herd with me. I also collected water from a pond several miles away from our village. But nowadays people get water inside the house', she expresses her wonder. She continues, 'As the cattle grazed around I would sing songs, narrate stories and enact scenes from the Bible to my friends'. She asserts, 'I learnt everything from nature'. With a sparkle in her eyes, she recalls her childhood days, when she led a carefree life – one with Mother Nature.

Apart from agriculture, Innasiamma has also tried her hand as a mason. As she reminisces, one is able to understand her mental strength as well as her physical strength, Shakthi, which she gained from nature. 'I've never felt that a woman is weaker than man. I worked with men, building walls and even digging wells'. Talking about her food habits, she comments, 'Today most of the people prefer nonvegetarian food, *keerai* is long forgotten'. She also suggests a recipe of *keerai* (greens) soup. With a lot of enthusiasm, she talks about medicinal herbs that she grows in the Home for the Aged. She had even brought seeds of *theenichi pachilai* – a medicinal herb, used to purify blood – all the way from her village, A. Vellodu. As she explains, suddenly she gets up, moves to the garden, unmindful of the scorching sun, plucks a few leaves from *theenichi* plant and hands them

INTRODUCTION

over to the researcher. 'This smells like Tulsi, but it is a different *moolikai* (medicinal herb) variety', she clarifies with a smile.

Jayanthi has been selling *keerai* and vegetables for the past fifteen years. She travels all the way from a village called Peria Obulapuram, near Gummidipindi, to Chennai everyday by the local train, the MRTS. Her day begins at 2.30 a.m. She goes around the village, collecting greens and vegetables from different farms and gardens. She reaches Chennai by 5.30 or 6.00 a.m. The greens and vegetables that she sells are cultivated in organic farms. She explains that the farmers use cow dung and goat droppings as manure. Chemical fertilisers are not in vogue. The description of her village was definitely appealing to city-dwellers caught in pollution, population, confusion and disorder. She described her village as a place of peaceful environment with fresh air and clean water that tastes like 'tender coconut', with greenery all around. 'In *Aippasi* we sow, in *Karthigai* we weed and in *Thai* we harvest the crops. We grow *kambu, keppai*, rice, greens, vegetables like brinjal, lady's finger, drumstick, flowers such as rose and jasmine'.

Jayanthi explained the medicinal value of *keerai* and hands them over to people with maternal care. For example, '*manathakkali keerai* has detoxifying value, memory power is enhanced by *vallarai keerai*, diabetic people need *venthaya keerai*, for healthy eyesight eat *ponnanganni keerai*'. Jayanthi recollected an interesting episode that happened in the month of June. On a sunny morning, she had left the basket in front of a building and gone upstairs to give *keerai* to a regular customer. When she came down, she saw a cow eating away the mangoes she had brought all the way from her village. The people who witnessed the scene started chasing the cow. But on that day, Jayanthi decided to feed the cow with some more mangoes. Joyfully, she recalled, 'I felt that the goddess had come down and I got an opportunity to feed her'. The rural women deify nature and understand the sacredness of life. They excel as vanguards of earth-based spirituality.

Earth tutelage

Nature is the supreme teacher, with her own pedagogical tools and techniques. An indigenous prayer confirms the role of Mother Nature in a person's life. Mother Earth teaches human beings to be calm and composed like the green grass filled with sunlight; patience in times of suffering like the rocks and stones; humility like the flowers; caring as mothers nurture the young ones; and courage like the tree rooted to the ground. The tiny ants teach about limitations on one side and the soaring eagle teaches freedom on the other. The leaves that fall down in autumn teach acceptance and the new seed that arises in the spring teaches renewal. The melting

INTRODUCTION

snow teaches forgetting and the rain that falls on dry land teaches kindness to humankind. Ecofeminist Pedagogy is inspired by the pedagogy of Mother Nature. It is characterised by calmness, patience, tolerance, humility, care, courage, aspiration, rejuvenation, kindness and simplicity of thought and action.

What is the scope of Ecofeminist Pedagogy? Ecofeminist Pedagogy believes in and encourages a 'heterarchical' (Gaard and Murphy 1998: 204) dialogical approach to education. It challenges indoctrination and monopolised thinking systems. The *New Oxford Dictionary of English* defines 'pedagogy' as 'the method and practice of teaching, especially as an academic subject or theoretical concept' (1367). Greta Gaard's *Ecofeminist Literary Criticism* provides insights for academicians to integrate the movement with the curriculum and understand Ecofeminist Pedagogy as an instrument for social change. It facilitates teaching and learning from a multidimensional perspective. In his essay *Deep Response: An Ecofeminist, Dialogical Approach to Introductory Literature Classrooms*, John Paul Tassoni emphasises the importance of Ecofeminist Pedagogy. The relationship between the world and the consciousness is an important factor in bringing about social change. Ecofeminist Pedagogy remains open 'to conflicting viewpoints' and does not 'perpetuate the very monologic conceptions of truth and hierarchy they seek to resist' (Gaard and Murphy 1998: 204). Tassoni explains that, 'by remaining open to opposing viewpoints, ecofeminists can continually examine and re-examine their own goals' (Gaard and Murphy 1998: 204). The Mother Earth Discourse is identified as a vital tool to realise Ecofeminist Pedagogy in the classrooms.

Maria Mies identifies *conscientizacao* as a process of establishing woman's rights and nature's rights. The word 'consciousness-raising' indicates the critical consciousness of a group. According to Paulo Freire, 'critical consciousness' helps end the 'culture of silence'. Ecofeminism amalgamates with Paulo Freire's theory of conscientisation in different ways. 'First, one becomes conscious of one's individual suffering as a woman, which is a subjective precondition for liberating action. Then women make a collective conscientisation . . . sharing and formulating of problems' (Mies and Shiva 2010: 11). As Maria Mies puts it:

> If women scholars begin to understand their studies as an integral part of a liberating struggle and if they focus their research on the processes of individual and social change, then they cannot but change themselves also in this process, both as human beings and as scholars. They will have to give up the elitist narrow-mindedness, abstract–thinking, political and ethical impotence and arrogance of the established academician. They must learn

INTRODUCTION

that scientific work and a scientific outlook is not the privilege of professional scientists, but that the creativity of science depends on it being rooted in living social processes.

(Mies and Shiva 2010: 41)

The thrust on ecofeminist research as a social obligation guides scholars to be responsible in understanding their research subjects. Hence, the growth of the ecofeminist-linguistic frame in this research has fostered an interest in the indigenous wisdom of women and men who live close to nature. Deborah Slicer, in her essay *Toward an Ecofeminist Standpoint Theory*, quotes philosophers Karen J. Warren and Jim Cheney, 'Centralizing women's voices is important methodologically and epistemologically to the overall critique and revisioning of the concept of nature and the moral dimensions of human-nature relationships' (Gaard and Murphy 1998: 53). Ecofeminism proposes an approach that reverses anthropomorphic, androcentric positions found in Western culture. Both anthropomorphism, which is human-centred, and androcentrism, which is male-centred, are questioned by ecofeminist thought. Students are encouraged voluntarily to 'embrace ecofeminism as more conducive to healthy human and nonhuman relations' (Gaard and Murphy 1998: 204).

Ecofeminists are open to 'conflicting viewpoints' (Gaard and Murphy 1998: 204), thereby motivating an ongoing dialogical process. A dialogical method allows each and every member in the class to be active, conscious and responsible in enhancing the teaching–learning process. Ecofeminist Pedagogy is a dialogic pedagogy, which promotes a democratic environment in the classroom and challenges the 'banking method of education', which treats the student's mind as tabula rasa and 'effaces student's own cultural experiences' (Gaard and Murphy 1998: 207). It also respects the sociocultural identity of each and every student in the classroom. The students and teachers are considered as learners and there is not one 'correct' interpretation of the text, but different interpretations that are accepted and sanctioned by all the participants, based on their sociocultural background. Moreover Tassoni explains:

> As an alternative to the banking model, the dialogical approach to literature encourages students to see 'others' as speaking subjects, not merely the objects of their attention. In the dialogical classroom, knowledge is not represented as static, but as determined between people within a given culture or situation. Dialogic teachers do not merely inform students that knowledge is determined interindividually.
>
> (Gaard and Murphy 1998: 209)

INTRODUCTION

Tassoni affirms that the dialogical approach in classrooms reiterate the importance of knowledge systems that, in turn, inspire them to lead better lives. Ecofeminist Pedagogy reverses the teacher–student positions. As ecofeminism cares for Mother Earth and her children, the teacher as ecofeminist-linguistic facilitator shows care and concern to the students and provides a favourable environment to grow.

This chapter introduced the aims and objectives of the book, folktales as promising seeds of silence into words of consciousness, the metaphor of Mother Earth as the crux of ecofeminist thought, definition and characteristics of ecofeminist theory, the scope of integration of nature and woman in select folktales from India. This ecofeminist praxis connects the text with the context, imagination with reality, environmental rights with women's rights and human rights, culture with nature and the classroom with the world. Thus, environmental movements, ecofeminist literary theories, indigenous ecofeminist experiences and ecofeminist pedagogies that care for flora, fauna, land, water and other forms of creation uphold the woman–nature proximity, spirit of interconnectedness and interdependence shape the Mother Earth Discourse framework for the analysis of folktales from India.

1
MOTHER EARTH DISCOURSE

> Come forth into the light of things, Let Nature be your teacher.
> — William Wordsworth

Interweaving woman–nature lore

Folktales show the interdependent relationship between human beings and the natural environment. In these tales, animals, birds, plants, trees and other objects in nature are acknowledged, respected and at times, worshipped, most often by women and children. Each and every living creature in nature has a special role to play in these folktales. In order to respect the inherent worth of nature and women, it is important to comprehend their voices. In the oral tales, nature communicates with women in different ways. Hence, folktales illustrate not only women's voices, but also nature's voices. What is the scope of an environmental tale? The Chipko Movement is a women's movement for the conservation of trees. It is said that 300 years ago in Rajasthan, a woman named Amrita Devi led a group of 300 people in a nonviolent protest to save the 'sacred *khejri* trees by clinging to them' (Shiva 2010: 67). The tree-hugging movement has inspired people to explore the significance of environmental folktales all over the world. For example, *The People Who Hugged the Trees: An Environmental Folk Tale*, adapted by Deborah Lee Rose (2001), is from a Rajasthani version of the story which describes a girl called Amrita who attempted to save trees by hugging them. This folktale, meant for children, has been translated into eleven languages and is prescribed for schoolchildren in South Africa.

Folktales convey that Mother Earth is sacred and it is the duty of human beings to respect her. *Amrita's Story* is a folktale that has been adapted by various writers in the West to communicate their concern for Mother Earth, and especially, the trees, to the children – for example, *The Barefoot Book of Earth Tales* by Dawn Casey and Anne Wilson, published in 2009 by

Barefoot in Cambridge. The author narrates, 'Sometimes, Amrita climbed her tree. Sometimes the wind swayed her and she was a forest queen. Sometimes she talked to her tree, sharing her daydreams and her secrets, but today was so peaceful that she sat in silence' (Casey and Anne Wilson 2009: 72). When the woodcutters decide to cut down trees for the Maharaj, Amrita boldly fights the ordeal, which is very much evident in the story.

> A woodcutter brushed past Amrita, toward her own special tree. 'No! No! Please don't!' she cried, tears springing to her eyes. 'Please don't cut down my tree.' The woodcutter advanced. The sharp tang of bleeding trunks was stinging her eyes. Amrita stepped in front of him, blocking his path. Her voice shook as she spoke: 'I will not let anyone harm my tree.'
> (Casey and Anne Wilson 2009: 77)

The integration of ecofeminism, folklore and discourse propagates a holistic view of life. The study of folklore as discourse has been carried out by several scholars in recent times. Professor Jawaharlal Handoo has collected and edited the conference papers of International Society for Folk Narrative Research (ISFNR). He has named one of those volumes as *Folklore and Discourse* (1999). The volume consists of papers 'discussing and analyzing the relationship between folklore the material, and other discourses such as nationalistic discourse, gender discourse, and other discourses that allot folklore a place in their scheme of organization' (Muthukumaraswamy 2006: ix).

According to Richard M. Dorson, there are different types of folklore theories. They are: Comparative Folklore Theory, National Folklore Theories, Anthropological Theory, Psychoanalytical Theory and Structural Folklore Theory. The Comparative Folklore Theory makes use of indices and motifs, but the 'function, style and structure remain outside their sphere' (Dorson 1963: 110). Anthropologists concentrating on oral tradition study the tales as a reflection of their culture and their values. Nationalist folklorists concentrate on the folklore of high civilisations and tend to ignore other subaltern cultures. The latest is the structural model of folklore used by the social sciences. The psychoanalytical school probes into the emotional meaning of the fairy tales and dreams (Dorson 1963: 110). As a result, a pragmatic theory of folklore is identified as the need of the hour.

Folklore as Discourse (2006), edited by M. D. Muthukumaraswamy, is a comprehensive collection of essays on topics such as 'Discourse of Folklore the Discipline', 'Folklore and Historical Perspectives', 'Discourse of Language and Identity', 'Folklore and the Discourse of Gender', 'Discourse of Ideology, Religion and Worldview', and so on. According to the folklorist

Peter Claus, 'discourse links us to others' (Beck et al. 2006: 8) and this aspect is vital in shaping the ecofeminist-linguistic framework to uphold the interconnectedness of life. In this study, the folktale is identified as a narrative discourse that communicates ecofeminist motifs that are favourable to Mother Earth.

Kamil Zvelebil's study of myths and folktales provides insights on nature–culture relationships in Tamilnadu. For example, in the story of Murugan, the Tamil god, Valli, the female protagonist, derives her name from a tuber plant in the *Kurinji* hills. According to the folk versions, she is the daughter of a deer who lives amidst nature and marries the hill-god Murugan (Zvelebil 1986: 40–46). Avvaiyar is a great devotee of Lord Murugan. There are number of mythical oral tales about Murugan and Avvaiyar. Women's tales offer alternative perspectives in each and every aspect of life. Brenda Beck and Peter J. Claus, in their introduction to *Folktales of India*, comment on the significance of women's roles in the narratives. Women 'appear in semi-magical roles . . . shift back and forth between human, vegetal, animal, and divine forms' and 'their basic sexual identity is also often linked to hidden psychological strengths, to their willingness to act on impulse, and to their courage to stick to their personal convictions' (Beck et al. 2006: xxx–xxxi). The women's tales weave the multifarious living organisms into their canvas with admiration and reverence.

In his book *Morphology of the Folktale*, Propp, the Russian folklorist, proposed that a tale has sequences determined by 31 functions, which begin with 'absentation' (where a member of a family leaves home) and end with 'wedding'. This classification is very methodical in understanding the plot. But the focus is more on structure rather than on content. The motif-index suggested by Thompson also does not favour the holistic approach to discourse. As a result, the Labovian paradigm of narrative structure is identified as a sociolinguistic tool to analyse ecofeminist motifs in the discourse. Folklore begins at home or *akam*, the woman's space. The stories and songs (lullabies) that children hear from their mothers and grandmothers at mealtimes (in Indian culture) and at bedtime (Western tradition) mould their childhood and shape their personality. Folklore is considered as a 'symbolic language' (Ramanujan 2009: xiii) of indigenous people. The figurative tales interconnect the world of fantasy with the world of reality. The allegorical meaning of the folktales shapes the consciousness of children.

Folktales are illustrations of rural people's mindscape that are in close proximity with their landscape. In Tamilnadu, folktales are told and folk songs are sung (in *puram*) to keep adults awake when people struggle up the high hills to fetch honey and tuber (*kurinji* landscape); when men and women probe into the forest for hunting and food gathering (*mullai* landscape); when farmers strive hard in the agricultural fields (*marudham* landscape); when fishermen go into the sea (*neythal* landscape); and when people travel through the arid regions (*palai* landscape). From the ancient times, women have accompanied men to work as seed gatherers. The *akam* and *puram* in Sangam literature complement one another in reinforcing the holistic principles of life as understood by Tamil people.

In Sangam literature, the central personae, *Kizhavan* and *Kizhathi* (man and woman), have claim over time and space. They are also known as *Talaivan* and *Talaivi*. Both woman and man had the responsibility to build their home, their community, their country and the world at large. *Nattrai* (meaning 'good mother') refers to the biological mother. *Sevili Thaai* is the foster mother who nurses and takes care of the child. *Sevili Thaai*'s daughter is *Thozhi* (friend) to the female protagonist. The spirit of sisterhood and conviviality is quite elaborately illustrated in Sangam poetry. The unique qualities of the personae are: *perumai* (meaning 'greatness', 'renown' and 'might'); *uram* (meaning 'strength'); *atcham* (meaning 'fear'), '*Kilatti* fears only what ought to be feared . . . fears god . . . dreads vice' (Selvamony 1998: 86); *niraivu* is contentment and is related to fidelity in relationships; *arul* is graciousness, sympathy and fellow-feeling, which also denotes compassion to human and nonhuman living beings in one's environment. Some of the characteristic features of the five landscapes represented in Sangam poetry are as follows: the flora (trees and plants) in *kurinji* – jackfruit, bamboo and *vengai* (kino) trees; *mullai* – *konrai* (*cassia*); *marudham* – mango; *neythal* – *punnai* (laurel); *palai* – *omai*, cactus; the fauna (birds and animals) in *kurinji* – peacock, parrot, monkey, elephant, horse and bull; *mullai* – sparrow, jungle hen and deer; *marudham* – stork, heron, buffalo and freshwater fish; *neythal* – seagull, crocodile and shark; *palai* – dove, eagle, fatigued elephant, tiger or wolf and lizard; the water bodies in *kurinji* – waterfall; *mullai* – rivers; *marudham* – pool; *neythal* – wells; *palai* – waterless wells and stagnant water.

Folklore as a cultural component has nature at its centre. Women believe and narrate stories that integrate nature and culture. They represent the indigenous knowledge systems which have been ignored and sidelined by academicians for many centuries. The tales narrated by women to children at mealtimes are said to have a healing effect on both the speaker and the listener. The food nourishes the child's body and the stories nurture the child's mind and soul. As a result, the storytelling sessions become a holistic form of education. During the storytelling sessions, women use their intuition and imagination to convey their beliefs and convictions spontaneously without any restraint. Besides entertainment, the folk discourse communicates the wisdom and knowledge of indigenous women and their understanding of the world around them. These oral tales shape the children's consciousness and mould their worldviews. The children who listen to the folktales grow up with a sense of abundance and contentment. Oral tales, communicated from one generation to another, by women to children during mealtime in insignificant villages, ascertain the worldview of anonymous human beings who were considered 'silent', but were actually 'silenced' by the patriarchal system from ancient times. The stories are figurative expressions that communicate in-depth psychological implications of women's thought processes. Nature exists along with human beings in folktales from India. Oral tales are characterised by a wide variety of patterns and motifs, which differ from one rendering to another. According to A. K. Ramanujan, a folktale is 'a poetic text' (Ramanujan 2009: xi) and 'a travelling metaphor' (Ramanujan 2009: xi). It highlights the symbiotic relationship between human and nonhuman beings on this earth. They typify indigenous beliefs that revere the spirituality of all life forms. Folktales are multifaceted expressions of ordinary people which communicate extraordinary understanding of nature.

Folktales highlight a circular pattern in terms of themes and techniques. This pattern symbolises the spherical shape of Mother Earth. It denotes a holistic approach to life and emphasises interdependence. The folktales defy the binary opposition of day/night, life/death and good/evil. Those bipolar opposites coexist in Indian women's folk culture and confirm the transient nature of existence. Alice Walker has emphasised yet another indigenous ecofeminist belief – the importance of perceiving and understanding the dynamics of the world in the form of circles. To quote Delveaux,

> How central the image of the circle is to Walker's work becomes obvious by one of her letters to Quincy Jones, co-producer of the film *The Color Purple*, in which Walker (1996: 143) points out that she didn't want to see Albert sit on a horse at the end, being separated from the others, because 'The feeling of the people is *circle*, not hierarchy'. It is exactly this image of a circle which would also mirror her view of a healthy ecosystem in which the circle brings people and other elements of nature on a same plane.
> (Delveaux 2012)

Folktales are thematically and technically constructed in the form of circles. As Mother Earth herself goes round and round in a circular fashion, the beliefs of the indigenous people confirm their proximity with nature. This ecofeminist belief interrogates the authoritative systems that dominate the world through different forms of hierarchy. Folktales are shaped by the circular principles in nature. In Indian homes, the children are made to sit in the form of a circle during mealtimes and the stories are narrated by an elder – most often by a woman. The circular pattern challenges hierarchical structures and provides a democratic outlook. The narration of folktales to children by grandmothers or the cooks in the household reiterates the significance of those relationships that are characterised by love and care and not power relations.

As writing was consigned to man's realm in ancient days, women chose to communicate through this oral discourse in the form of folk songs and folktales. A folktale is a cultural vehicle that carries a set of beliefs, convictions and thought processes, shaped and moulded by the environment in which women live. These multidimensional forms of informal discourse educate children on various aspects of life and the world they grow up in. A. K. Ramanujan is of the opinion that 'the aesthetics, ethos and worldview of a person are shaped in childhood and throughout early life, and reinforced later by these verbal and nonverbal environments' (Ramanujan 2009: xiii). The folktales are from seven collections, such as *Folktales from India: A Selection of Oral Tales from Twenty-Two languages* (2009), selected and edited by A. K. Ramanujan; *A Flowering Tree and Other Oral Tales from India* (1997), translated by A. K. Ramanujan, and edited by Stuart Blackburn and Alan Dundes; *First There Was Woman and Other Stories: Folktales of the Dungri Garasiya Bhils* (2007), selected and retold by Marija Sres; *Feminist Folktales from India* (2003) by Qiron Adhikary; *Folktales of India* (1987), edited by Brenda Beck, Peter J. Claus, Praphulladatta Goswami and Jawaharlal Handoo; *Earth Care: World Folktales to Talk About* by Margaret Read Macdonald and *Fearless Girls, Wise Women and Beloved Sisters: Heroines in Folktales from Around the World* by Kathleen Ragan. This research also includes a translation and analysis of a tribal tale of the Pulaiyar community from Palani Hills, Tamilnadu.

Folktales are the unique forte of women that authentically represent 'nature-culture'. In his lecture in 1991 at the University of Minnesota, A. K. Ramanujan discussed a Kannada folktale, *A Flowering Tree*, as 'A Woman's Tale'. He felt that, of the many dimensions in the story, one was very significant, that is, 'it resonates with our present concerns with ecology and conservation' (Ramanujan 1997: 219). He classifies certain stories as 'women-centred tales'. According to him, 'the women-centred tales counter and complement the attitudes of the male-centred tales' (Ramanujan 1997: xxxi). In these tales, the heroines are witty and clever women who solve the riddles and save people and other living beings in their environment. The Indian translator's observation has guided the researcher to explore themes and motifs of woman–nature proximity in folktales from India. A woman's perception of her environment is different from a man's perception. In his essay on 'Women's Tales', A. K. Ramanujan uses the term 'counter-system' to denote that 'these stories present an alternative way of looking at things. Genders are genres. The world of women is not the world of men' (Dharwadker 2004: 446). Women's sensitivity to the environment finds authentic representations in folktales from India. The folktales considered for the present study are *Tell It to the Walls, Bopoluchi, A Story in Search of an Audience, Sukhu and Dukhu, The Kite's Daughter, A Flowering Tree, Heron Boy, The Serpent Mother, Nonviolence, Hanchi, A Story and a Song, Acacia Trees, A Golden Sparrow* and *The Pomegranate Queen* from A. K. Ramanujan's *Folktales from India: A Selection of Oral Tales from Twenty-Two Languages* and *A Flowering Tree and Other Oral Tales from India*.

Oral tales of indigenous women epitomise their deep understanding of a culture integrated with nature. Marija Sres, a religious missionary, has lived among the Bhil tribal people for the past forty years and documented the stories of women. She explains that when she came to Gujarat in the 1970s, the land was characterised by feudalism and patriarchy. But the women had stories, oral tales with alternative worldviews characterised by abundance, care, concern for other living beings and a sense of contentment. The folktales selected and retold by Marija Sres in *First There Was Woman and Other Stories: Folktales of the Dungri Garasiya Bhils* (2007) are authentic representations of the folk beliefs of Bhil tribes in Gujarat, India. They exemplify indigenous belief systems and worldviews of those people, which are akin to an ecofeminist philosophy of life. The Bhil folktales chosen for study are *First There Was Woman, The Golden Age and the Deluge, How Kava Deceived Kavi, Fulwanti, the Flower Princess* and *Those Clever Crows*.

According to ecofeminist spirituality, the goddesses of nature empower women with *Shakthi*. *Feminist Folktales from India* (2003) is a collection of stories by Qiron Adhikary, which reiterates woman–nature proximity. The feminist folktales project positive, self-affirming images of women who think and act. They interconnect women's understanding of nature and culture. The folktales are labelled feminist and the stories emphasise the feminine strength or Shakthi in women who live close to nature. Adhikary's feminist folktales analysed in this research are *How the Mahi River Married the Sea, The Woman Who Was Loved by a Tree Spirit, The Rain God's Bride, The Girl Who Understood Birds, The Tiger Woman* and *The Porcupine Daughter*.

The diversity of Indian culture is represented by several collections of folktales translated into English across different ages. *Folktales of India: A Selection of Oral Tales from Twenty-Two Languages* (1987), edited by folklorists Brenda Beck, Peter J. Claus, Praphulladatta Goswami and Jawaharlal Handoo, is a collection of ninety-nine tales collected by eighteen regional folklorists across different states in India. The folktales selected for the study are *The Goddess of Mahi River, The Boy Who Could Speak with Birds, The Girl Who Was Loved by a Tree Spirit* and *The Rain Prince's Bride*.

Bhoomi Tales is a collection of folktales translated from Tamil to English by Dr P. Mary Vidya Porselvi and published in July 2015. Twenty folktales in the book were collected through fieldwork by volunteers of an NGO called Mact India and five stories were translated from Ki. Rajanarayanan's *Nattupura Kathai Kalanjiyam*. The folktales chosen for analysis in this book are: *The Gift of Truth, Fruits of Annadhaanam, A Life of Contentment, Leaders Are Sown, Nature Woman, Elephant and the Hunter, A Poet and His Song, What the Tree Said!, What the Cloud and the Stars Wished For, God's Gift, The Princess and the Parrots, Do Good unto Your Enemies, The Greedy Man, It Is Raining Snacks!, Who Is Greater!, A Missed Shot, A Man Is . . ., The Monkey and the Woodcutter, Where Do the Sparrows Live!, Good Things Happen to Good People, The Child Who Taught a Lesson to the King* and *Respect for Life*.

Reinventing the ecofeminist discourse

This study aims at analysing and synthesising folktales as ecofeminist discourse. Narrative/Discourse analysis arises from the field of sociolinguistics. 'Sociolinguistics' is a term that connects the beliefs of the linguists with the views of sociologists. It is the scientific study of language in a society. As Suzanne Romaine puts it, 'The question of language and gender seen from a feminist perspective must address two fundamental questions: how do women speak? And how are they spoken about?' (Cameron 1998: 101) The twin themes of Speech and Silence have been studied by sociolinguists in the context of marginalised and oppressed groups. The feminist praxis to identify women's silences is a predominant goal in this research. The metaphors of speech and silence are studied in the context of women's environment.

> Feminism is both 'theory' and 'practice' (i.e. praxis). Feminist researchers start with the political commitment to produce useful knowledge that will make a difference to women's lives through social and individual change. They are concerned to challenge the silences in mainstream research both in relation to the issues studied and the ways in which study is undertaken.
>
> (Letherby 2003: 4)

The analysis of folktales using the ecofeminist-linguistic frame is a way of identifying the 'unvoiced' and the 'unexpressed' in women–nature–culture. In other words, it aspires to interrogate the 'silences' in conventional research.

Women and silence are of concern to feminist linguists such as Deborah Cameron. An ecofeminist-linguistic approach challenges anthropocentric, androcentric discourse that overlooks, dominates and, at times, erases the voices of the voiceless groups. The quest for women's voices in nature–culture offers new meanings. In this study, a folktale is identified as a narrative discourse that redefines cultural formations. Narrative discourse is a holistic form of expression with different levels of meaning that shapes and moulds individuals in an environment. Discourse analysis is an analysis of language in use. It is identified as a tool in building up a society by establishing a paradigm that links the environment and woman's voice to form the Mother Earth Discourse. It is also an instrument of the social construction of reality.

> The research contrasting women's and men's approaches to discourse suggests, in fact, that women may be especially well suited to producing significantly new meanings. Because this possibility depends on the development of a shared new outlook, it might be better promoted in the cooperative mode of discourse than in the competitive, where less attention is paid to the other.
> (Mcconnell-Ginet and Eckert 2003: 208)

This research is an attempt to identify new meanings that emerge from women's tales. This study reiterates the feminist standpoint that men and women have different perceptions, different perspectives and different expressions of understanding the environment.

Having defined the ecofeminist concepts relevant to this study, the researcher seeks to identify the sociolinguistic/feminist linguistic concerns. The twin themes of speech and silence are explored by the feminist linguist Deborah Cameron. She motivates the quest for women's voices in culture and society, where language becomes a feminist issue. As an extension of Cameron's argument, the present study explores an alternative quest for women's voices in 'nature-culture', where language becomes an ecofeminist concern. Through the analysis of folktales, the researcher wishes to offer an ecofeminist critique of language. 'Is language a feminist issue?' asks Deborah Cameron in her book *The Feminist Critique of Language*. She explains, '"Speech" and "silence" have been powerful metaphors in feminist discourse, used to figure all the ways in which women are denied the right or the opportunity to express themselves freely' (Cameron 1998: 3). Hence, it is important to ask the following questions: Is language an ecofeminist issue? What is the significance of woman's language of the environment? The framework has evolved from the integration of ecofeminist ideologies and sociolinguistic concerns. Sociolinguist William Labov proposed the model of narrative structure to analyse 'natural narrative' or 'personal experience narrative' at Martha's Vineyard, New York, in the 1960s. According to his paradigm, a narrative consists of six important components: abstract, orientation, complicating action, resolution, evaluation and coda. The

MOTHER EARTH DISCOURSE

Labovian model of narrative structure is an effective method of sociolinguistic understanding for the following reasons: first, it provides space for questioning. Second, it is a systematic approach to narrative. Hence, it becomes the root of the ecofeminist-linguistic framework as this research attempts to integrate ecofeminist thought with sociolinguistic inquiry, the thrust being woman's language of the environment.

How does the Labovian paradigm of narrative analysis become the starting point of the ecofeminist-linguistic framework? In the narrative analysis, 'Abstract' is a short introduction to the story. It states the main theme or the predominant motif in the story. 'Orientation' describes the setting, people (characters) and their environment. 'Complicating action' gives an account of the actual events happening in the narrative. 'Resolution' suggests the result or conclusion of the tale. 'Evaluation' refers to the aim of the narrator in communicating the particular story. 'Coda' is a way of stating the relevance of the story to the day-to-day life. The proposed framework emerges from the seeds of ecofeminism and sociolinguistics. The seeds of silence are believed to have words of consciousness that spread their roots into the ecofeminist quest and sociolinguistic quest. The ecofeminist quest motivates the understanding of woman–nature relationships and the sociolinguistic quest inspires the comprehension of woman–language connection. The plant that emanates from the interface branches out into motifs, relationships, concerns, worldviews, consciousness and expressions and flowers forth into the Mother Earth Discourse. As an integrated framework, the ecofeminist–linguistic interface provides a space to connect, interconnect and reconnect with the life-affirming narratives of the rural, the indigenous and the native people. Women who narrate tales incorporate nature in their cultural discourse to provide a new definition of reality. The Mother Earth Discourse brings into line the beliefs of people who have a holistic approach to life.

In the Labovian model, six pertinent questions are raised. They are: What was this about? (Abstract) Who or what are involved in the story, and when and where did it take place? (Orientation) Then, what happened? (Complicating Action) What finally happened? (Resolution) So what? (Evaluation) and How does it all end? (Coda) Ecofeminist-linguistic questioning is recognised as a method of revealing the power of the conscious mind. In order to facilitate the analysis of folktales from an ecofeminist-linguistic perspective, the researcher revisits the Labovian questions and reframes them as, what is the Mother Earth Motif found in the story? What type of Mother Earth Relationship do we find in the tale? What happens to Mother Earth and her children? What are the Mother Earth Worldviews of women and men in the story? How do the characters communicate Mother

Earth Consciousness in the folktale? How does the story motivate the listener or reader through the Mother Earth Lingua Franca?

The integration of ecofeminist theories with the sociolinguistic framework is represented in Table 1.1, which forms the basic analytical structure to analyse folktales from India. The table consists of four columns. Column I has information on the different narrative categories proposed by Labov. Column II provides space for narrative questions. Column III presents the narrative questions that are revisited and reframed to form ecofeminist-linguistic questions. Column IV demonstrates the various categories such as motifs, relationships, concerns, worldviews, consciousness and expressions that, together, form the Mother Earth Discourse.

Table 1.1 The integration of ecofeminism with Labovian discourse structure

(I) Narrative category	(II) Narrative question	(III) Ecofeminist–linguistic question	(IV) Mother Earth Discourse
Abstract	What was this about?	What is the Mother Earth Motif found in the story?	MOTIFS
Orientation	Who or what are involved in the story, and when and where did it take place?	What type of Mother Earth Relationship do we find in the tale?	RELATIONSHIPS
Complicating action	Then, what happened?	What happens to Mother Earth and her children?	CONCERNS
Resolution	What finally happened?	What are the Mother Earth Worldviews of women and men in the story?	WORLDVIEWS
Evaluation	So what?	How do the characters communicate Mother Earth Consciousness in the folktale?	CONSCIOUSNESS
Coda	How does it all end?	How does the story motivate the listener or reader through the Mother Earth Lingua Franca?	EXPRESSIONS/ LINGUA FRANCA

Source: Prepared by the author

Beehive cosmos: Mother Earth Discourse

The ecofeminist-linguistic framework facilitates us to explore woman–nature–language relationships in folktales from India. This section throws light on the formulation of the ecofeminist–linguistic interface and the development of the Mother Earth Discourse model. The six ecofeminist–linguistic questions correspond to six categories that contribute to the Mother Earth Discourse. In other words, this study aims to answer the ecofeminist–linguistic questions through motifs, relationships, concerns, worldviews, consciousness and consciousness-raising expressions/Lingua Franca.

It is visualised in the form of a beehive with hexagons that symbolise the different components of the Mother Earth Discourse. Figure 1.1 resembles

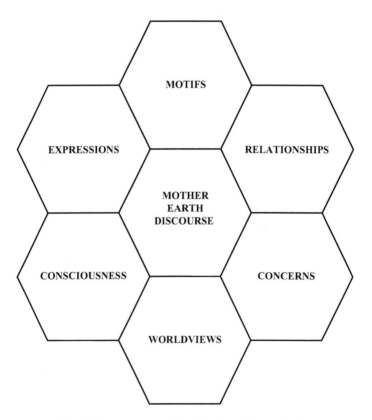

Figure 1.1 Mother Earth Discourse visualised by the author in the form of a beehive
Source: Prepared by the author

the cells of a honeycomb, which symbolises interconnectedness and collective strength. The ecofeminist–linguistic framework visualised in the form of a beehive is emulated in nature's likeness.

Why is the ecofeminist–linguistic paradigm represented in the form of a beehive? The ecofeminist belief in interconnectedness is symbolised by a beehive. In a beehive, bees work together to create the rich source of honey. They symbolise inspiration of both thought and action. Beehives promote organisation, indefatigable strength and intelligence. They represent a worldview of abundance. Bees work together to achieve one common goal through collective effort. Ecofeminism believes in the combined growth of all life forms. A beehive symbolises an integrated structure that promotes interdependence. It signifies positive energy and hope. Besides, a busy beehive offers hope and opportunities to positive minds and emphasises the power of a group. The Mother Earth Discourse, as a symbol of motivation, promises alternative thinking that aids sustainable development and gender equity. Ecofeminist philosophy is open to ideologies that respect, revere and care for living beings on this earth.

Bees in a honeycomb denote collective strength and can be understood as a perfect symbol of grassroots movements that believe in thought transformed into action, through consciousness-raising. In Greek mythology, Aphrodite, goddess of love, worshipped bees which create perfect hexagon cells in the honeycomb. Hence, she is also called Melissa (meaning the Queen Bee) and her priestesses 'melissae' or 'bees' (the worker bees are all females). The Mother Earth Discourse promotes the collective power of people who work for the well-being of nature. Besides, Western science confirms that bees are one of the more intelligent creations in the animal kingdom, which commune effectively through a dance form. 'When a worker bee finds a source of nectar and returns to the beehive, it can perform a complex dance routine to communicate to the other bees the location of this nectar' (Yule 2014: 9). Bees harmlessly gather honey, contributing to the harmony of the planet. Mother Nature has a particular order and a set of organising principles. In the beehive model of narrative analysis, the first question raised is: what is the Mother Earth Motif found in the story? In order to answer this question, themes, metaphors, patterns, images and symbols are identified in folktales from India. Motifs are a unique feature in women's art forms. Women's thought processes are characterised by multiplicity and diversity, as identified in their rangoli, embroidery and quilting. Mother Earth Motifs derive inspiration from *kolam* in the Tamil culture, *kalam* in the Kerala tradition and rangoli in the northern parts of India and are represented in the form of flowers. The floral patterns also draw attention to the understanding of women's expressions in the domestic space which are otherwise considered as mere rituals.

Mother Earth Motifs

The twelve types of Mother Earth Motifs are: 'The Creator and the Created' – *Isis Panthea, Amma-I-Appan*; Silence and Speech – *Her-Meta, Athena's Wit*; 'Food, Household and Sisterhood' – *Annamangai* and *Sis-Tie*; 'Trees and Forest' – *Woody-Woman, Vana-Devi*; 'Land and Water' – *Tellus-Ma, Aqua-Stree*; and 'Birds and Animals' – *Aves-Eve, Fauna-Fem*.

Isis Panthea literally means 'Isis the Supreme Goddess' who symbolises motherhood, fertility and nature. She is the first daughter of Geb, god of the Earth and Nut, the goddess of the omnipresent sky. Stories that deal with the formation of the earth and the creation of the first human beings are categorised under *Isis Panthea* themes. The **Amma-I-Appan** motif celebrates the complementary nature of masculine and feminine principles. In Tamil, *Amma* is mother and *Appa* is father. The tales that recognise the intrinsic value of life beyond the gender differences are classified as tales with *Amma-i-Appan* motifs. **Her-Meta** is a motif identified in the ecofeminist-linguistic framework that explores women's silences and expressions. It deals with tales about women's storytelling tradition. *Her-Meta* story is a woman's story about a story. Another collection of folktales belongs to the category called **Athena's Wit**. Athena is the Greek goddess of wisdom, inspiration, courage and skill. *Athena's Wit* motifs underscore the power of woman's speech, wit and humour. The tales about women and food are classified as **Annamangai** tales. *Annam* means 'food' and *Mangai* means 'woman' in Tamil. These motifs help one to view the problematic connection between woman and food beyond the nature–nurture proposition. Folktales that bring to light the realistic picture of women involved in cooking amidst the environmental problems are also identified in this section. The **Sis-Tie** motif refers to the depiction of sisters, sisterhood and bonding in folktales from India. *Sis-Tie* tales also highlight the concerns of beauty and health of women that are associated with the spirit of sisterhood and consciousness-raising.

The oral tales that explicate tree–woman relationships are termed as **Woody-Woman** tales. These narratives highlight the proximity between the 'woods' (trees) and women. The collective strength of trees and women are emphasised by these stories. **Vana-Devi** means goddess of the forest. Unlike the European fairy tales such as *Hansel and Gretel* that depict the forests as homes of witches, Indian folktales have tree goddesses living in the forests. **Tellus-Ma** tales are stories associated with the earth, soil and land. *Tellus* is the goddess Earth and *Ma* signifies mother. Soil sustains life. Indigenous people revere the soil, the land as the soul of Mother Earth. The folktales that illustrate water–woman association are identified in **Aqua-Stree** stories. The word 'aqua' refers to water. *Stree* is a term that denotes 'woman' in India. The interconnectedness of water and woman is highlighted by *Aqua-Stree* tales. The bird–woman bonding is reiterated in tales that are termed as **Aves-Eve**. Birds are also called 'aves'. 'Eve' is another word for 'woman', which also denotes the first woman on earth, according to the Bible. The interdependence of birds and women is exemplified in *Aves-Eve* narratives. The folktales that represent animal–woman motifs are called **Fauna-Fem** narratives. Fauna refers to the world of animals. The root word 'fem' from female, feminine and feminist corresponds to woman. In order to understand the intrinsic value of life, animal–woman relationships are studied as *Fauna-Fem* tales.

Mother Earth Relationships

The second question raised in the ecofeminist-linguistic analysis of a folktale is: what type of Mother Earth Relationships do we find in the tale? Mother Earth Relationships are characterised by: spirituality, where human beings and other living beings are acknowledged as the children of Mother Earth; proximity of women and nature to bring about harmony; sensitivity of women towards nature to unravel the mysteries of earth; productivity of earth-centred practices that contribute to nature-culture; simplicity of life that arises from the intimacy of human–nature relationships; and practicality of women reflected in their responsible conscious, purposeful living. Like the leaves of a plant, Mother Earth Relationships are organically connected to one another and provide nourishment to all living beings in the environment.

The indigenous people's belief in the sacredness of life contributes to the understanding of Mother Earth 'spirituality'. The ecofeminist belief in earth-based spirituality throws light on the communication process between nature and human beings. The union of the sacred with nature and culture constitutes ecofeminist spirituality. Women worship the nature goddesses and derive power from them. Women understand life as sacred through the power of procreation. Women who live close to nature recognise consciousness in plants, trees, birds and animals through this unique maternal quality characterised by the recognition of earth-based spirituality. Spirituality is the unique relationship between the human and the divine. Ecofeminist spirituality interweaves the spirituality of the human with the spirituality of nature and the divine. The closeness of the woman–nature association suggests that woman power influences nature power and nature power influences woman power. In Western culture and philosophy, binary opposition is a system that identifies two theoretical opposites, set off against one another. Culture is set against nature, man against woman, day against night, black against white, body against mind, civilisation against savagery. Eastern philosophies advocate holism, dissolve dichotomy and identify the opposite theories as complementary principles to reinforce woman–nature 'proximity'. Woman–nature proximity does not stop with essentialism. Rather, it sanctions women to explore their inherent worth in relation to the intrinsic value of nature and people around them.

Woman–nature proximity is an affirming principle in the consciousness of indigenous people across the world. Rural woman's innate understanding of her environment and eco-sensitivity is reinforced by the folktales. Woman's ecological awareness and 'sensitivity' are part of her consciousness. Her eco-sensitivity and eco-consciousness emerge out of the need to fulfil her responsibilities in day-to-day life. She understands the needs of fellow human beings on the one hand, and the needs of nonhuman living organisms on the other hand. Sensitivity towards nature helps women to be genuine and honest towards their environment and fellow living beings in that environment. The word 'productivity' is related to the sustainable growth of all living beings on this planet. The texts chosen for analysis, including the case studies, offer scope to understand the degraded state of the environment in a patriarchal consumerist society and the attempts taken by women to 'healing all our relations' (Plant 1989: 49). Women in the folktales do not see the world as inanimate. They communicate with all the living organisms around them, be it a bird, a tree or a snake. Women share the spirit of sisterhood with other forms of life on this earth.

'Simplicity' is a rare blessing in this modern era, yet an important asset of ecofeminist thought. To be simple in thoughts, words and deeds requires enormous strength on the part of the individual in this extremely modernised, globalised world. The indigenous women's relationship with the natural environment provides a simple way of life that contributes to subsistence perspective and sustainable development. Maria Mies discusses the importance of 'voluntary simplicity' (Mies and Shiva 2010: 253), promotes self-sufficiency, interrogates consumerist culture and encourages an eco-friendly lifestyle. Simplification as against modernisation paves way to peaceful coexistence. 'Practicality' is a fundamental principle of ecofeminism. Women are practical in identifying the environmental issues immediately. Ecofeminist thinkers believe in transforming thought into action, theory into practice. The ecofeminist belief in praxis, i.e. blending of theory and practice, contributes to the movement–theory–experience–pedagogy paradigm. In the ancient times, women were specialists in food gathering, childcare, cooking, pottery, weaving, construction of temporary or permanent shelters, tool-making and knew medicinal application of plants and herbs. This contributes to ecofeminist practicality.

Mother Earth Concerns

In the ecofeminist-linguistic framework, the third question, 'what happens to Mother Earth and her children?' attempts to find answers through the ecofeminist issues and concerns in the folktales. They throw light on Mother Earth Concerns in the indigenous stories. Mother Earth Concerns is comprehended in terms of the needs–rights relationship of nature and women. Based on Abraham Maslow's theory of self-actualisation, the five different types of needs are identified. They are physiological needs, safety needs, need for belonging, self-esteem needs and need for self-actualisation. Abraham Maslow, in his theory of self-actualisation, proposed that human needs exist in the form of an 'ascending hierarchy'. They are basic physiological needs – food, sleep, protection from extreme hazards of the environment; the needs for safety and security needs; the third need, to belong and to love; the need for self-esteem for both self-respect and esteem from other people and the fifth and highest need, the need for self-actualisation, or the desire to become everything that one can become (Marshall 1998: 590).

Mother Earth Concerns are related to the fundamental needs of human beings and nonhuman living beings. According to Max-Neef, there are different types of fundamental human needs. They are 'subsistence (for example, health, food, shelter, clothing); affection (self-esteem, love, care, solidarity and so on); understanding (among others: study, learning, analysis); participation (responsibilities, sharing of rights and duties); leisure/idleness (curiosity, imagination, work); identity (sense of belonging, differentiation, self-esteem and so on); freedom (autonomy, self-esteem, self-determination, equality)' (Mies, Bennholdt-Thomsen and von Werlhof 1988: 255). The realisation of women's needs–rights relationship provides an insight into ecofeminist issues. However, the Inherent Rights of Mother Earth, according to the Declaration of Rights of Mother Earth, are:

> (1) Mother Earth and all beings of which she is composed have the following inherent rights: (a) the right to life and to exist; (b) the right to be respected; (c) the right to regenerate its biocapacity and to continue its vital cycles and processes free from human disruptions; (d) the right to maintain its identity and integrity as a distinct, self-regulating and interrelated being; (e) the right to water as a source of life; (f) the right to clean air; (g) the right to integral health; (h) the right to be free from contamination, pollution and toxic or radioactive waste; (i) the right to not have its genetic structure modified or disrupted in a manner that threatens it integrity or vital and healthy functioning; (j) the right to full and prompt restoration for violation of the rights recognized in

this Declaration caused by human activities; (2) Each being has the right to a place and to play its role in Mother Earth for her harmonious functioning. (3) Every being has the right to wellbeing and to live free from torture or cruel treatment by human beings. (http://therightsofnature.org/universal-declaration/)

The understanding of the different kinds of needs and rights helps one to identify the ecofeminist concerns in society and culture. Many women in our society – rich or poor, urban or rural – are always chained to the destiny of fulfilling basic needs. They take care of their family, and at times, an entire community. Quite ironically, the same basic needs, such as food, shelter, safety, security, love and concern, are denied to women. Hence, in this connection, at the sociological level, Maslow's hierarchy of needs is integrated with ecofeminist thought to study the issues of women, children, nature and marginalised men.

The eco-critical theory of *oikos* is also used to identify Mother Earth Concerns in folktales from India. The Greek word 'oikos' means home, which also refers to planet earth or *Bhoomi*. As an eco-critical theory, Dr Nirmal Selvamony's theory of *oikos* is used in the analysis of folktales from India. According to him, there are three types of *oikos*: integrated, hierarchic and anarchic. In the integrated *oikos*, nature, culture and the sacred remain united with the human beings. The primitive societies are said to follow and experience this type of *oikos*. Human beings respect and revere the ancestral spirits and the elements in nature. The power relations are governed by both love and authority. The hierarchic and the anarchic *oikos* are characterised by domination and power relations and there is no unity between nature, culture and the sacred (Selvamony and Alex 2007). Dr Nirmal Selvamony's *oikos* theory provides an insight into the different kinds of environments in which we live. In this research, attempts have been made to integrate the *oikos* theory with feminism, which results in 'oikofeminist' approach to folktales from India, where the *oikos* of the silenced and the oppressed women and nature are considered for study. The folktales abound in the sacred–nature–culture relationship that indicates the integrative *oikos*. However, an oikofeminist reading of the stories reveals that women and nature suffer a great deal in the hierarchic and anarchic *oikos*.

Once every twelve years in spring this wondrous hill region, bewitchingly beautiful like a nubile maiden, stands resplendent in blue, shyly averting her eyes from her beloved, the sky. As far as the eye can see, everything is blue. The buzzing of bees eager to suck honey from the *kurinji* flower can be heard from every side.

MOTHER EARTH DISCOURSE

The gurgling waterfalls create their own music. The sky seems to descend every twelve years to embrace this beloved mountain damsel, who has been waiting for him since the beginning of time. The blue of the sky is reflected in the new buds that cover the joyous maiden. Mother Nature too awaits the bridegroom having spent twelve years weaving a garment of blue flowers for her dear daughter. The rising sun smiles warmly at the maiden with the tantalizing smile, who stands half veiled by clouds, as if to say, 'You foolish creature, I am your lover, not the sky. I give life to the sky. Look at me!'

(Krishnan 2002: 59)

The passage from *When the Kurinji Blooms* by Rajam Krishnan exemplifies an integrative *oikos* with the union of nature, culture and sacred. The novel in the end also gives an account of the anarchic *oikos* when the consumerist minds take over the land from tribal people and set up tea plantations. The ecofeminist concerns deal with the issues and problems that the marginalised and the oppressed people face on this planet. Women who live in the rural areas and slums in the cities bear the brunt of industrial growth, environmental degradation and ecological disasters.

Mother Earth Worldviews

The fourth question in the ecofeminist-linguistic framework is: what are Mother Earth Worldviews of women and men in the story? This stage of Mother Earth Discourse serves as a phase of transition from analysis to synthesis. The Sapir–Whorf hypothesis emphasises the relationship between the language of the speaker and her/his view of the world. Wardhaugh confirms language 'determines how speakers perceive and organize the world around them, both the natural world and the social world . . . the language you speak helps to form your world-view' (Wardhaugh 1992: 221). In this section of the narrative analysis, Labov asks the question, 'So what?' And the researcher attempts to rephrase the question, 'So, what is the worldview of the people in the story?' Worldview is defined as 'System of ideas of the objective world and a person's attitude towards surrounding reality and to himself, and also corresponding points of view shared by people, their convictions, ideals, principles of cognition and activity and value orientations' (Wardhaugh 1992: 370).

The predominant worldviews identified in the folktales are care for Mother Earth, concern for a holistic outlook, respect for inherent worth, appreciation of nature's abundance, acknowledgement of interdependence, emphasis on circular principles, recognition of nature's power, affirmation of woman power, assertion of pluralism and belief in synergising knowledge. Life on earth is viewed as a subject in the integrated web of life, which calls for the realisation of their inherent worth. The celebration of the intrinsic value of life results in the appreciation of nature's abundance and acknowledgement of interdependence. The interdependence of life on this earth reinforces the circular principles in the universe. The cyclical patterns in nature reiterate nature's power as woman power and vice versa. The multifarious hues in the canvas of nature promote pluralism and belief in synergising the indigenous wisdom from culture across the planet.

Caring and nurture are the fundamental qualities of a woman's feminine self. However, a strategic form of ecofeminist thought emphasises the need to be aware of exploitation of women in the name of nature–nurture proposition. And in this way, ecofeminism seeks to counter essentialism. Human beings living close to nature understand the interconnectedness of life. Sangam poetry communicates the holistic worldview of Tamil people. The *Purananuru* song by Kaniyan Punkunran, for instance, exemplifies the ancient belief in the cyclical nature of life.

> Every town our home town
> every man a kinsman.
> Good and evil do not come
> from others.
> (Hart 2002: 122)

These lines signify the worldview of Tamil people during the Sangam period. The people of Tamilnadu believe that all human beings are their relatives. Even today, they are renowned for hospitality characterised by warmth and generosity. The *Tirukkural* (*Kural*) elucidates this worldview of the Tamils in great detail. However, it would be more appropriate to use the word 'humans', 'persons' or 'relatives' instead of the sexist term 'man'. In the folktales from India, the narrators and the narrated communicate care and concern for earth as a living being. They are sensitive to their natural environment. They are kind towards plants, birds and animals. On the contrary, there are certain characters insensitive to the needs of their fellow human beings and their environment. The word 'care' is central to ecofeminist thought. It implies care for one's self and his/her environment around. The Greek word 'holos' in *holism* means wholeness or totality, in contrast to reductionism. The former looks at the whole, which is made up of minor units, whereas the latter observes the importance of understanding the smaller units. In the Mother Earth Discourse, holism is understood in terms of society, language, women and environment. When they are intertwined to form a meaningful whole, they constitute an alternative form of learning in the form of holistic pedagogy. The folktales represent the holistic worldview of women and men living close to nature. A plant, a bird, an insect or a pebble exist in this universe with an *intrinsic value* of its own. A deep ecological understanding of life, combined with ecofeminist ideology, suggests that a woman, a man or a child can have their inherent worth in them, independent of any hierarchical systems. Indigenous people believe that there is a spiritual element in all living creatures.

> Honor the sacred.
> Honor the Earth, our Mother.
> Honor the Elders.
> Honor all with whom we share the Earth:-
> Four-leggeds, two-leggeds, winged ones,
> Swimmers, crawlers, plant and rock people.
> Walk in balance and beauty.
> (https://educationforjustice.org)

According to these indigenous people, a tree, an animal or a river exists not for the sake of human beings, but because of its innate value as a part of Mother Earth. Though folktales tend to be anthropomorphic, on closer reading, some of these oral tales try to capture the consciousness of nonhuman living organisms and speak for the well-being of the natural environment. The respect for the *inherent worth* of nature is apparent in the writings of environmental movement poets. For example, a poet of the Chipko Movement, Ghanshyam 'Shailani', wrote a song in which human beings in rural areas respect Mother Earth as a living being. 'A fight for truth has begun / At Sinsyaru Khala / A fight for rights has begun / In Malkot Thano / Sister, it is a fight to protect / our mountains and forests / They give us life / Embrace the life of the living trees / And streams to your hearts / Resist the digging of mountains / Which kill our forests and streams / A fight for life has begun at Sinsyaru Khala' (Gottlieb 2004: 467). The song communicates collective conscientisation through the use of words 'our' and 'us', signifying group identity. The word 'sister' conveys the theme of sisterhood in the feminist context that yields strength to the critical consciousness of women as a group who find it a 'problem-formulating method' (Mies and Shiva 2010: 42). The song highlights the importance of attaining sustainable growth. Sustainable development is a form of augmentation that fulfils the basic needs of the present generation without compromising the needs of the future generations. The Chipko song emphasises sustainable development and voices out concerns against the exploitation of nature. Chipko songs exemplify the language of *Ahimsa* or nonviolence. They also reiterate woman power derived from nature. The life-affirming values of the tribal people and the destructive mentality of the materialists are juxtaposed in the Chipko songs.

In the Mother Earth Discourse, words that indicate *interconnectedness* are a significant feature. The holistic view of life is characterised by 'interdependence' among living creatures. 'Cohesion' signifies the intricate relationship among living beings in the 'web' of life. Web symbolises the common destiny of all living and nonliving creatures. 'Holistic' is a common term used by eco-critics, deep ecologists and ecofeminists who believe in the completeness of being. The word 'organic' also suggests wholeness.

> Many people have been asking, 'What is the connection between democracy, the environment and peace?' Those people are used to thinking of these three themes separately. If they are talking development, they only talk about development. If they are talking about peace, they talk only of peace and they don't talk about development. If they are talking about development they only talk about development and they don't talk about the environment or even about democracy! But many of us, when we are out there in the field, do recognise that when you are trying to do this work to really have a long lasting impact you need to have a holistic approach.
> (Maathai 2004)

The above passage is taken from Wangari Maathai's Nobel Prize Acceptance Speech, where she explains that the relationship between democracy, environment and peace lay concurrent in her act of planting trees. In this way, she tried to emphasise a holistic approach to development. In the folktales from India, the woman or the male protagonist always exhibits the sense of *interdependence* with a nonhuman living being. Hence, folktales speak for the interconnectedness of life on this earth. The Declaration of interdependence confirms the reciprocal relationships and peaceful coexistence of birds, animals, plants, land, water and human beings on this Earth:

> We, the people of planet Earth,
> In recognition of the interconnectedness of all life
> And the importance of the balance of nature,
> Hereby acknowledge our interdependence
> And affirm our dedication
> To life-serving environmental stewardship,
> The fulfillment of universal human needs worldwide,
> Economic and social well-being,
> And a culture of peace and nonviolence,

To insure a sustainable and harmonious world
For present and future generations.
(http://www.wetheworld.org/
declaration.htm)

The spirit of interconnectedness and interdependence is found in different tribal cultures across the planet. In Hinduism, it is called *Vasudhaiva Kutumbakam* (meaning *Vasudha* – Earth, *Kudumbam* – family). This notion awakens a common consciousness of the inhabitants of Mother Earth.

A circle is symbolic of the *cyclical pattern* of life. A circle symbolises the spherical shape of the earth. A circle denotes a holistic approach to life. A circle emphasises interconnectedness and interdependence. A circle indicates pattern of six seasons believed by the Tamil people. They are *muthu-venil* (summer), *kar-kalam* (rainy season), *kutir* (autumn), *mun-pani* (early winter), *pin-pani* (late winter) and *ila-venil* (spring). On the other side of the world, the Native American Lakota Sioux prayer *Mita Kuye Oyasin*, which means 'all my relations', emphasises not just the universal sisterhood/brotherhood among human beings, but also among plants, animals, rocks and mountains. 'All my relations. I honor you in this circle of life with me today. You are all my relations, my relatives, without whom I would not live. We are in the circle of life together, co-existing, co-dependent, co-creating our destiny... One, not more important than the other... All of us a part of the Great Mystery' (http://nhpeacenik.livejournal.com/).

Pluralism denotes diversity in beliefs, convictions and thought processes among human beings. Worldviews of adivasis are pluralistic in terms of religion, society, culture and occupation. For example, the indigenous knowledge of women farmers are definitely pluralistic with rich ideas contributing to biodiversity. This variety is captured in fine detail in folktales from India. The pluralistic dimension challenges binary opposition and the hierarchical structures and promotes multiple viewpoints, synergy decisions, thereby enhancing the collective strength of people. The term 'synergy' emerges from the Greek word *syn-ergos*, meaning 'working together'. The Chipko women and the women of the Narmada Bachao Andolan believe in synergy of thought and action. The Mother Earth Discourse enables earth-centred knowledge systems that help one to reconnect with culture and tradition to bring about transformation.

One of the most important worldviews of people who live close to nature is *Hope and Goodwill*. Modern literature centred on urban locales and highly civilised societies often represents disillusionment and depression. The main reason for this cynicism is the undue importance given to individualism. In contrast, the indigenous people believe in collective strength and spirit of interconnectedness. In moments of trouble, they gain strength from their environment and the people around them. Natural phenomena, such as the sunrise, seasonal changes, rainfall and the song of the birds, signify unprecedented optimism in their minds and hearts. It contributes to the well-being of nature and human beings on this planet. Human beings who live in close association with nature acknowledge the fact that *small is beautiful* and less is more. Indigenous people respect the intrinsic value of an ant, a spider or a honeybee. They value the tiny flowers on earth and the stars in the sky. They are contented with what life has to offer every moment. Ilam Peruvaluti's song 182 of *Purananuru* goes thus:

> This world lives
> because
> Some human beings
> do not eat alone,
> not even when they get
> the sweet ambrosia of the gods;
>
> they've no anger in them,
> they fear evils other men fear
> but never sleep over them;
>
> give their lives for honor,
> will not touch a gift of whole worlds
> if tainted;
>
> there's no faintness in their hearts
> and they do not strive
> for themselves.
>
> Because such human beings are,
> this world is.
>
> (Hart 2002: 117)

The worldview of women is the worldview of abundance. Vandana Shiva describes 'the worldview of women in India who leave food for ants on their doorstep, even as they create the most beautiful art in *kolams*, *mandalas*, and rangoli with rice flour. Abundance is the worldview of peasant women who weave beautiful designs of paddy to hang up for birds when the birds do not find grain in the fields' (Shiva 2000: 16–17).

Mother Earth Consciousness

How do the characters communicate Mother Earth Consciousness in the folktale? What are the predominant features of Mother Earth Consciousness found in the folktales from India? Consciousness is being aware, being awake and a diligent understanding of the self and the environment around. This research identifies three types of consciousness in folktales from India. They are *Shakthi Consciousness, Ahimsa Consciousness* and *Shanthi Consciousness*.

In essence, *Shakthi Consciousness* reiterates feminine power as opposed to feminist power. *Shakthi* is an embodiment of feminine energy, fertility and creativity. *Shakthi* is also known as *Prakriti*, the cosmic primordial energy that pervades the universe. Mother is represented and worshipped as a goddess in various indigenous tribes and cultures. She is worshipped as Aditi, the goddess of abundance and 'primordial vastness, the inexhaustible' (Shiva 2010: 39). She is Demeter, the Greek goddess of harvest; Cybele, the Phyrgian concept of Mountain Mother. She is Durga, the Indian goddess with ten arms, an embodiment of *Shakthi* with a contemplative smile. *Gaia* is the Greek term for Mother Nature; Ceres is the goddess of agriculture, crops and fertility. Panchamama is the equivalent of Mother Earth, worshipped by the indigenous people of the Andes. The word *Mata* or *Amma* signifies both the universal Mother and the earthly mother. The goddess worship in indigenous cultures across the world promote *Shakthi Consciousness*. In South India, the *Shakthi* goddesses are called *Amma*, e.g. *Mariamma* (goddess of rain). *Prakriti*, the feminine principle, is said to spread through the entire universe, blessing the tiny pebbles and grass. Thus, *Shakthi Consciousness* is identified as the inherent power of every living organism. In the postmodern era, an ecofeminist reading of the *Kural 56 Chapter 6*,

> *Tharkaaththuth Tharkontaan Penith Thakaichaantra*
> *Sorkaaththuch Chorvilaal Pen* (Thiruvalluvar)

reveals that a woman has the *Shakthi* to take care of herself, her husband, along with the people around, her environment, which includes other living and nonliving organisms and has the capability to find ways to express herself in times of need with an indefatigable spirit in her. Tamil poet Bharathiyar invokes the supreme power or energy as *Parasakthi*.

> We sing the glory of Parasakti.
> How did she originate?
> We just don't know that.
> She is our great mother, autogenetic,
> Born of the Supreme Being, 'the Self'.
> Whence did she appear?
> How did she appear from the Supreme Being called 'Self',
> That we don't know.
>
> (Sebastian 1995)

Shakthi Consciousness denotes the universal power that empowers each and every living being on this earth; there is a connection between the power of the cosmos and the power of living beings within the cosmos.

Ahimsa Consciousness is the consciousness of living beings who respect and care for other beings living around them. *Ahimsa* literally means avoidance of violence. Nature is also said to have *Ahimsa* principles inherent in it. A wild beast in the jungle attacks the prey only when it is hungry; otherwise, it remains calm. It does not store food in tins and cans for future use. *Ahimsa* is the principle of nature and philosophy of Mother Earth. People who live close to nature practice *Ahimsa* in their day-to-day life. *Ahimsa Consciousness* of a person is reflected in her/his thoughts, words, deeds and way of life. Ecofeminist activisms such as the Chipko Movement and Narmada Bachao Andolan uphold *Ahimsa* as a powerful instrument of protest. Environmental movements across the world assert that *Ahimsa* or nonviolence is the necessary tool for liberation. This underscores the fact that *Ahimsa* is not just the characteristic of people who work for the well-being of nature, but the essence of Mother Earth and *Prakriti*.

Alice Walker believes that all creation living on this earth belongs to one family. She also believes in worshipping Mother Earth as God, as She protects, nurtures and provides autonomy to be what we are. Walker explains, 'Mother Earth is such a good choice . . . Mother Earth will do all that She can to support our choices . . . For they are of Her, and inherent in our creation is Her trust' (Walker 2005: 31). As a victim of slavery, violence and exploitation, Alice Walker had led a painful life. However, her belief in nonviolence is a comforting revelation to people who live in a world of suffering and indifference. In an *Ahimsa* way of life, human beings tend to understand the personal space of their neighbours in their environment. Hence, the principle of *Ahimsa* is central to ecofeminist philosophy. In her poem on nonviolence, she affirms:

> When they torture your mother
> plant a tree
> When they torture your father
> plant a tree
> When they torture your brother
> and your sister
> plant a tree
> When they assassinate
> your leaders
> and lovers
> plant a tree
> When they torture you

too bad
to talk
plant a tree.
When they begin to torture
the trees
and cut down the forest
they have made,
start another.

(Walker 2005: 112)

Alice Walker's poem juxtaposes the worldviews of destruction of the dominant systems and the worldviews of creation of people living close to nature. This poem provides a glimpse not only of violence that exists in the battlefields, but also of the violence that exists in the minds of people.

Subtle forms of violence in the day-to-day life, such as consumerist culture and accumulative lifestyle, encourage *himsa* behaviour, according to thinkers such as Usha Jesudasan, a spokesperson of the *Ahimsa* way of life. In her article titled 'About Respecting Personal Spaces', she explicates the idea of how people's personal space is sacred and the intrusion into that personal space is violence. What is the relationship between *Ahimsa* and *Shanthi* or peace? According to Usha Jesudasan, the *Ahimsa* way of life can be realised by using words of peace, by building a bond and having a dialogue. She writes, 'The ahimsa way of life embraces simple living – is nonaccumulative life; when we avoid accumulating things, possessive relationships and try to live in harmony and fairness with everything and everyone around us' (Jesudasan 2008). Simple living is closely associated with the belief in *Ahimsa* ideology. *Ahimsa* as the quintessence of nature is highlighted by indigenous women in India. As Maria Mies and Vandana Shiva in their book *Ecofeminism* explain,

> For Third World women . . . the divorce of the spiritual from the material is incomprehensible for them, the term Mother Earth does not need to be qualified by inverted commas, because they regard the earth as a living being which guarantees their own and all their fellow creatures' survival. They respect and celebrate Earth's sacredness.
>
> (Mies and Shiva 2010: 19)

The concept of *Ahimsa* and the practice of *Satyagraha* bestow courage on women, children and men to campaign against the cutting down of trees. The dynamism of nature offers a prototype to the women who combat injustice done to nature and environment. Mahatma Gandhi's belief in

Ahimsa has been an inspiration to the Chipko Movement from the early 1970s. His words, 'the earth has enough to sustain everyone's need. But it has got too little to satisfy everyone's greed' (Sharma 2009: 114), motivated the Chipko activists to fight against deforestation. The concept of *Shakthi* has a direct bearing on the lives of simple women who strive hard to protect their environment. It is perceived as a dynamic force that guides their minds and motivates their spirits in achieving what they want to achieve. Hence, this research is an attempt to identify *Shakthi* as a universal force that guides not only women, but the whole of humankind to lead a better life, characterised by nonviolence and peace.

Shanthi Consciousness is the power of the conscious mind, especially of human beings who strive to maintain harmony and peace in their environment. T. S. Eliot's *The Wasteland*, published in 1922, ends with the famous line 'Shantih, shantih, shantih', which not only communicates world peace, but peace within each individual. It is distinguished by a life of contentment, magnanimity and satisfaction as against selfishness and greed. *Shanthi Consciousness* promotes peace within and peace without. Mother Earth has been considered a symbol of peace right from the ancient times. However, the globalised world that exists today represents a place of turmoil, disorder and chaos. Being conscious of the ecological crisis and undertaking steps to change the situation is a positive sign for the well-being of the future generations. *Shanthi Consciousness* begins with the individual. But it gains power with the synergy of fellow beings who are ready to share the consciousness of peace with the environment.

Ecofeminist thinkers painstakingly incorporate the language of contentment in their works. Ecofeminism expounds an alternative view of life that challenges the greed of the consumerist society. People who live close to nature fetch food only for survival and do not store anything for future use and exemplify a life of contentment and gratitude. They uphold the feminine quality of gratification that assists women to care for their environment. The principle of nonviolence or *Ahimsa* encourages a simple harmonious way of life. People who live close to nature believe that contentment motivates *Shanthi* or peace. Alice Walker emphasises the importance of gratification in her poem 'Expect nothing. Live frugally on surprise'. The poem underscores the importance of leading a simple and contented life. However, on the contrary, there are circumstances where the tribal people do not even get their basic needs fulfilled.

In Mother Earth Discourse, the connecting factor between motifs, relationships, concerns and worldviews is undermined by the consciousness of people who live close to nature. Through the proposed model, the researcher identifies three important dimensions of Mother Earth consciousness, which are *Shakthi*, *Ahimsa* and *Shanthi*, as represented in folktales from India. This research studies folktales and the importance of the relationship between the unconscious, the subconscious, the conscious mind of the individual and the collective conscious of groups. If consciousness can shape or reshape the world, it is necessary to be aware of things happening around us, by being conscious of the environmental needs. It is the responsibility of each and every individual to adopt environmental values that would help *Gaia* to lead a healthy life. Ecofeminist thought is integrated with the ancient wisdom of Indian philosophy, as reflected in the folk literature. And this has given birth to the identification of the three significant concepts – *Shakthi*, *Ahimsa* and *Shanthi*.

Mother Earth Lingua Franca

How does the story motivate the listener or reader through Mother Earth Lingua Franca? Re-reading folktales from the ecofeminist-linguistic perspective motivates a process of consciousness-raising. Psychologist Velmans defines 'consciousness' in this way. 'Anything that we are aware of at a given moment forms part of our consciousness, making conscious experience at once the most familiar and most mysterious aspect of our lives' (Velmans 2009: 3). The relationship between science and spirituality is underscored by the awareness and raising of consciousness. According to Lynne McTaggart, the cutting edge in research concentrates on the 'nature of human consciousness', which has rewritten the significance of 'scientific certainty that consciousness may be central in shaping our world' (McTaggart 2009).

Consciousness-raising is the final stage of the ecofeminist-linguistic framework. At this point in time, it is necessary to ask the question, how does the story motivate the listener or reader to understand Mother Earth *conscientizacao* for attaining gender equity and sustainable development? It is definitely a mammoth task to realise a world of gender balance and ecofriendly society. Yet, a conscious beginning, a collective goal, constructive planning and a positive vision are sure to transform society. Bell Hooks describes the dynamics of consciousness-raising among women. 'Women came together in small groups to share personal experiences, problems and feelings. From this public sharing comes the realization that what was thought to be individual is in fact common: that what was thought to be a personal problem has a social cause and a political solution' (Hooks 2000: 48). In this way, women learnt to develop self-esteem and self-worth and to realise the value of collective strength.

Mother Earth consciousness-raising is considered as a dynamic process that interlinks motifs, relationships, concerns, worldviews and consciousness. It is identified as ecofeminist praxis, to study the connections between prevalent theories and existing practices. Hence, the Mother Earth Discourse is perceived as a pedagogical tool for consciousness-raising, not only among women, but also among the oppressed, the silenced and the marginalised groups. Like the wings of a bird, Mother Earth Lingua Franca as *Terra Mater Lexis* and *Bhoomi Register* provides hope to life and a promise to the planet. Ecofeminist terms, phrases and syntax are studied using the discourse of ecofeminist writers and case studies gathered using fieldwork. The ecofeminist-linguistic framework provides an opportunity to classify the sociolinguistic elements, which might be termed *Terra Mater Lexis* and *Bhoomi Register*.

Terra Mater Lexis

The identification and understanding of the indigenous words, phrases and expressions will pave an alternative way of looking at the world. *Terra Mater Lexis* in ecofeminist thought can be defined as the use of vocabulary that motivates care for Mother Earth and realisation of the interdependence of life. For example, in the Mother Earth Discourse, words that indicate interconnectedness are a significant feature. The holistic view of life is characterised by terms such as 'interdependence' and 'interrelatedness' among living creatures. 'Cohesion' signifies the intricate relationships between living beings in the web of life. The web symbolises the common destiny of all living and nonliving creatures. 'Holistic' is a common term used by eco-critics, deep ecologists and ecofeminists who believe in the completeness of being. The word 'organic' also suggests wholeness. People who think and act 'ecofeminist' make use of words with prefix 're-,' which is identified as a characteristic of the Mother Earth Discourse. The word 'reproduction' denotes creation in the ecofeminist context in different ways. Nature produces and reproduces; so do women. 'Regeneration' suggests revival of nature, culture, society and spirituality. *Reweaving the World* by Gloria Feman Orenstein metaphorically states the role of women in connecting the broken threads of existence, characterised by chaos and confusion. The unravelling of the knots and the rebuilding of a new world is one of the goals of ecofeminist praxis. Cassandra Kircher believes in 'rethinking dichotomies' (Gaard and Murphy 1998: 159) in the Western philosophy. An ecofeminist approach to literary texts calls for 'revisiting' and 're-reading', which explicate the unread, the unexpressed and the undiscovered. 'Revisiting' one's culture and tradition also promises richness and abundance for the future generations. 'Rebuilding' or 'restoring' the sociocultural structures that have been demolished by androcentric, anthropomorphic norms are necessary to bring back the wealth of the planet. 'Re-visioning' a new world based on equality, simplicity, care and concern is necessary to restore the security of all living creatures on this earth. 'Re' signifies hope for the future generations. The recognition of the linguistic features which the researcher chooses to name *Terra Mater Lexis* grants an answer to the question, 'how is Mother Earth Discourse presented?' The naming of women in folktales from India, for instance, is a case in point.

Bhoomi Register

By exploring the language of women who are involved in agriculture and farming, an ecofeminist-sociolinguistic category called the *Bhoomi Register* has been identified in the process of this research. *Bhoomi Register* is a category that arises from the Mother Earth Discourse to recognise the language of people who live close to nature. It reinforces the power of words with positive energy that add to the well-being of Mother Earth. From the sociolinguistic perspective, attempts have been made to identify the *Bhoomi Register*. A register 'is a conventional way of using language that is appropriate in a specific context which may be identified as situational (e.g. in church), occupational (e.g. among lawyers) or topical (e.g. talking about language)' (Yule 2014: 210–11). Register in this study is a variety of language used for a specific purpose or particular social setting favourable to the well-being of Mother Earth and all her children. The *Bhoomi Register* may be defined as a topical kind of register that is found in indigenous people's discourse who voice their concerns for *Bhoomi Thaai* or Mother Earth. Mother Earth or *Bhoomi Register* is classified into different types, based on the alternative worldviews and consciousness studied through the Mother Earth Discourse model. 'Discourse is shaped by People's Purposes . . . Thinking about purpose, and about interpretations of purpose, means thinking about speech acts intended and understood, about the strategic, rhetorical aspects of texts and text-builders, about "registers", or ways of speaking and writing that key speaker's intentions' (Johnstone 2000: 126).

The *Bhoomi Register* emerges from the sociocultural aspects vividly represented in the novel *When the Kurinji Blooms* by Rajam Krishnan; environment, shelter and clothing confirm their simplicity of life: *hattis* are rows of thatched or tiled houses; *edumane* is an outer room; *ogamane* is an inner room; *hagottu* is a milk-house. Men wear a *dhoti*, a long piece of thick, special weave of cotton and the *dupatti*, a turban. Women wear a *thundu*, which is a piece of white rectangular cloth wrapped around the body and reaching the knee, *mundu*, a piece of finer cotton cloth worn like a shawl over the shoulders and *pattu*, a scarf-like piece of white cotton cloth worn across the forehead and tucked at the back of her head. They worshipped gods and goddesses; *Isan* was the Supreme Being and *Hethappa*, the divine ancestor. Jogi, the protagonist of the novel called his grandmother, *hethai* and the mother, *ammai*. The Badagas ate *samai* (little millet), *tinai* (millet), *poriurundai* (a sweetened ball made of puffed rice) and *porimavu* (roasted gram flour). They stored food in *honai*, a long cylindrical vessel made out of bamboo, *palapetti*, a wooden box where they keep their fruits of their labour and *kalam*, a vessel to store milk.

In Part I, Chapter four of the novel, Lingayya moistens baby Girijai's tongue with milk and utters a traditional blessing, 'May you be married into a good house . . . May you reap a thousand fold whatever you sow . . .' (Krishnan 2002: 21). Badagas exemplify a nature-centric way of life, characterised by closeness to nature, abundance and contentment, and the spirit of well-being found among indigenous communities all over the world. Deep Ecology underscores a deep understanding of the environment around us. The Badaga blessings communicate their worldview of abundance. In the first text given below, an elder blesses a youth that he would be endowed with one that becomes a thousand, live a hundred years, visit nations all over the world and be a gifted person who returns to his homeland with all his wealth.

> *Ollithagi, ondhu saaviraagi, ko endu korasi, bo endu bokki, nooru thumbi, naadu jaradu, dheera p(b)oorana aagi, baddukki ba*
> [Let everything become good, let one become a thousand (wealth), let 'ko' be the call, let it boil as 'bo', let 100 (years) be completed, visit all [over] nation(s), be a great and enlightened person and come back with all these.]
>
> (Jayaprakah 2015)

In another blessing, the elder teaches the complementary principles in nature, where the good and the bad moments coexist in the cyclical pattern of life.

> *Ollitha Aethi, Hollava Thalli, Olagodho Ellava Geddu Ba*
> [Leave all that is bad, take all that is good, come back winning all/everything in this world]
>
> (Jayaprakah 2015)

Odhidhama Niddhana, Oddidhama Erandina is a Badaga proverb, which means 'a person who spends time learning and pondering (over a problem) is better than the one who runs away (in a hurry) and thus trips over. [*Odhidhama* – learned one, *Niddhana* – stops to ponder over[think] a problem, *Oddidhama* – one who runs away or is in a hurry, *Erandina* – trips over' (Jayaprakah 2015).

MOTHER EARTH DISCOURSE

The *Bhoomi Register* highlights the deep ecological principles found in the traditional Badaga blessing, *ondhu, ompaththu aagali*, meaning 'Let prosperity/good deeds increase nine folds', given below.

Let prosperity/good deeds increase nine folds,/Let a prosperity increase a thousand times,/Let good health and happiness be bestowed/Let the cattle wealth/livestock (number of buffalos and cows) increase/Let wealth increase . . . Let the (sown) crops increase/Let the milk (yield) increase . . . Let the fruits increase/ May you build (your own) a house/May you get married/Let one house become a thousand . . . Let grass turn to flowers and stones to fruits when touched/ . . . Let the strength of Elephant be bestowed (on you) . . . Let you live to be a full hundred with lots of wisdom so as to make others wonder (envious)/ . . . Let your name and fame spread wide and far and called by all and overflow/Let your home be filled with children/and let there be many daughters in law/May you look after your dear and near ones/Earn a great name in this world/And live with PROSPERITY

(Jayaprakah 2015)

From the original version of the song, the researcher lists the vocabulary that exemplifies the *Bhoomi Register*. In line 1, *aagali* is positive change; in line 2, *haracha* is health, *soga* is happiness, *kodali* is given; in line 20, *bala* is strength; in line 21, *siri* is happiness; in line 22, *budhdi* is intelligence and *bevara* is wisdom; in line 24, *sippathi* is manifold; in line 25, *olliththu* is goodness; in line 26, *poorana* is complete; in line 28, *geddhu* is to win. The song not only reveres the culture and tradition of Badaga people, but also welcomes the positive influence of education. An integrative approach to life is vividly represented in the Badaga song of prosperity. The *Bhoomi Register* in Rajam Krishnan's *When the Kurinji Blooms* explicates native people's concern for Mother Earth, their belief in interconnectedness and interdependence, the worldview of abundance and contentment and the cyclical pattern of existence. They reinforce their belief in the intrinsic value of all life forms.

This chapter includes the ecofeminist-linguistic paradigm called Mother Earth Discourse in the form of a beehive model and the identification of motifs such as *Isis Panthea, Amma-I-Appan, Her-Meta, Athena's Wit, Annamangai, Sis-Tie, Woody-Woman, Vana-Devi, Tellus-Ma, Aqua-Stree, Aves-Eve* and *Fauna-Fem*; relationships such as spirituality, proximity, sensitivity, productivity, simplicity and practicality; concerns related to physiological, safety and security, belonging, self-esteem and self-actualization needs; worldviews of care and nurture for Mother Earth, call for a holistic outlook, respect for the intrinsic value and inherent worth, appreciation of nature's abundance, recognition of interdependence, emphasis on circular principles, appreciation of nature power, affirmation of woman power, assertion of pluralism and belief in synergising knowledge systems; the identification of *Shakthi*, *Ahimsa* and *Shanthi* Consciousness and Mother Earth lingua franca that includes *Terra Mater Lexis* and *Bhoomi Register*. In the following chapter, the ecofeminist-linguistic framework is used to analyse folktales from India that deal with, first, woman, and then, her environment. It focuses on the theme of 'the Creator and the Created' in folktales entitled *Isis Panthea* tales and *Amma-I-Appan* tales. The folktales are studied in terms of motifs, relationships, concerns, worldviews, consciousness and the lingua franca.

2
THE CREATOR AND THE CREATED

Blessed are the Sons and Daughters of Light who know their Mother Earth. She is the Giver of Life. Acknowledge that you are a part of your mother and she is part of you. She generated you and gave you life . . .

— An Indigenous Prayer and Blessing

Did God create man as the first human being? The *Isis Panthea* motif attempts to find an answer to this question. Indigenous stories portray alternative versions of the conception of universe, and woman is deemed the first human being born on this earth. At the same time, indigenous worldviews confirm their belief in the concept of interconnectedness. *Amma-I-Appan* tales integrate the masculine and feminine principles represented in the folk discourse of indigenous tribes in different cultures across the world. These are tales that challenge the binary opposition of man–woman, day–night, nature–culture, intuition–reason and so on.

Isis Panthea tales

Any indigenous tale that believes in the creation of woman as the first human being can be classified under *Isis Panthea* tales. Some of the characteristic features of *Isis Panthea* tales are as follows: they deal with an omnipotent Creator and mortal beings; they represent primitive ways of life; they show a close understanding of human–nature relationship; most often, the women are empowered beings who represent the qualities of Mother Nature. The Biblical Adam and Eve story is challenged by various myths that recount woman as the first creation on this earth. For example: in the Australian Aboriginal creation myth, the Sun Mother creates life on earth. She walked in all directions, and everywhere she walked, the plants and trees grew. She melted the ice and created the rivers and streams of the world. She awoke the spirits of the birds and animals and they burst into sunshine in a glorious array of colours. Finally, she gave birth to two children and they became the first parents (Smith 2003: 23–31). *Prakriti, Aditi* or *Parasakthi* of the Indian tradition are identified as equivalents to *Isis Panthea*. As Rosalind Miles in *The Women's History of the World* explicates, these alternative stories reinforce ecofeminist belief in earth-based spirituality.

Isis Panthea tales are Creation tales. Every society and culture in the world has a Creation story. Creation stories are of different types, influenced by social, cultural, economic, geographic and political systems. A matriarchal system considers woman as the first creation, whereas the patriarchal system deems man as the first human being born on this earth. Some people believe that a divine being was responsible in creating the earth through His/Her thoughts, words and dreams while others believe that God sent a bird or an animal into the world that was responsible for creating life. The origin story differs from one indigenous tribe to another. Certain indigenous tribes suppose that world was formed from the cracking of a cosmic egg. Alternative worldviews promote 'World Egg' as a popular myth found in the Creation stories of different cultures and civilisations. World Egg signifies hope for the future, an ever-increasing need to understand indigenous knowledge and the significance of Mother Earth as a living entity.

In *Isis Panthea* stories, the creation of woman as the first human being is studied from an ecofeminist perspective. Understanding the Isis myth guides the ecofeminist thinker to appreciate three significant facets in the women's world of creation: first, the origin of earth; second, the formation of life and third, the conception of stories. An authentic parallel between the reproduction of a child and the creation of tales is identified as a common streak in folktales from India. In this context, the researcher also explores alternative forms of procreation in the stories selected for analysis. In the Hopi story from Arizona, called *The Four Creations*, there is a reference to the 'Creator' and the Creation song, where the Spider Woman is the first woman born on this earth. 'Sotuknang went to the world that was to first host life and there he created Spider Woman, and he gave her the power to create life. First Spider Woman took some earth and mixed it with saliva to make two beings. Over them she sang the Creation Song, and they came to life' (*Creation Stories from around the World* 1). The Spider Woman is the creator of life, and also the Creation song representing the different forms of procreation. The Spider Woman symbolises interconnectedness and propagates the ecofeminist belief in bringing together the various threads in the web of life.

Woman is the first creation, according to the beliefs of native people across the world. The indigenous belief in 'the great goddess', 'the universal

THE CREATOR AND THE CREATED

mother' and 'the great mother' (Miles 1989: 36) confirms the significance of *Isis Panthea* themes. Mother Earth was worshipped as the great feminine being nurturing and sustaining life. Feminist thinkers believe that the great goddess myth of the tribal people was overthrown by the God the Father image of monotheist religions such as Christianity and Islam. *Isis Panthea* motifs facilitate an understanding of woman–nature relationships in folktales from India. Woman is considered as the first creation in these tales, and for this reason; the folktales are named after *Isis Panthea*, the first daughter of the Greek god. She represents the qualities of Mother Earth. She has care and concern for her environment. *First There Was Woman* is a folktale that illustrates the *Isis Panthea* motif. This Garasiya Bhil folktale deals with the creation of Mother Earth. The title denotes that the first human being born on this earth was a woman. The narrative gives an account of woman's environment as a land filled with peace and harmony. Kudrat, the omnipotent being, creates Pruthvi (earth) out of love. Love, care and concern are significant values in ecofeminist thought. On another level, Sati, the first woman/human being created on this earth, symbolises fullness and truth. The first woman born on this earth symbolises the self-regulating *Gaia* and the omnipresent feminine principle *Prakriti*.

The metaphor of Mother Earth in the story *First There Was Woman* suggests the magnanimity of feminine power that creates, sustains and nurtures life on this earth. As Vandana Shiva explains, 'at one level, nature is symbolized as the embodiment of the feminine principle and at another, she is nurtured by the feminine to produce life and provide sustenance' (Shiva 2010: 38). The title of this story can be understood in different ways from an ecofeminist standpoint. The story deals with the creation of feminine principle, the earth mother called Pruthvi, who is a replica of the Indian *Prakriti* and the Greek *Gaia*. The folktale also provides an insight into the making of the first human being – Sati, the complete woman. In the folktale *First There Was Woman*, Pruthvi is identified as the greater 'Self', which symbolises the cosmos, and Sati, the lesser 'self', the microcosm. Women who become conscious of their true self through a process of self-realisation and self-discovery attain self-actualisation to form a higher 'Self'.

In the folktale *First There Was Woman*, the storyteller demonstrates three types of Mother Earth Relationships: Sati's relationship with the natural environment, the relationship between Kudrat and Pruthvi and the relationship between Sati and her son, the first man. In this Bhil folktale, Pruthvi represents a feminine space, characterised by interconnectedness and interdependence. Kudrat, the male principle, and Pruthvi, the female principle, are not seen as opposite forces. Instead, they are represented as complementary principles that aid a harmonious functioning of the natural system in the world. This tale of Creation asserts *Shakthi* as the inherent power of every woman who lives close to nature. The indigenous people believe that 'woman's bones' (Sres 2007: 11) were first created and the first feminine form was called 'Pruthvi, the Earth' (Sres 2007: 11). Sati, the first human being, embodies the qualities of Pruthvi, the Earth Mother. The storyteller narrates

> Finally one night, on the eve of the *aamli-melo*, when the whole forest was silent and bathed in the light of the silvery moon, Kudrat took some soil into his hands, weighed it carefully, and shaped a *murti*, an image. So although there were birds and beasts and flowers before, this was the first living human being, the most beautiful shape Kudrat could think of- and it was a Woman. Yes, the *murti* was complete and perfect.
>
> (Sres 2007: 15)

Sati epitomises the supreme qualities of the Earth Mother in this tale. Her relationship with the environment represents an integrative *oikos* where every living and nonliving thing is in perfect order. The word *murti* symbolises precision and perfection of the creator and the created, in the story. Sati is described as a contented, peaceful and complete person who radiates her good qualities to the world around her.

Sati symbolises the woman in the forest. In India, forests have been worshipped since ancient times and the goddess of the forest is called *Aranyani*. She symbolises fertility and life. The forest as the feminine principle is characterised by order, diversity, harmony and perfection, as exemplified in the folktale *First There Was Woman*. 'I will call her Sati, because that's what she is, whole, intact, perfect', says Kudrat (Sres 2007: 15). The bond between Kudrat and Pruthvi symbolises an ideal man–woman relationship. It is not based on hierarchy or power politics. Instead, it is characterised by love, concern and understanding. In this context, women's milieu is an environment based on *Ahimsa Consciousness* and *Shanthi Consciousness*. Sati symbolises the integration of woman power and nature's power. She acknowledges the sacredness or spiritual power of all living organisms created on this earth. The inherent worth of each and every creature in the lap of Mother Earth is recognised by Sati. Indian feminism believes in woman power or *Stree Shakthi*, which is, in other words, the power of *Ahimsa* or nonviolence. Sati is an epitome of *Shakthi Consciousness*. The connection between Sati and her son represents maternal caring. Mother Earth provides everything to all the living creatures under her care. In the same way, Sati emulates her mother in providing nurture to her first-born son. Sati is a creator like her mother Pruthvi. The power of procreation reinforces woman power as nature's power and contributes to proximity. A mother respects the sacredness of her child and continues to revere the spiritual element in her/him till the end.

Women intuitively understood the inherent worth and the needs of the child, in olden days when Western science was not developed enough to show the foetus in the womb through ultrasound scanning methods. A mother not only fulfilled basic needs, but also, fulfilled the psychological needs of caring, belonging, security needs, self-esteem needs, and also inspired her/him with seeds of motivation to attain self-actualisation later in her/his life. *Isis Panthea* sensitivity is reinforced by Sati's care and concern for her environment. According to the Bhil folktale, in the beginning, when Sati was created, she communicated with all the living creatures. 'True, there were birds and insects of all kinds, and many kinds of animals moved among the trees and followed her wherever she went, but there was none like her, none to talk to her' (Sres 2007: 16). Sati's world is a woman's world. She is sensitive to the dewdrops on leaves and the patch of grass. Sati 'would be awakened by the twittering of the birds, and soon she had learnt exactly which bird had what kind of song' (Sres 2007: 16). The word 'talk' is quite significant in highlighting the issues of speech and silence in the context of women's tradition. The first woman, Sati delivers the child in wilderness. Like Sati, women who live close to nature derive *Shakthi* from the environment. Chipko women celebrate forests as they help them to fulfil not only their basic needs but also their self-esteem needs, and at times, their self-actualisation needs, characterised by collective efficiency. These women are conscious of their selves and conscious of their environment and help other women in their neighbourhood to be awake and to be aware. As Anees Jung describes,

> The forest is awake. And the women in the forest are awake. Each one now has a name. Also an identity realized and shared. Despite isolation and dire poverty these women have acquired a collective power that stems from a felt need. Their voices have soared above the hills, finding echoes in distant corners of the country.
> (Sres 2007: 107–08)

The significance of consciousness-raising is reiterated in the passage given above. It emphasises the dynamics of women's groups, which strive at a collective goal rather than an individual's quest for self-actualisation.

The story exemplifies Mother Earth Relationships characterised by spirituality and sensitivity. Pruthvi is an epitome of earth-based spirituality represented in each and every living creature. Pruthvi is a manifestation of *Prakriti*, the all-pervading life-affirming principle recognised by indigenous ecofeminist thought. The first woman believes in the worldviews of interdependence and interconnectedness of life and communicates with all the nonhuman living beings on this earth. She reveres Mother Earth as a living being. In *First There Was Woman*, the ending suggests the life-affirming quality of the feminine principle that pervades the whole world and illustrates a mother's unconditional love for her son. 'Sati was very happy looking at her son, and she nursed him and spoke to him, and helped him grow tall and sturdy ... And Kudrat loved her so that now he became one with her, and she must never forget that first it was Woman's Kingdom' (Sres 2007: 17). From this passage, the reader or the listener understands that Sati, the first woman, had a 'voice' as she 'spoke' to her son. The first man, according to this simple Bhil tribal tale, was the offspring of woman and nature. This story reverses the Eurocentric myth of Adam and Eve, where man is considered as the first human being created on this earth. Indigenous tribal tales across the globe reiterate the *Isis Panthea* belief highlighted in this folktale, *First There Was Woman*. The serpent or *sapsi* is a symbol of constructive power in this Garasiya Bhil folktale. The first man is a child of the woman and nature, where the serpent signifies Kudrat's power. This reverses the Western conventional symbolism of serpent as evil. In this tale, the serpent denotes procreation and new life as against the popular association of snake as an agent of evil and destruction.

In the Creation stories, the forest is at the centre. Nature is personified as a maternal spirit that showers care, concern and love to all living beings. Human beings live together in unity by understanding the connection between nature and culture. Their cultural beliefs and practices are guided by natural principles. Human nature is shaped by the harmony in nature. *Isis Panthea* themes can be identified in myths and stories about the origin of the planet. They communicate alternative worldviews of indigenous people across the world. In *Isis Panthea* stories, there is a clear evidence of woman as the first creation, yet at times treated as a silent human being. The Garasiya Bhil folktale *First There Was Woman* suggests the possibility of an ideal space for universal parity, characterised by feminine principles. Sati in *First There Was Woman* emerges as a human counterpart to Pruthvi or Mother Earth, representing the spiritual qualities of the nature goddess, closeness with the natural cycles adhering to the seasons, sensitivity towards the living beings around, exemplifying constructive consciousness, simple living and practical approach to life. In the Bhil folktales, the land of Sabarkantha exemplifies a place characterised by interdependence and interconnectedness. The birth of the firstborn son to Sati exemplifies an event of celebration of both nature's power and woman power.

A Kurumba tribal tale from the Nilgiris gives an account of a strong and courageous woman called Peechi, who climbed mountain peaks along with men of her tribe to fetch honey. Tribal people narrate that since she challenged men, she was killed by them, and even today, people are afraid of going to a particular place for fear of being punished by her spirit. The story illustrates the innate power or shakthi of women, on the one hand, and the constraints laid by the patriarchal society on her, on the other hand. In *Isis Panthea* stories, the characters are aware of the presence of the living earth. Kudrat, the creator, exclaimed, 'Ah, beautiful Earth, Pruthvi, my Woman' (Sres 2007: 12). The *Isis Panthea* motif is rendered not only through the narrative voice in the story, but also through the voices of the narrated. In the Bhil stories considered for study, the narrator Marija Sres effectively traces the origin myth in *First There Was Woman*. Ecofeminist spirituality is exemplified in the relationship between Kudrat and Sati. Sati's relationship with her environment is an instance of *Isis Panthea* sensitivity. Sati giving birth to the first male child on earth is a demonstration of *Isis Panthea* productivity.

In *Isis Panthea* tales, women's relationship with the natural environment is characterised by power, a sense of abundance and contentment, peace and harmony. On the contrary, activist writers such as Mahasweta Devi contend that today, in the world of modernisation, with the culture of exploitation and destruction, the indigenous people do not even get the basic necessities fulfilled, and this results in a number of casualties during childbirth. According to ecofeminist thought, romanticising the tribal existence does not offer a healthy trend. It is necessary to understand the predicament of women who live in inhuman conditions during pregnancy and childbirth in forests or deserts. Instead, a realistic approach to the indigenous people's way of life is indispensable. In *Isis Panthea* stories, the creation of woman as the first human being is studied from an ecofeminist perspective. Understanding the Isis myth guides the ecofeminist thinker to appreciate three significant facets: first, the origin of earth; second, the formation of life and third, the conception of stories. An authentic parallel between the reproduction of a child and the creation of tales is identified as a common streak in folktales from India. In this context, the researcher also explores alternative forms of procreation in the stories selected for analysis.

The belief in the sacredness of the environment is reinforced in the folktale *Avvaiyar's Rest*. Avvaiyar is a poet of the Sangam period in Tamilnadu. The legend from Tamilnadu is retold by Cathy Spagnoli and Paramasivam Savanna in the book *Earth Care: World Folktales to Talk About*, authored by Margaret Read MacDonald. One day, the famous Sangam poet Avvaiyar was walking down near a village. As she was very tired, she searched for a place to rest and found a temple. She sat down under a tree and stretched her tired legs out. Seeing this, the temple priest came running up to her and cried that her legs pointed right towards the statue of a god. Avvaiyar calmly asked him, 'My son . . . I will be delighted to move them away from the god.

Simply tell me in which direction there is no god, and there will I point my feet' (Macdonald 2005: 92). This story exemplifies the value of the omnipotent, omnipresent nature, which represents both the creator and the created as a unified whole. This tale communicates the worldview of Tamil people during the Sangam period, who hailed the entire earth as sacred. This particular rendering of the story in English also suggests the importance of Eastern philosophies that the Western audience is trying to comprehend for a holistic view of life. *Avvaiyar's Rest* also thrusts upon the nature of the Divine as a transcended being who is beyond a human being's understanding of time, space, gender and class. Avvaiyar, the Sangam poet, is one of the early exponents of ecofeminist thought, who propagated the spirit of interconnectedness and respect for the intrinsic value of life in her poetry. The story *Avvaiyar's Rest* communicates her belief in earth-based spirituality.

Isis Panthea tales redefine the stereotypical notions of womanhood. The *Isis Panthea* concerns cater to the understanding of woman's basic needs at the time of childbirth, security and safety needs in the process of creation, the love and belonging needs of women transcending the power politics of man and woman, the need for self-esteem established by alternative forms of procreation, ecofeminist view of individual and collective self-actualisation. The predominant *Isis Panthea* worldviews identified in the select folktales are: care for Mother Earth with reference to the character of Pruthvi, a holistic outlook of life and a sense of completeness perceived by Sati, reverence to the value of the intrinsic value of all living beings in the forest, the land of Sabarkantha signifying abundance, Sati and Kavi epitomising woman power drawn from nature. *Isis Panthea* consciousness is typified by *Shakthi–Ahimsa–Shanthi*. The privilege of recognising the First Woman with the qualities of *Shakthi*, *Ahimsa* and *Shanthi* principles is identified in *Isis Panthea* stories. Stories told by the indigenous people across the world, which differ from and challenge the Eurocentric, androcentric myths and fables, are categorised as *Isis Panthea* stories. They affirm woman as the first creation on this earth. As represented in *First There Was Woman*, Pruthvi or the earth is considered the first feminine form created by God. Woman–nature proximity is reinforced by Sati and Kavi in the Bhil folktales. These folktales throw light on the origin of the first woman, her close association with Mother Earth and the distance created between nature and culture by the first man, Kava in *How Kava Deceived Kavi*. *Isis Panthea* tales reiterate woman power and the consciousness of *Shakthi* derived from nature. The identification of *Isis Panthea* themes in folktales reiterates the significance of feminine strength to recreate a world based on *Shakthi Consciousness and Ahimsa Consciousness*. The innate strength of women is underscored by these stories. *Isis Panthea* themes empower womanhood by revisiting the first woman and the celebration of the 'great goddess' (Miles 1989: 36).

THE CREATOR AND THE CREATED

Shakthi Consciousness emphasises the constructive power of people who live close to nature and believe in what the modern-day self-help literatures call the win-win situation. By being aware of one's *Shakthi*, a person such as Sati is able to identify the *Shakthi* in her neighbour in the immediate surroundings. When human beings are able to recognise and respect the *Shakthi* of their neighbours, they are also endowed with *Ahimsa Consciousness*. *Ahimsa* thinkers believe that the most important characteristic of a person's culture is when s/he gives least trouble to her/his neighbour. When there is an integration of *Shakthi* and *Ahimsa* consciousness, as reflected in the folktales, *Shanthi Consciousness* is experienced by nature and human beings. Thus, ecofeminism believes in respecting the complementary principles that govern the planet. The *Purusha–Prakriti* relationship in Hindu mythology and its equivalent, the complementary yin-yang principles in Chinese philosophy, are recognised as *Amma-I-Appan* motifs in folktales from India, discussed in the next section

Amma-I-Appan tales

The *Amma-I-Appan* motif communicates the importance of respecting man and woman alike and paves ways towards a society that believes in peaceful coexistence. In her poetry *Konrai Vendhan*, Avvaiyar said, '*Annaiyum Pithaavum Munnari Deivam*' (meaning 'mother and father are the first known gods'). In Hindu mythology, the image of the androgynous Arthanareeswara synthesises the masculine and feminine principles. There are folktales in India that glorify the complementary nature of masculine and feminine principles. The Tamil devotees of Siva praise him in the prayer to *Arthanareeswara* as half-male and half-female, 'Her body is dance preparing for the creation of differentiation, his is the dance of destruction that destroys everything, I bow to Siva (which includes *Shakthi*), mother of the universe, I bow to Siva, father of the universe' (Goldberg 2002: 105). *The Golden Age and the Deluge* and *How Kava Deceived Kavi* are two folktales prevalent among the Bhil tribes that centre on the first man, Kava, and the first woman, Kavi, which can be classified as *Amma-I-Appan* tales. The stories highlight twin concepts, which are considered as binary opposites in Western ideology, but seen as complementary principles in Eastern philosophy, governing the cyclical pattern of life. They are 'golden age' and 'deluge'; happiness and sadness; Kudrat, the god of creation and Deva, the god of destruction; Kava, the man and Kavi, the woman; the worldviews of abundance versus scarcity, authenticity and trickery. In the Eastern philosophy of life, these dimensions are not considered as bipolar opposites; rather, each element has a role to play in the functioning of the planet.

THE CREATOR AND THE CREATED

The Golden Age and the Deluge is an origin story, which begins with the description of Sabarkantha as a place of peace, order and harmony, where animals, birds and human beings celebrated interdependence. The forests provided the adivasis with abundant resources. The story takes on a different turn when the people stopped worrying about the increase in population. A natural calamity in the form of floods killed many people in the Bhil land. During the floods, two people found refuge in trees. They were Kava and Kavi. The story ends with the meeting of Kava and Kavi. As Deva, the darker side of Kudrat (the creator) proclaims, 'You Kavi, will be called *Stree* (woman) and you Kava will be named *Purush* (man)' (Sres 2007: 6). In the folktale *The Golden Age and the Deluge*, the woodland of Sabarkantha, according to the narrator, Marija Sres, exemplifies a land of tranquillity and harmony, 'flowing with milk and honey' (Sres 2007: 2). The interdependence of human and nonhuman living beings is revealed in the lines 'Animals and adivasis, both came to the silent pools and watering holes to drink and bathe, and both did this in comfort' (Sres 2007: 1). In Sabarkantha, nature is characterised by *Ahimsa Consciousness* and *Shanthi Consciousness* where 'the animals never killed for pleasure' (Sres 2007: 1). The worldview of indigenous people is a worldview of abundance. Vandana Shiva draws the distinction between the culture of people living close to nature and culture of the greedy consumerists. 'The end of consumerism and accumulation is the beginning of the joy of living. That is why the Indigenous people of contemporary India are resisting, leaving their forest homes and abandoning their forest culture . . . And it is the forest that can show us the way beyond this conflict by reconnecting to Nature and finding sources for our freedom' (http://www.resurgence.org/magazine/article3390.html). The tribal people who live in the forests have a worldview of abundance, which reflects the qualities of Mother Earth. 'The earth yielded its fruit at the slightest touch of the spade or hoe . . . they lived in plenty' (Sres 2007: 2).

In *The Golden Age and the Deluge*, a flood brings about change in the earth's surface, parallel to the story of floods in the Bible. This tale delineates the cyclical pattern of life and the complementary nature of existence as perceived by the indigenous people of India. In the Bhil folktale, the golden age is followed by deluge only for a short time. It is followed by the creation of Kavi and Kava and a new world is promised to them by the Creator. Mother Earth has the 'self-regulating' quality within herself with which she brings about stability and equilibrium after a chaos, as witnessed after a volcanic eruption or an earthquake. The use of the phrase 'ever-renewing' in the discourse also suggests a similar idea of renewal and restoration. The words 'remedy' and 'restoring' are also synonymous with the replenishing power of the Earth Mother. Ecofeminism believes in the revival of a life-affirming culture. *The Golden Age and the Deluge* traces the transition from the land characterised by motherly care to the world of insensitive patriarchal domination.

How Kava Deceived Kavi is a sequel to *The Golden Age and the Deluge*. This tale gives an account of a competition between the first man and first woman. Deva tries to complicate the woman–man relationship in this story. Kavi is a strong woman who is ready to run a race with Kava. However, Deva informs Kava that 'if not by strength, then Kava must win by trickery' (Sres 2007: 7). First, he drops a pair of silver earrings; then, a nose-ring; then, bangles and so on. When Kava, the man, is not able to win the race, he 'distracts' Kavi, the woman, with jewels. He gives Kavi a pair of earrings (*butti*) and thinks, 'Right. This will distract her, and I'll win the next race' (Sres 2007: 8). In the same way, he gifts her with a nose-ring (*chuni*), bangles (*bangdi*) necklace (*handi, haydi*), breastplate (*hansda*), and finally, the 'heavy' anklets (*payal*). All those jewels did not distract Kavi. She won the race all the time. At last, Kavi gets defeated when 'Kavi felt pulled down [sic] by the weight of her jewellery' (Sres 2007: 9). *How Kava Deceived Kavi* is a fable of power politics, which is representative of the patriarchal systems that restricts women from realising their true potential, the inherent worth or Shakthi.

How Kava Deceived Kavi is a tale that depicts the trickery played by Deva, who is considered the darker side of Kudrat, on the first human beings to create confusion and chaos in this world. This simple folktale is a parable of the power struggle that has existed between man and woman from ancient times till date. This story traces the origin of the patriarchal system and the domination of man over woman. According to Marti Kheel, 'The image of the earth as a living organism and nurturing mother has historically served as a cultural constraint restricting the actions of human beings. One does not readily slay a mother, dig into her entrails for gold, or mutilate her body' (Kheel 2008: 212). The failure of Kavi is the result of the plot created by Deva and Kava for complicating the relationship. A woman becomes a construct when she craves for material needs, such as gold and silver. Kavi outwits Kava so many times before the invention of jewels in the story, and in the end, she succumbs to Kava's trickery. The ecofeminist belief in simplicity offers a solution to the complexities that arise due to power politics in the folktale.

In the beginning of this story, Kavi personifies indigenous woman's power. 'Kavi was a very vibrant girl with a great sense of fun, and she knew she could outmatch the boy any day. So they ran a race, and she was much ahead of him and won' (Sres 2007: 7). In the natural environment, Kavi expresses her true self, she was 'lithe and speedy as a gazelle' (Sres 2007: 7). Deva upholds the patriarchal laws when he remarks, 'he (Kava) must be better than the girl, and not to settle for defeat' (Sres 2007: 7). His recommendations to win the match by trickery go in vain for a long time. The ornaments symbolise the various forms of restrictions that hinder women in their challenging routine of day-to-day life. Kavi, in contrast, is portrayed as a victim of patriarchy. Kavi's defeat in the man-centred race indicates the beginning of patriarchal domination. Sati's landscape is a space filled with *Shakthi–Ahimsa–Shanthi* consciousness contributing to an integrative *oikos*, whereas Kavi's *oikos* is identified as hierarchic *oikos* in the folktale *How Kava Deceived Kavi*. In the tale *How Kava Deceived Kavi*, when Kavi accepted the gifts from Kava, she moved away from her Earth Mother, essentially and spiritually, and she lost her Shakthi in the man-centred race. During the transition from nature to patriarchal culture, women have not only lost their strength, but also their voice and they have become silent or been silenced.

In the ecofeminist-linguistic structure, the ultimate questions raised are: How do the characters communicate their consciousness in the story? And how does the story motivate the listener or reader to understand ecofeminist *conscientizacao*? Folktales do not stop with entertainment. A deep understanding of the folk discourse reveals the consciousness of the narrator and the narrated. Marija Sres describes the status of woman in ancient times, 'Ever since, men have used gifts, little and big, to distract women, and to make them do their bidding. Women, like Kavi, are happy to receive gifts, not realizing that like this they often lose their freedom. This is how even now the Dungri Garasiya tribe pays for the bride a dapu, a bride price which shows how a woman becomes a man's property' (Sres 2007: 10).

In the folktale *How Kava Deceived Kavi*, one is able to infer the fact that women need not aspire to run a race as the competition is designed by the patriarchal systems for the benefit of men. Women and men are shaped and moulded in different ways in nature. The competition between them is a fruitless exercise. The difference between Kavi in *How Kava Deceived Kavi* and Sati in *First There Was Woman* is the difference between an urban woman who is moulded by the patriarchal society and is shaped by male-dominated thinking and the rural woman who still values her culture and tradition and continues to exhibit her intrinsic values, which she derives from nature. Kavi becomes a construct in the hands of patriarchy whereas Sati symbolises the native woman with the *Shakthi* derived from nature. The women goddesses epitomise woman power as nature's power. In the Japanese story *The Origin of Japan and Her People*, there are three creators – 'The Spirit Master of the Centre of Heaven', 'The August Wondrously Producing Spirit' and the 'Divine Wondrously Producing Ancestor' (Donald 1962: 561). The eight main islands of Japan were born in the union of Izanagi and Izanami. The first parents signify the harmonious nature of

THE CREATOR AND THE CREATED

male and female principles. Many cultures across the world consider the Sun as a male principle in nature. But the Japanese Creation tale gives an account of the goddess of the Sun.

The origin story differs from one indigenous tribe to another. Certain indigenous tribes suppose that the world was formed from the cracking of a cosmic egg. Alternative worldviews promote the 'World Egg' as a popular myth found in the Creation stories of different cultures and civilisations. The World Egg signifies hope for the future, an ever-increasing need to understand indigenous knowledge and the significance of Mother Earth as a living entity. According to Chinese myth, *Pan Gu and Nü Wa*, Pan Gu, a giant, developed and slept in an egg for 18,000 years. One day, he woke up and felt the need to separate heaven and earth. 'As the two continued to separate, Pan Gu grew to hold them apart. For 18,000 years he continued to grow, until the heavens were 30,000 miles above the earth' (Walls and Walls 1984: 135). The first woman Creator or the creation goddess, according to Chinese mythology, is Nü Wa. 'From the edge of the pond she took some mud and shaped it in the form of a human being. At first her creation was lifeless, and she set it down. It took life as soon as it touched the soil, however, and soon the human was dancing and celebrating its new life' (Walls and Walls 1984: 135). The Pan Gu and Nü Wa relationship confirms the idea of interdependence in Yin-Yang theory.

The Golden Chain is an origin story of the Yoruba people of Nigeria. They believe that Olorun, the Supreme Being who transcended the male and female, created the world. 'Gathering gasses from the space beyond the sky, Olorun sparked the gasses into an explosion that he shaped into a fireball. He sent that fireball to Ife, where it dried the lands that were still wet and began to bake the clay figures that Obatala had made. The fireball even set the earth to spinning, as it still does today. Olorun then blew his breath across Ife, and Obatala's figures slowly came to life as the first people of Ife' (David 1991: 31). According to a Maori story, *The Separation of Heaven and Earth*, the first parents of the human race were Rangi and Papa, also called heaven and earth. They had six sons: Tane-mahuta, the father of the forests and their inhabitants; Tawhiri-ma-tea, the father of winds and storms; Tangaroa, the father of fish and reptiles; Tu-matauenga, the father of fierce human beings; Haumia-tikitiki, the father of food that grows without cultivation; and Rongo-ma-tane, the father of cultivated food (George 1956: 250). The Maori people believe that the six sons intended to separate heaven and earth, and in the process, created the world. When the sons are in distress, it is nevertheless Papa or Mother Earth with her feminine principles who takes good care of them.

Identifying the *Amma-I-Appan* motif is a significant premise in myths and legends around the world that deal with the first woman and man.

THE CREATOR AND THE CREATED

They are Adam and Eve (Christian/English), *Adi Sakthi* and *Siva* (Hindu), *Izanagi* and *Izanami* (Japanese) and *Pan Gu* and *Nü Wa* (Chinese). *Amma-I-Appan* motifs can be identified in Tamil sayings and beliefs. For example, the first *Kural* written by Valluvar is '*Agara Mudhala Ezhuthellam Aadhi / Bhagavan Mudhatre Ulagu*', which means 'Just as the alphabet "A" is the beginning of all letters, so also, God (the father and mother) is the beginning of this universe', where God is the omnipotent God, representative of both woman and man. Tamil poet Subamaniya Bharathi celebrates the eternal power as *Parasakthi*. In the stories chosen for study, the Creator is either a goddess, or at times, a supreme being who epitomises both male and female principles. The women goddesses represent constructive consciousness. The Spider Woman in the Hopi tale, the goddess of the Sun in the Japanese tale, Nü Wa in the Chinese mythology, Papa in the Maori myth, Pruthvi and Sati in the Bhil folktale create, procreate, protect and sustain life. They reinforce the belief in the intrinsic value of all life forms. They uphold interconnectedness and interdependence. They reinforce woman power and nature's power. The male and female principles in these stories are complementary in nature. Revisiting *Amma-I-Appan* tales, the gods and goddesses of earth fulfils the ecofeminist goal of 'reweaving' our planet.

Across the world, different cultures have multifarious varieties of Creation stories that represent Mother Earth as *Gaia* and *Terra Mater*. The principle of *Prakriti* is identified in each and every living creature which acts as a unifying principle of Mother Earth. Sati, the first woman in the Bhil folktale, symbolises a complete being who understands the importance of interconnectedness and interdependence as they exemplify the microcosm of Planet Earth. The cyclical pattern of life is represented through the creation motifs in *The Golden Age and the Deluge*. The holistic outlook of life guides the indigenous people to remain rooted to the ground in times of happiness or sadness. They are sensitive to the grey areas in between binary opposites in the sociocultural systems. They consider opposite forces as complementary in nature. They view living beings as independent parts of the larger whole. These worldviews provide sustenance to ecofeminist-linguistic thought. *Amma-I-Appan* stories emphasise the creation of Mother Earth as a living being. Woman–Nature proximity empowers women, children and the marginalised people. The Creation stories reconstruct the bridge between nature and culture. The respect for the inherent worth of the unborn, the living and the dead is reinforced by these tales. These folktales communicate the interconnectedness and interdependence of life governed by the feminine principle called *Gaia* or *Prakriti*.

The concept of binary opposition and dualistic thinking poses a problem for Western ecofeminists, whereas the ecofeminists from the Eastern part of the world are aware of the opposite forces as complementary principles. According to Ynestra King, ecofeminism should recognise the woman–nature connection,

> as a vantage point for creating a different kind of culture and politics that would integrate intuitive/spiritual and rational forms of knowledge, embracing both science and magic insofar as they enable us to transform the nature/culture distinction itself and to envision and create a free, ecological society.
>
> (Diamond and Orenstein 1990: 67)

Hence, integration is the fundamental premise of ecofeminist thought. 'A family is like a forest, when you are outside it is dense, when you are inside you see that each tree has its place' is an African proverb. People who understand the value of family contribute more to their society, and in turn, to the planet, which they consider as an extended family. They learn the qualities of tolerance and sharing from family members. They understand the meaning of diversity. *Amma-I-Appan* motifs inspire us to respect the space of each individual in the family. Family is a microcosm where one identifies the inherent worth of life, explores the spirit of caring and sharing and discovers the spirit of interdependence and peaceful coexistence. The consciousness-raising process begins at home or *akam,* which disseminates into seeds of hope to the larger home, *puram,* contributing to the welfare of Planet Earth.

Though ideally speaking, women and men have equal rights on this earth, women as human persons have been silenced since ancient times. Silence in this context does not mean absence of a voice. The voices were either not heard or not listened to. In this ecofeminist quest, one is able to identify women's unvoiced, unheard expressions about their environment. Nevertheless, as ecofeminism propagates an alternative to a 'hierarchical' approach to life, it is inclusive of environmental/subaltern concerns of children, men and other marginalised groups. The next chapter seeks to explore the folktales that deal with women's silences and speech, called *Her-Meta* tales and *Athena's Wit* tales.

3

SILENCES AND SPEECH

> We need to find God, and he cannot be found in noise and restlessness. God is the friend of silence. See how nature – trees, flowers, grass – grows in silence; see the stars, the moon and the sun, how they move in silence . . . We need silence to be able to touch souls.
>
> — Mother Teresa

In this chapter, *Her-Meta* motifs and *Athena's Wit* motifs reveal two important aspects in women's stories. They are 'her' stories in contrast to history or 'his' stories. Two, they are meta narratives or 'stories about stories'. In this case, the twin themes of speech and silence are interrogated in the context of woman and her environment. *Her-Meta* stories and *Athena's Wit* tales provide answers to questions such as: Do women remain silent always? Who are those silenced women? What are the ways in which they are silenced? How are they silenced? When are they silenced? Why are they silenced? What is the significance of women's language 'of' the environment? What is the significance of women's language 'for' the environment?

Her-Meta tales

In folklore, scholars such as A. K. Ramanujan suggest that folktales about storytelling are classified as 'meta' folk narratives, where the 'tellers reflect on tales' (Ramanujan 2009: xxxiii). Since the focus of this research is woman's tales, the researcher coins a term, called *Her-Meta* stories, to refer to those types of tales. To put it differently, *Her-Meta* motifs in the ecofeminist-linguistic frame communicate the importance of understanding worldviews and consciousness of woman's 'nature–culture', principally expressed through the power of the spoken word. *Her-Meta* stories considered for analysis in this research are *Tell It to the Walls*, *A Story and a Song* and *A Story in Search of an Audience*. Quite specifically, *Her-Meta* stories trace the silenced, the marginalised and the oppressed women's voices. A woman's story about stories, about silences and alternative forms of discourse can be categorised under *Her-Meta* stories. The richness of oral tradition can be studied through this dimension. An ecofeminist critique of woman's language is a necessary tool in this age of ecological chaos and *Her-Meta* tales finds answers for the woman–environment–language issues.

Her-Meta motifs promote the understanding of woman's meta stories of her environment, which are characterised by the following dimensions. Women who are silenced by the patriarchal system and other forms of oppression communicate through alternative forms of expression – for example, oral tales narrated to children. Listening to women and nature is a conscious attempt towards realising sustainable growth and well-being of Mother Earth. These folktales ensure that *Her-Meta* voices are heard by people. Human beings in an environment need to be sensitive to the silences in women and nature. *Her-Meta* tales are expressions of women's imagination that indirectly communicate their experiences in day-to-day reality. These tales also have the scope of expressing nature's experiences. These oral tales reiterate the need to identify women's *Shakthi Consciousness* in terms of expression. By respecting the inherent worth of the silenced women, these oral tales promote *Ahimsa Consciousness*. As a result, *Her-Meta* narratives pave the way towards *Shanthi Consciousness*.

Tell It to the Walls is a Tamil folktale told by Kanakkamal in Srirangam and translated into English by A. K. Ramanujan, which appears first in his collection called *Folktales from India*, first published in 1991. This story exemplifies the *Her-Meta* motif. The central woman character in the story is a poor widow with two sons and two daughters-in-law. The children did not respect her intrinsic value. They reproached and ill-treated her. 'As she kept all her woes to herself, she grew fatter and fatter. Her sons and daughters-in-law now found that a matter for ridicule. They mocked at her for growing fatter by the day and asked her to eat less' (Ramanujan 2009: 1). The therapeutic effect of storytelling has often been underscored by psychologists. The importance of expression as opposed to silence is highlighted by this story. The story *Tell It to the Walls* with the *Her-Meta* motif emphasises the importance of speech and listening in the context of aged women. The title of the story denotes the conditions in which old women, particularly widows, exist in our society. Such women are alienated from their family members and the community, and at times, forcefully transported to urban areas by their children and treated as domestic help or 'nanny', and made to live in miserable conditions.

In most of the Indian folktales from India, old women are depicted as domineering mothers-in-law. However, there are quite a few stories of beggared mothers. Sarah Lamb in her essay, *The Beggared Mother: Older*

Women's Narratives in West Bengal, gives an account of stories narrated by older women who live in poverty and face a loss of identity. *Tell It to the Walls* is a parable that communicates concern for the aged.

> When she started narrating the stories the walls came down one by one. Standing in the ruins, with bricks and rubble all around her, she felt lighter in mood and lighter in body as well. She looked at herself and found she had actually lost all the weight she had gained in her wretchedness. Then she went home.
>
> (Ramanujan 2009: 1)

In this story, the old woman finds an emotional outlet by narrating the story to the walls and the last line suggests that she went back home with a peaceful mind. A feminist interpretation of the tale would suggest that the old woman had a sense of relief once she broke down the four walls of the house, which symbolise the traditional space for a woman in patriarchal society. In order to explore silences, it is necessary to practise conscious listening. The conscious listener of these folktales has the major responsibility of unravelling the implications of the woman's discourse that finds a cure through storytelling. These stories help the narrators to re-create an alternative space in their mental landscape where worldviews, beliefs and convictions are appropriated by the consciousness of *Shakthi*.

Mahasweta Devi's depiction of Jashoda in *Stanadayini* provides a realistic account of woman's pain and suffering in her old age and at the time of her death. 'One must become Jashoda if one suckles the world. One has to die friendless, with no one left to put a bit of water in the mouth' (Guha 1987: 276). An ecofeminist reading of Jashoda's story outlines the following dimensions. If Jashoda represented feminine principles like Mother Earth and nourished all her children with care, why did the children not understand her suffering in the end? Why did they not reciprocate her concern and love? As Sarah Lamb discusses the *Older Women's Narratives in West Bengal*, she comments,

> In the stories that older women tell . . . there is almost always a breakdown in mother-child reciprocity. A recurrent theme in the narratives of older women is that of mothers who have given everything they have to their sons-birth, breast milk, food, and material wealth-but who ultimately receive nothing in return.
>
> (Raheja 2003: 69)

Mahasweta Devi's *Stanadayini* can be read as a parable of the dominant patriarchal consumerist society that treats women as objects and commodities and exploits the natural resources, particularly in third world countries such as India. The 'suckling' metaphor in the story communicates the nature–nurture proposition that is misappropriated by Western science, technologies and industrial growth in this era of globalisation.

How do we understand the implications of woman's silence in the folktales from India? *Her-Meta* motifs provide the tools to unravel the folk tradition that gives a voice to the unspoken and the unheard. *Her-Meta* motifs can be defined as themes and symbols that uphold women's tales about storytelling. They are 'Her' stories that deal with women's environment, her understanding of life, her approach to the world at large, her concerns, worldviews and consciousness. They are meta stories that offer a commentary on the form of storytelling, highlight the importance of expression and reiterate discourse of power, nonviolence and peace. *Tell It to the Walls*, *A Story and a Song* and *A Story in Search of an Audience* are considered as 'metastories' or 'stories about stories'. According to Patricia Waugh, 'Metafiction is a term given to fictional writing which self-consciously and systematically draws attention to its status as an artefact in order to pose questions about the relationship between fiction and reality' (Waugh 1984: 40). In the same way, 'meta stories' underscore the relationship between woman's imagination and the reality. Folktales mirror the worldviews of the narrators, the narrated and the translator. It is necessary to identify the voices and comprehend their worldviews of the narrator, the narrated and the translator. This research inspires an ecofeminist quest to identify women's silences. An Oriya poet Reba Ray's poem reads thus in translation,

> In silence I came to this world
> And my life will sing unceasing,
> In silence will my life forever
> Her songs of silence sing
> (Kamala 2009: 72)

Unravelling the silences and re-reading the indigenous oral discourse leads to a sustainable growth of nature and humankind. The ecofeminist-linguistic quest offers a tool that explores 'her stories' of silence and 'her songs' of silence in folk discourse from India.

A Story and a Song is a meta story from Karnataka, translated by A. K. Ramanujan in his collection, called *A Flowering Tree and Other Oral Tales from India*, published in 1997. The tale begins with the following words: 'A housewife knew a story. She also knew a song. But she kept them to herself, never told anyone the story or sang the song' (Ramanujan 1997: 1). It is the story and a song of the woman. In the nature-culture-specific tale of South India, the flames of the lamps from various houses are also personified as living characters. The flames from the house of the protagonist inform the other flames in the temple, 'The lady of our house knows a story and a song. She never tells the story, and has never sung the song to anyone. The story and the song got suffocated inside; so they got out and have turned into a coat and a pair of shoes. They took revenge. The woman doesn't even know' (Ramanujan 1997: 2). The story raises the question, what happens to those untold stories and unsung songs of women? The tale ends with these words, 'The husband, lying under his blanket in the temple, heard the lamp's explanation. His suspicions were cleared. When he went home, it was dawn. He asked his wife about her story and her song. But she had forgotten both of them. "What story, what song?" she said' (Ramanujan 1997: 2). The transformation of the story and song can be interpreted in different ways. On the one hand, the woman is punished by the 'story' and the 'song' for not letting them out. On the other hand, the patriarchal society restricts women from voicing out their creativity and imagination, and hence, the housewife is punished because she 'knew' a song and 'knew' a story.

In this meta story, the story and the song 'wanted release' (Ramanujan 1997: 1). This situation raises the feminist linguistic concerns of speech and silence. The story and the song seem to have metaphorically fallen out without the woman's knowledge. 'The woman didn't understand what was happening' (Ramanujan 1997: 1). At this juncture, it is imperative to ask why the story and the song get transformed into a man's coat and shoes. Keeping women in the dark and in ignorance is a patriarchal strategy, which needs to be interrogated from an ecofeminist perspective. The right to information, the right to education and the right to expression are the essential tenets one needs to observe from such *Her-Meta* folktales. When the husband realises the truth after listening to the lamp flames in the monkey god temple, he returns home and asks for 'her story and her song' (Ramanujan 1997: 2). The woman's forgetting of the story indicates an erasure of traditions, of women's cultures. Hence, *Her-Meta* stories seek to identify themes of silence and expression through the Mother Earth Discourse. This story draws attention to ecofeminist productivity, which attempts to explore *Her-Meta* stories.

According to Ramanujan, the worldview of these simple storytellers is that 'nothing is ever lost, only transformed' (Ramanujan 1997: 228). In the story *A Story and a Song*, when the lamps are put out at night, they move to the temple. This worldview on the level of ecofeminist praxis offers hope to the affirmative thinker that silences could be transformed into significant expressions. The significance of listening is reiterated by another *Her-Meta* tale, called *A Story in Search of an Audience*, which gives an account of an old lady who wanted to tell a story, but found it very difficult to find an audience. Her sons and grandsons did not have time to listen to the story. 'Wherever she went, to whomsoever she approached, she couldn't find a single listener' (Ramanujan 2009: 31). At last, she found a pregnant woman who was very hungry. The old woman made *payasam* and fed her. And before she could tell the story, the pregnant woman fell asleep. When the old woman was upset, the girl child in the womb spoke, 'Why don't you tell me the story? I will listen to it' (Ramanujan 2009: 32).

The respect for inherent worth is indicated by the earnest listener in the unborn girl child. When the girl child in the womb listened to the story, the old woman blessed the child with these words, 'Wherever you go, deserted villages will become prosperous towns, cotton seeds will become pearls, dry trees will be covered with fruit, even old cows will give milk, barren women will have children, lost jewels will be found and dead men will come back to life' (Ramanujan 2009: 32). The girl child in the womb symbolises a microcosm of Mother Earth radiating the qualities of tolerance, care and concern. Later in the story, the girl child epitomises the spirit of nature power or *Shakthi* as she grows up in the lap of Mother Nature and the trees and the birds take care of her. She marries a king as the old woman had wished and their country becomes a land of milk and honey, signifying abundance. In the folktales selected for study, the women characters are named or 'un-named' in different ways. The first category is women without names. The 'poor widow' in *Tell It to the Walls*, 'A housewife' in *A Story and a Song*, the 'old woman', 'the pregnant woman' and the 'girl child' in *A Story in Search of an Audience*, the 'mother' are women characters with no names. They are named according to the social identity in a patriarchal setup.

Her-Meta motifs are recognised in 'her' stories narrated by women, about women and for women in relation to her environment. There is a search for the woman's voice and a quest for the 'listeners' in these stories. Women's tales which are considered taboo by a patriarchal society are also classified under *Her-Meta* stories. *Her-Meta* stories are read as Mother Earth Discourse, with the ecofeminist principles of sacredness and respect for the intrinsic value of women and nature in mind. The identification of *Her-Meta* stories has initiated the ecofeminist linguistic quest for women's voices in mainstream culture. The old widow in *Tell It to the Walls*, the housewife in *A Story and a Song* and the old woman in *A Story in Search of an Audience* are silenced women in search of a voice. *Her-Meta* tales are conscious expressions that attend to the devices and strategies of women's storytelling. The old widow finds solace after narrating her woes to the walls. The story and the song trapped inside a woman find a way to escape from the silent housewife in *A Story and a Song*. The value of an unborn girl child is reiterated in *A Story in Search of an Audience*. A girl child in her mother's womb listens to the old woman's story, which communicates the intrinsic value of life.

In folktales with *Her-Meta* motifs, the study shows that it is necessary to respect the voice of every living creature on this earth. *Her-Meta* relationships affirm the significance of identifying and recognising the silenced voices, such as the poor widow in *Tell It to the Walls*, the housewife in *A Story and a Song* and the old lady in *A Story in search of an Audience*. When human beings respect the spirituality in other living creatures, *Her-Meta* motifs emphasise the need for conscious listening. This is enhanced by being sensitive to the needs of women and their stories, calling attention to the woman's power of expression. While *Her-Meta* concerns basically define the need for women's expression as against women's silence in our society, the motifs that underscore women's freedom of expression through different forms of discourse characterised by wit, irony and humour, at times suppressed by the patriarchal culture, are classified as *Athena's Wit* in the following section.

Athena's Wit tales

Athena's Wit motifs are characterised by *Shakthi* when an environment provides women the right to expression, *Ahimsa* when her voice is accepted and respected without any hindrance and *Shanthi* in harmonious relationships. A. K. Ramanujan has delineated the significance of discovering alternative worldviews that lie hidden in darkness and silence in an oral tale. The story given below metaphorically suggests the importance of integrating alternative worldviews with the mainstream, which fulfils one of the goals of ecofeminist pedagogy.

> one dark night an old woman was searching intently for something in the street. A passer-by asked her, 'Have you lost something?' She answered 'Yes, I've lost my keys. I've been looking for them all evening.' 'Where did you lose them? 'I don't know. Maybe inside the house.' 'Then why are you looking for them here?' 'Because it's dark in there. I don't have oil in my lamps. I can see much better here under the streetlights.
>
> (Ramanujan 2009: xiv)

Folktales can be likened to cornucopia, a symbol of abundance and 'nature-culture'. There is a wealth of knowledge and wisdom unexplored in our culture and tradition. Like the old woman, many people look for keys under the streetlights and tend to ignore the fortune lying in the dark. The identification of *Athena's Wit* motifs in folktales illuminates the darkness and throws light on the silences.

Women's 'literal power of the spoken word' (Muthukumaraswamy 2008: 1) is captured in the Telugu folktale titled *The Princess in the Big Rock*. In this tale, a girl who is trapped within the rock is rescued by the power of maternal love and caring words. 'A mother went up to the rock and said, "Oh princess in the rock, come outside. Serve the ghee. Suddenly, from inside the rock a splendid, radiant woman came out. Everyone was amazed and gasped: "Ah!" The prince, smiling, took her hand' (Muthukumaraswamy 2008: 7). The story confirms the importance of woman's speech in a community, group and the society at large. The cyclical pattern of life is reinforced by this worldview. Transformation is another important characteristic in folk discourse and indigenous people believe in the transient nature of life, death and rebirth, as reflected in the folktales from India. The princess gets transformed from a passive rock to an active living being through the power of the word in the tale.

It Is Raining Snacks! is a folktale narrated by Nallu from Rasalipatty. The story throws light on the presence of mind and witty talk of rural women that reflects their understanding of the environment. The mother exemplifies a witty village woman who excels in crisis management. The mother and daughter find some treasure in the forest. The mother did not want her daughter to reveal this truth to the villagers.

> When she opened the box, she found gold coins glittering. The daughter looked at that. The mother thought that the daughter might tell this to the village people. She got an idea. She looked at her daughter and said, 'Hey look up.' The daughter looked up. She threw the snacks she had brought from home. She also showered the water she carried with her. The little girl asked her mother, 'What is this ma?' Amma replied, 'It is raining snacks.' The girl felt happy and cried, 'Hey, it is raining snacks, it is raining snacks.'
> (Porselvi 2015: 77)

When they returned to the village, the curious villagers asked the little girl about the source of wealth. The little girl replied 'When it rained snacks we got the treasure!' (Porselvi 2015: 77) The village people laughed at her and sent her away. The clever mother was proud of her witty plan that saved them. The tale throws light on the unique type of discourse that characterises mother–daughter relationships. In ancient times, women were specialists in food gathering, childcare, cooking, pottery, weaving, and construction of temporary or permanent shelters, tool-making and knew about the medicinal application of plants and herbs. The talented hardworking mother also has a worldview of abundance. She goes to another village with her daughter, builds a house and lives happily. She helps the poor people with gold coins she got from the forest. She buys some land and works hard in the fields. She also encourages her neighbours to work hard. She does a lot of charity. She becomes very popular in that country. The king hears this and marries her daughter. As she had the heart to share the treasure with the people around her, she received a lot of blessings in her life.

A *Poet and His Song* is a tale that highlights the theme of simplicity in rural woman's discourse. The tale emphasises the therapeutic quality of music. One day, Ramu the singer was walking down the road. Suddenly, he saw a rat on the way staring at him. Ramu looked at the rat and sang, as usual,

> 'Why are you blinking like that?
> ... blinking like that?'
> The busy rat started digging the soil. Ramu saw that and sang,
> 'Why are you digging like that?
> ... digging like that?'
> The frightened rat hurriedly ran away from the place. Ramu laughed and sang,
> 'Why are you running away like that?
> ... running away like that?'
>
> (Porselvi 2015: 35)

Ramu thought for a moment and realised that he had composed a funny song. He decided to sing the song to the king and get a prize from him. But ironically, the king became furious with Ramu. But when the king had a sleepless night, he finds refuge in Ramu's song, which yields him lot of benefits. Metaphorically speaking, the music and the song of a simple poet-singer restore a chaotic situation and create an integrated *oikos* or an environment of peace and harmony. The tale emphasises the therapeutic quality of music and reinforces *Shanthi Consciousness*.

The Crookened Back is an Irish folktale about Grandmother Peggy Barrett, a storyteller telling a story. This tale confirms the significance of storytelling as a form of procreation. She was known for her humorous tales. 'Peggy, like all experienced story-tellers, suited her tales, both in length and subject, to the audience and the occasion' (Ragan 2000: 21). Grandmothers pass on the lore from one generation to another. In *The Crookened Back*, Peggy Barrett gave 'full scope to her memory, or her imagination, or both' (Ragan 2000: 22). *Whuppity Stoorie* is a tale from Scotland that projects the vulnerable position of women, especially single mothers in a patriarchal society. When the husband abandons her, the woman who is named Goodwife is manipulated and exploited by people in her society. Like the heroine in *Rumplestiltskin*, Goodwife discovers the fairy's name, and as a result, saves herself and her child. 'Little kens our goodwife at home/That WHUPPITY STOORIE is my name!' (Ragan 2000: 30).

The Importance of Lighting is a tale popular in Tamilnadu, India about the goddesses Lakshmi and her sister. The story is about a young woman who brings prosperity to her home by replacing the goddess of poverty with the goddess of wealth through her wise words and deeds. One day, when the king of the town was having his bath, an eagle took away his ring and dropped it in the businessman's house. The young woman took the ring and tied it to the end of the sari and handed it over to the king. The king made an announcement that whoever brings back the ring to him, s/he will receive whatever s/he asks for. The young woman told her husband, 'Let us go and give it to the King. One thing I may tell you that I will never ask for riches. Whatever I ask from the king, you must be satisfied with that and will never get angry with me' (Ragan 2000: 190). Her husband agreed.

The woman used her intuition to bring perpetual wealth to her house. She went to the king and said, 'Your majesty! I do not want riches. My only wish is that on one Friday, nobody should light lamps in their houses. Even in the palace there should be no lamp. Only I will light lamps in my house' (Ragan 2000: 190). The king agreed to this. The young woman's family borrowed some money and bought oil, earthen lamps and cotton. The young woman and her two sisters-in-law observed fasting on Friday and lit the lamps all over the house. Goddess Lakshmi went around the town and found the houses in complete darkness. Then, she spotted the businessman's house fully lit and entered the house. 'Goddess Lakshmi's sister couldn't live there any longer . . . She promised that she would not enter it again and left the house through the back door' (Ragan 2000: 191). The family regained all the riches the next day. The story confirms the popular belief of Tamil people, who light lamps on Friday and welcome Goddess Lakshmi into their houses.

On the contrary, the famous Ambai chose her pen name for two reasons. One, she was not interested in the practice of 'Friday rituals' and the name of goddess 'Lakshmi' associated with it. Two, she borrowed the name Ambai from the character of a woman writer in Devan's novella *Parvatiyin Sangalpam* (Sangalpam means 'a determined vow'). The name 'Ambai' has its source in *The Mahabharatha* in the character of the androgynous 'Amba-Shikandin'. From this example, one is able to understand that women in the modern world appreciate the rituals to a certain extent in the right sense, but transcend beyond that for holistic development.

In the recent times, women writers such as Ambai and Bama have integrated folktales and folk songs in their fiction. *A Deer in the Forest* is a short story by Ambai which deals with a woman called Thangam Athai who could not bear a child. Ambai, in the introduction to the short story, explains,

'Thangam Athai emerged out of many women I knew. It is possible that she rewrote her body at that very moment when she was narrating the story to the children' (Ambai 2003: 10). The story begins, 'Those nights are unforgettable, nights when we listened to stories. It was Thangam Athai who told them. They were not the usual ones about the crow and the fox, the hare and the tortoise. These stories were her own' (Ambai 2003: 69). Thangam Athai narrates the story of the deer which loses its way into the forest. Later, the deer gets accustomed to the new environment and attains peace.

> Suddenly, as if a magic rod had been laid upon it, the deer's terror disappeared entirely. It began to like this forest. It began to learn all its nooks and crannies. Even though it was a different place, this forest, too, contained everything . . . The Deer understood all the secrets of this new forest. And after that it walked around the entire forest without fear. The deer's terror had all gone and it was at peace.
>
> (Ambai 2003: 79)

The symbolism of the deer in an alien environment reinforces the position of a woman who has gained critical consciousness. Through her storytelling sessions, Thangam Athai, as a conscious individual, resists the implications of the 'institutionalized motherhood' by suggesting an alternative form of procreation.

Folktale patterns have influenced writers such as Ambai. She experiments with different kinds of narrative techniques in her short stories. The above story is narrated from a child's point of view and 'the story inside the story' is rendered by Thangam Athai. The fable belongs to the Indian oral tradition of storytelling, where a grandmother or aunt tells stories to children at bedtime or mealtime, in a way passing on wisdom and knowledge to the younger generation of the family. 'As we children listened to the story, we imagined that the dark parts of the room were the forest; we made friends with the deer, and now we too were at peace' (Ambai 2003: 79). Affirmation of woman power calls for the celebration of womanhood in terms of body, mind and soul. *A Deer in the Forest* signifies the transition from silence to speech. Lakshmi Holmstrom, in her introduction to *A Purple Sea*, commenting on Ambai's works, states, 'Most of her stories, are, above all, celebrations of women, who are not seen as victims but rather as human beings coping with great courage and resourcefulness in the face of gender oppression and the bondage of ideologies' (Ambai 1992: 3).

Thangam athai in *A Deer in the Forest* represents the embodiment of an alienated self. As a 'childless' woman, she becomes 'an outsider'. She is defined as 'hollow' and one who 'had never flowered'. 'Valli's mother had once told Valli. "Hers is just a hollow body." Where was the hollow? Could it be that, like the broken wing of a bird, it was not visible?' (Ambai 2003: 71) Thangam Athai breaks the image of hollowness by narrating the symbolic story of the deer in the forest. In the 'deserted, friendless place. The deer trembled.' This indicates Thangam athai's position in a state of exile, a 'self' alienated from her own society. Alienation is 'a state of estrangement from oneself, or society' (Humm 1992: 6). Thangam Athai destroys her alienated self by re-creating a world of her own. Thus, the place gets 'transformed'. Thangam athai narrates, 'The moonlight fell softly, on everything and as if touched by a magic wand, the deer shed all fear. It liked the forest' (Ambai 2003: 76). The deer has transcended the reality of exile. So has Thangam Athai. The fable can be studied using Maslow's theory of the hierarchy of needs. The need for self-esteem and self-respect is fulfilled. On the one hand, Thangam Athai is a symbol of empowerment; on the other, she symbolises the transcended 'self'. In the process of telling the story, she attains self-actualisation by proving herself that she is a 'creator'.

Anecdotes, personal experiences, folktales, folk songs, riddles and proverbs that reflect the culture of Dalit women are recorded in Bama's novel *Sangati*. It explores the silences and celebrates the culture of Dalit women. It is a sociocultural document of Dalit women who live close to nature. In her 'preface' to the novel, Bama writes, 'Even in times of trouble, boredom, and depression, the urge grew to demolish the troubles and to live happily' (Bama 2005: vii). The novel begins with the lines, 'If the third is a girl to behold, your courtyard will fill with gold" When I was born, it seems that my grandmother, Vellaiyamma quoted this proverb and rejoiced' (Bama 2005: 3). In her introduction to *Sangati*, Lakshmi Holmstrom recounts that in the novel, the 'language of women' is characterised by 'its vigour, and its closeness to proverbs, folk songs, and folklore' (Bama 2005: xx) and she quotes Bama, 'From birth to death, there are special songs and dances. And it is only the women who will perform them. *Roraattu* (lullaby) to *oppari* (dirge), it is only the women who will sing them' (Bama 2005: xx).

The goddesses known for wisdom and knowledge, speech and expression, music and arts are as follows: Athena, Isis, Sophia (Greek) and Minerva (Roman), Saraswati, Kalaivani (Indian), Benzaiten (Japanese-Buddhist-Hindu) and Nuwa (Chinese). On the one hand, the patriarchal society reveres women as goddesses. Even today, in many cultures, women are restricted within the four walls of the house and excluded from formal education. In the past, they were silenced for several centuries, but women had identified other forms of discourse to express themselves. In the modern world, young women have lost track of the indigenous knowledge systems. Revisiting folklore enables a pragmatic approach to the holistic development of an individual, community, society and the world at large.

Kolam and rangoli are very effective forms of communication by women. In India, rangoli/*kolam* is a folk art, considered auspicious, when drawn in front of the houses to invoke God's blessings. In the past, women used rice flour to draw beautiful patterns and designs at the entrance of their houses. *Kolam* signifies an auspicious beginning and hope for the day. It is an alternative form of discourse of women.

> Making Rangoli is a thing of joy,
> It would fill your heart with lovely pleasure,
> When you would watch the silent Poetry,
> Smiling in your house on the floor,
> And telling a lovely story, of your creative art,
> You would feel as if, you have found a treasure,
> A treasure of wealth and a way to pleasure
> . . .
> Just make it near the entrance point,
> From where the Goddess of wealth
> May come seeing these colorful drawings,
> Sitting on her favorite seat of Lotus,
> She would enter in your house
> With her blessings of wealth & pleasure
> (Ravindra 2010)

Kolam is a form of prayer, meditation and expression of the sacredness of life. According to Dr Nirmal Selvamony, the drawing of the floral designs (*kolam*) in the courtyard of the house dates back to the Sangam period, which is recorded in poetry such as *Kuruntokai* and *Perumpaanaarruppatai* (Muthukumaraswamy 2006: 166). Women in India create rangoli designs in geometric shapes, flower patterns and images of gods and goddesses. Hence, the identification of motifs becomes the starting point in understanding the Mother Earth Discourse. Susan Hawthorne, an Australian ecofeminist thinker and poet, visited India in 2009 and wrote a poem on the significance of *kolam* to women in Tamilnadu.

> where they are drawn and when
> is all important
>
> early morning is auspicious
> it sets the shape of the day
>
> I watch as a watered driveway
> scrubbed clean
> has a few points of white grain sprinkled

the woman works quickly
she knows her design for the day
runs the powdered grain
from point to point

it is a mandala
a yantra
a sign

so that the forces of the universe
align themselves
with her intentions
 (Hawthorne 2009)

In the recent times, mathematicians have identified *kolam* as scientific representations in nature-culture. Mathematicians have identified the Fibonacci number sequence (0, 1, 1, 2, 3, 5, 8, 13 . . .) in traditional *kolams*. *Kolam* connects spirituality with science. The different reasons for drawing a *kolam* are listed by Peter Claus in *South Asian Folklore: An Encyclopedia*:

> Tamil women say there are six major reasons why the Kolam is created: 1) to create a space of auspiciousness, goodwill and luck; 2) to show the presence of the woman householder; 3) to welcome the goddess Lakṣmi, the goddess of wealth, prosperity and alertness, and to banish the goddess Mudevi, the goddess of poverty, misery and laziness; 4) to show that the household is in the state of overflowing abundance and not in misery; 5) to feed a thousand souls – ants, insects and birds; and 6) to absorb the ill effects of the evil eye.
> (Claus 2003: 340–41)

Kolam is a powerful form of discourse that determines women's physical and mental space. It is usually drawn at three important spaces: the kitchen space around the hearth/stove where cooking takes place; the entrance of the house and the threshold of a temple. As A. K. Ramanujan puts it, 'What we separate as art, economics, and religion appear intermeshed as aspects of the same performance. The aesthetics, ethos and worldview of a person are shaped in childhood and throughout early life and reinforced later by these verbal and nonverbal environments' (Ramanujan 2009: xiv).

In *The Dead Bridegroom*, a folktale from Karnataka, a young prince named Jayasekhara tragically died of a sudden illness. The king wanted to get his son married even after his death. The king wanted a bride for his dead son. There was a poor Brahmin who had a daughter named Lalitha. He wished to get his daughter married to the dead prince. Though Lalitha's mother disagreed to this, the poor man thought that it would bring him some wealth. Lalitha was married to the dead prince. When she was about to enter the funeral pyre along with her husband, she had a voice. An old woman who stood there said that if she performed the Jyothi Puja, the Worship of light, he would come back to life. 'Lalita wasted no time. She cleaned the floor and placed a wooden plank on it. She decorated the floor around it with rangoli designs made of white powder. She spread rice on the plank and placed a pair of lamps on it, lit them and worshipped the Force of Light . . . The Prince took a breath, another, then sat up as though waking from deep sleep' (Sherman 2009: 297). The folktale reveals the spirit of hope and redemption.

Athena's Wit tales confirm the importance of understanding women's oral tradition. This is, at times, a story within a story, a tale which highlights the conventions of storytelling and/or a tale addressed directly to the reader. *Her-Meta* motifs redefine the significance of women's voices to create a better environment. By showcasing the voices of women, these stories reinforce the value of their *Shakthi Consciousness*. These stories are oral tales that accentuate the importance of speaking and listening in the context of woman and her environment. These folktales represent the silenced voices of women and their voiceless narratives. Apart from the identification of women's tales about storytelling, they also stress the need to listen consciously, which is an important way of acknowledging the intrinsic value of human beings in an environment. The analysis of folktales from India suggests that: Creation stories around the world confirm that Mother Earth originated with the help of the all-pervading feminine force. The relationship between the first woman and man indicate that they formed out of an organic whole. They represent complementary principles in nature. They upheld the spirit of interconnectedness and interdependence. Women were celebrated as goddesses from ancient times. However, this raises the problem of merely putting them on the pedestal, on the one hand, and trampling them under the feet, on the other. Nevertheless, goddess images empower young women of all cultures in different ways.

Food is an effectual form of discourse. Food and stories nourish the body, mind and soul. What is the relationship between food and stories? Why did mothers and grandmothers narrate tales at mealtimes to children in the olden days? How do we revisit and redefine women's food culture close to nature? How did women celebrate nature-culture? How did women recognise the spirit of sisterhood? These questions communicate the interdependence of nature, women, children, men and other nonhuman living beings on this earth. The themes of food, household and sisterhood are discussed as *Annamangai* tales and *Sis-Tie* tales in the following chapter.

4

FOOD, HOUSEHOLD AND SISTERHOOD

> We're connected, as women. It's like a spider web. If one part of that web vibrates, if there's trouble, we all know it, but most of the time we're just too scared, or selfish, or insecure to help. But if we don't help each other, who will?
>
> — Sarah Addison Allen

Indian ecofeminism integrates the social, the cultural, the natural and the spiritual into a holistic philosophy of life. Ecofeminists strongly believe in revisiting the pre-patriarchal societies, and as a form of pedagogical quest, learn from them. Starhawk is a believer of ecofeminist spirituality and cultural ecofeminism. In her book *The Spiral Dance* (Starhawk 1999), she explains that cultural feminism understands 'women are in essence more nurturing, peaceful, co-operative and closer to nature than men' (215). Social ecofeminism believes in equality of the sexes and aims at gender equity and sustainable development. Cultural ecofeminism aspires to study women and their relationship with nature-culture. The spiritual slant to ecofeminism has evolved into yet another school of thought, called ecofeminist spirituality. *Annamangai* motifs deal with the representation of nature-centred cultural representations of women and food in folktales from India. *Sis-Tie* reverberates the bonding among women that emphasises collective strength and peaceful coexistence. Food and other forms of culture in the rural household reiterate the spirit of sisterhood. The different nature-centred rituals and practices emerge as multifarious threads that bind women's nature-culture into an organic whole.

Annamangai tales

Folktales and food are inextricably bound to one another in *Annamangai* tales. The oral tales chosen for analysis in this section are: *Fruits of Annadhanam, The Clever Daughter-in-Law, Dolls, For Love of Kadabu, It Is*

FOOD, HOUSEHOLD AND SISTERHOOD

Raining Snacks! and *The Man Who Loved Two Women, Maya and Laya*. *Fruits of Annadhaanam* is a Tamil oral tale narrated by Kamatchi Ammal from Rasaalipatty, Pudukottai District. In this folktale, a poor mother and her son, Balan, live in a certain town. The mother worked as a daily labourer. In the evening, when she came back from work, she cooked food, and shared some of it with a needy person. Balan did not understand the reason for this gesture.

> 'It is alright if we have plenty. But Amma is struggling hard to earn the rupee. With that money why does she do charity.' Balan asked his mother. The mother replied, 'the best form of charity is *Annadhaanam* . . . giving food to others. Those who practice *Annadhaanam* would reap the fruits one day'.
>
> (Porselvi 2015: 13)

In order to find out an answer, he went into the forest to meet an ascetic. On the way, he meets a mango tree, a snake and a pond who had their own doubts and wanted answers from the ascetic. Balan finds out the answer for the questions of the mango tree, the snake and the pond, and also, finally understands the value of giving alms. Balan has a different level of consciousness in the beginning of the story. In the quest to meet the Siddhar, Balan undergoes a consciousness-raising process whereby his experience teaches new truths. At the end of the tale, he is convinced about his mother's worldview of abundance. He also understands the benefits of respecting the intrinsic value of life around him. Closely associated with *Annadhaanam* is the Tamil word called *Virunthombal* (which means hospitality/serving the guest), which is represented in *Tirukkural*. For example,

> Each day he tends the coming guest with kindly care;
> Painless, unfailing plenty shall his household share. (83)
>
> With smiling face he entertains each virtuous guest,
> 'Fortune' with gladsome mind shall in his dwelling rest. (84)

Virunthombal brings prosperity and a sense of well-being to the family that serves the guest with love and care. Mother Teresa narrates an 'extraordinary experience' in her Nobel Peace Prize Speech about her visit to a Hindu family who had eight children. When she took some rice and went to meet the poor family, the mother took the rice and divided into two portions and went out. Mother Teresa narrates,

> When she came back I asked her – where did you go, what did you do? And she gave me a very simple answer: They are hungry

also . . . What struck me most was that she knew – and who are they, a Muslim family – and she knew. I didn't bring more rice that evening because I wanted them to enjoy the joy of sharing. But there were those children, radiating joy, sharing the joy with their mother because she had the love to give. And you see this is where love begins – at home.

(Teresa 1979)

These tales and narratives explicate the nature-nurture proposition that unites women with Mother Earth. They are tales which deal with food, nurture, sharing and love. There are other folktales that showcase food as a source of conflict, crisis and a tool of power politics.

In *The Clever Daughter-in-Law*, the mother-in-law is 'a terrible tyrant' (Ramanujan 1997: 31). The daughter-in-law is made to do all the household chores, such as clearing the cowshed and carrying water from the well. But she is given 'leftovers and stale rice' (Ramanujan 1997: 31) to eat. There is a snake gourd plant in the backyard of the house. Whenever the mother-in-law prepared a big potful of snake gourd *talada*, she and her son would eat most of it and give very little to the daughter-in-law. One day, when the mother-in-law had gone out, the daughter-in-law prepared a potful of snake gourd *talada* and took it to the Goddess Kali temple. She sat next to the image of the goddess and ate the entire pot. When the mother-in-law came to know this, she abused her and beat her. However, Goddess Kali, who was a witness to the daughter-in-law, was said to be in a state of shock and 'the Kali image in the temple now had its hand on its mouth' (Ramanujan 1997: 32). This tale throws light on the power politics played by the mother-in-law in managing the household.

The villagers believed that somebody had polluted the goddess and her temple. The daughter-in-law understood the truth and went to the temple. She chastised the goddess image with a broomstick. The goddess image removed her hand from her face. The villagers appreciated her. But her husband and her mother-in-law were terrified by the incident. They decided to kill her. However, the daughter-in-law cleverly escapes from their trap, sets out into the forest, comes across a group of thieves, tackles them with her wit, and finally, returns home. The mother-in-law was appalled to see her daughter-in-law come back to life. The daughter-in-law narrated the story of how she came back to life from the dead (Ramanujan 1997: 35). From that moment, the mother-in-law realised the worth of her daughter-in-law and they led a happy life. The daughter-in-law emerges as an empowered woman, outwitting the thieves in the forest and her relationships at home. She exemplifies *Shakthi Consciousness*.

In this tale, there are three important women characters – the mother-in-law, the daughter-in-law and the Goddess Kali. The mother-in-law–daughter-in-law relationship is a political one. The mother-in-law expects her daughter-in-law to do all the work. The daughter-in-law brings water for the house, cleans the house and looks after the household, including the vegetable garden in their house. The mother and son exploit her labour and refuse to share the produce. One day, when she wishes to taste the fruit of her labour, she is punished. The daughter-in-law emerges as a heroine by using the mythical associations with Goddess Kali (goddess of power) and God Yama (god of death) in the end. She recreates her environment by empowering herself and raising the level of consciousness of people around her. She acquires *Shakthi Consciousness* in her life, exhibits *Ahimsa Consciousness* even when her husband, mother-in-law and the thieves inflict violence on her, and ultimately, brings about *Shanthi Consciousness* to her family in the end of the tale.

Dolls is a tale that 'teaches' a woman to control her desires to eat food. A husband brings a bushel of fish every day. But his wife would eat up 'all the middles of the fish' and leave him 'only fish heads and fish tails' (Ramanujan 1997: 50). He seeks the help of his sister, who lived in the same town. The sister asks him to make three dolls and place them 'one near the cooking fire, a second one among the pot, and another in the wall niche' (Ramanujan 1997: 50). Next time, when the wife begins to eat the fish, the dolls begin to speak. 'The doll in the wall answered . . . ' The woman gets scared, and from that day onwards, she fed her husband with all the fish. The husband thanks his sister for the idea. This tale highlights the use of wooden dolls as psychological tools to teach a lesson to the woman who craved food.

The Clay Mother-in-Law is a Tamil folktale about a naive daughter-in-law who follows her mother-in-law's orders every day. After the mother-in-law's death, the daughter-in-law is in a state of confusion. 'She could not see her way about the little house and she missed her mother-in-law's daily instructions' (Ramanujan 2009: 36). Like the three dolls in the previous tale, the husband prepares a clay doll of his mother. 'He went to the nearest potter and ordered a clay image of his mother, as large as life. He gave special instructions to the potter to make one hand show two fingers and the other three' (Ramanujan 2009: 36). Every day, the daughter-in-law cooked and served food for her clay mother-in-law. A wicked woman from the neighbourhood entered the house through a hole every day and stole the food spread in front of the clay doll. The innocent daughter-in-law believed that her mother-in-law ate the food every day. This simple tale throws light on the conditions in a patriarchal society in which many women are kept in a world of darkness and ignorance. Lack of education is one of the key factors that restrained women within the four walls of the house. The story also reveals the fact that the mother-in-law, as an agent of patriarchal society, never taught her daughter-in-law to be independent, skilful and clever. In such families, besides formal education, the young daughters-in-law did not receive the indigenous wisdom from elderly women in the family because of their prejudice and bias.

For Love of Kadabu is a famous oral tale narrated in many parts of India and also in China. A man visits her mother-in-law's house and falls in love with a dish called *Kadabu* (sweet puffs). He returns home to tell his wife muttering '*Kadabu* . . . *Kadabu*' on the way. But when he slipped and fell on the road, he screamed '*Badaku!*' He forgot the word *Kadabu*. When he reached home, he asked his wife to prepare *Badaku* for him. The wife did not understand what he meant and made fun of him. The furious husband 'slapped her cheeks and boxed her ears' (Ramanujan 2009: 69). When an elderly lady from the neighbourhood heard the news, she came home and said, 'You've have beaten up the poor girl so badly. Look at her, her cheeks have puffed up like a *Kadabu!*' (Ramanujan 2009: 69), and the man jumped up with joy and said that it was *Kadabu* and not *Badaku* that he wanted. In the Tamil version, *Kadabu* is replaced with *Kozhukottai*. Though the folktale is narrated often and is considered an amusing tale, the woman getting beatings from her husband reflects a society that overlooked domestic violence. In the Tamil version, he forgets the word *kozhukattai* when he jumps across a puddle and screams '*athiripachaa!*' (an exclamatory word). In another story, a *Patti* (grandmother) is cooking *kozhukattai*. It is evening time. She goes to the cowshed to give food and water to her favourite cow. She also spent time talking to her. After some time, when she returns, she finds the food was uncooked.

> So Patti asked, '*Kozhukkattai, Kozhukkattai*, why are you not cooked yet?' To which *Kozhukkattai* replied, 'the stove was not lit, so I am not cooked'. So Patti asked the stove, 'Oh stove, why were you not burning?' The stove said, 'Nobody kept firewood, so I did not burn'. Patti turned to her daughter-in-law, 'Oh dear daughter-in-law, why did you not put firewood in the stove?' Daughter-in-law answered, 'The baby was crying, so I did not put firewood'. Patti cooed to the baby, 'Oh my dear child, why did you cry'. The baby wept, 'Ants bit me so I cried'. Patti approached the ant, 'Oh ant, why did you bite the baby?' 'Will I not bite if somebody put their foot into the ant-hill?'
>
> (Ammupatti 2008)

It is a story to teach children not to play with ant-hills. Apart from that, this simple tale throws light on the responsibilities of women in the household.

The conflict arises when women try to balance domesticity and creativity in their everyday life. The patriarchal society frames laws, creates rules and prepares 'conduct books' for women. According to those laws, a woman's primary concern must be related to the domestic. A woman writer, a creative human being, struggles her way to create and express herself in different works of art. Women have a conflict with the traditional roles of mother, lover and wife. Only some women are able to transcend the limitations of the domestic space by speaking or writing about them. For example, in the short story *Gifts*, Ambai narrates, 'I've been cooking *dosais* since I was ten. Enough to feed twenty people a day, for forty years. How many does that make? Seven thousand and three hundred *dosais* a year. Two lakh and ninety-two thousand *dosais* in forty years. Besides *idlis*, *vadais*, *appams*, vegetable curries and *sambars*. How many times has she drained the rice? How many kilos of rice has she cooked? And she smiles' (Ambai 1992: 9). The household chores are usually unrecognised and unacknowledged. In the story *A Kitchen in the Corner of the House*, Ambai presents the details of the kitchen activities in a strenuous manner. 'Jiji kneaded mountains of Chappati dough. She sliced baskets of onions and kilos of meat. She sliced baskets of onions and kilos of meat. She roasted *pappads* in the evening [. . .] She made the *pakoras*, she fried entrails' (Ambai 1992: 237). By finding an expression to the 'unexpressed' and by creating an alternative space, the woman-narrator (the author herself or the persona representing the author) and the narrated woman discover the 'true self'. Moreover, in the process, they attain self-realisation, and finally, they reach the supreme state of 'self-actualisation'.

Food is always associated with one's faith and value systems. *A Life of Contentment* is a simple fable narrated by Saroja from Virudhapatti, which reiterates the age-old belief, 'East or west, home is the best'. It is a tale about the friendship between a cat in a village and a fox in the woods. The cat shares food items such as the *vadai* and the *appalam* with the fox. The fox is tempted to eat different types of food in the village. The fox thought, 'instead of eating one food everyday how it would be, if we eat all the varieties on the same day' (Porselvi 2015: 19). However, the cat discourages this idea. At midnight, the fox reached the house where the cat lived. The people at home were fast asleep. The cat wanted to make his friend happy. So, he served different kinds of food items. The fox ate to his fill and felt very sleepy. After some time, the fox suddenly woke up. He thought that he was in the forest and started howling loudly. The people in the house got up immediately and ran in all directions. The frightened cat saw that and went into hiding. The fox got beatings from the villagers. He ran away into the forest to save his life. The folktale underscores the ecofeminist belief in contentment and gratification as against greed and jealousy. A folklore enthusiast may be reminded of a similar motif in an Aesop's fable called 'The Country Mouse and the Town Mouse'. This tale emphasises contentment as a course to *Shanthi* or Peace.

The Man Who Loved Two Women is a Nagaland folktale. A man meets two young women; one is rich and another is poor. He did not know whom he should marry. His mother suggested a competition for the two. On a particular day, the mother and son took the two young women for a picnic lunch. The rich woman ate and drank very little, whereas the poor woman ate to her heart's content. The young man followed the rich girl to her house and hid himself near a window.

> 'I'm starving,' she snapped. 'Make me some dinner.' Her parents hurriedly cooked some rice and boiled some arum roots. 'Here you are dear,' they said, placing the food before her. 'I'm tired,' said the woman. 'Feed me.' Both her father and mother sat before her, peeling arum roots and stuffing them into her mouth as if she were a baby bird, and feeding her handfuls of rice.
>
> (Adhikary 2003: 16–17)

For every mouthful of food she ate, the man filled the same amount of sand and pebbles in a cloth sack. The next day, he showed the sack of sand and pebbles and asked the young women, 'who can eat as much rice and arum root as I have sand and stones?' The rich woman deceitfully said, 'do you think we are gluttons?' But the poor woman honestly replied, 'If I had that much food, I would probably eat it all' (Adhikary 2003: 17). The young man came to a conclusion. He chose the poor young woman as his wife for her sincerity.

Fasting is an important aspect that connects women with the environment. In her article 'Food Is Everything', Vandana Shiva explains,

> Fasting has been used for the purification of the body, mind and soul. The body is purified by letting it rest and allowing it to cleanse itself through self-regulation. The mind is purified by the cultivation of self-control. The discipline of eating is not just a biological discipline, it is also a mental discipline. Above all, it

makes us aware of the sacredness of food, the sacredness of our body and the connection of our food and body to the universe.
(http://www.resurgence.org/magazine/article 2690-food-is-everything.html)

Fasting is practised in almost all cultures and religions across the world. Buddhists practise nineteen-day fasting; in Christianity, people fast for forty days during Lent, especially on Ash Wednesday and Good Friday. In Islam, people fast during the holy month of Ramadan. In Jainism, there are different kinds of fasting, promoting the *Ahimsa* way of life. Fasting is also a form of *Satyagraha*, a nonviolent form of protest used by environmentalists in different cultures.

The goddesses of food, cooking and home in different cultures are *Annapoorani* (Tamil), *Edesia* (Roman), *Ukemochi* (Japanese), *Hestia* (Greek) and *Shakambari* (Indian). Women in the domestic sphere spend an enormous amount of energy to fulfil the expectations of the other members of the family. Nevertheless, quite ironically, they lack self-identity. The young girl in 'Gifts' is 'socialized' by the patriarchal society. The woman writer asks: 'Then what do you do at home?' (Ambai 1992: 13). The young girl replies, 'O, I've got masses to do. How can amma do all the work by herself? Anni and I help her. We have to feed the cows, grind the rice for dosais, make the chutney. . . .' (Ambai 1992: 13). Similarly, another 'woman in the house' takes on the enormous labour.

The household chores are usually unrecognised and unacknowledged.

A Tamil proverb goes, 'The skill of women goes as far as the fireplace'. Do women feel contented to be Hestia's heir? This position raises the problem of restricting women within the four walls of the house. In *Therigatha*, the earliest known anthology of songs written by Buddhist *theris* or nuns, which dates back to the 6th century BC, Sumangalamata's song 'A Woman Well Set Free! How Free I Am' reads:

> A woman well set free! How free I am,
> How wonderfully free, from kitchen drudgery.
> Free from the harsh grip of hunger,
> And from empty cooking pots,
> Free too of that unscrupulous man,
> The weaver of sunshades.
> Calm now and serene I am,
> All lust and hatred purged.
> To the shade of the spreading trees I go
> And contemplate my happiness.
> (Tharu and Lalita 2011: 69)

Trees offer an alternative form of shelter that allows women to breathe freely, compared to the patriarchal space that suffocates them. The woman feels that she wants to be set free from the 'kitchen drudgery' and the 'empty cooking pots' and 'To the shade of the spreading trees I go' and contemplate her 'happiness' (Tharu and Lalita 2011: 69). The woman finds peace under the trees. The poet persona draws the distinction between the physical space that restricts her and the spiritual space that promises to redeem her. She finds peace and happiness under the trees. The feminist concerns of enclosure and escape are represented in Sumangalamata's song. It is important to realise the role of women at home (family) and also Home (the world at large).

In olden days, women who lived close to nature believed in the spirit of sisterhood. Women are connected together in the web of life, experiencing the same anxieties, troubles and difficulties in life. 'Sisterhood includes the idea and experience of female bonding, and the self-affirmation and identity discovered in a woman-centred vision and definition of womanhood' (Humm 1992: 268). In the next section, *Sis-Tie* motifs are identified in folktales from India.

Sis-Tie tales

Sis-Tie tales have the following characteristics: there are sisters who are loving and sisters who are jealous; a clever sister and a foolish sister; a rich and evil sister and a poor and kind sister; sisterhood among women from different families; sisterhood among women and trees, birds and animals; sisterhood that raises the level of consciousness of people around them and sisterhood that empowers and transforms the society in which they live. Neera Desai (2006) in her book, *Feminism as Experience: Thoughts and Narratives*, studies the use of terms associated with women and feminism. According to her, in the Gujarati language, which is her mother tongue, there are three terms used to refer to women. They are *stree, nari, mahila*, each with different connotations. The first two words have a biological connection whereas the third term refers to women in groups. In Tamil, women are classified according to their age, *pedhai* (5–7 years), *pedumbhai* (8–11 years), *mangai* (12–13 years), *madanthai* (14–19 years), *arivai* (20–25 years), *therivai* (26–31 years) and *perilam penn* (32–40 years). There are a number of folktales that deal with sisters and sisterhood of all ages and their concerns of immediate and the larger environment.

Maya and Laya is a Nagaland folktale about two friends belonging to an agrarian household. Folktales all over the world have the rich family–poor family motifs in different languages. In the Nagaland tale, Laya's family is rich and Maya's family is poor. Every day, the two women shared lunch with each other. In times of famine, Laya's family helped Maya's family. Woman's ecological awareness and sensitivity is part of her consciousness. Her eco-sensitivity and eco-consciousness emerge out of the need to fulfil her responsibilities in day-to-day life. She understands the needs of fellow human beings, on the one hand, and the needs of nonhuman living organisms, on the other hand. Folktales reveal woman–nature relationships that are characterised by care and concern for Mother Earth and her children. The story also underscores the value of a girl child. In many villages across India, even today, female infanticide is a common practice. The patriarchal system is strongly rooted in the minds of women who consider the girl child a burden. In Usilampatti, a village near Madurai, a woman remarked, 'I will keep this one, only if it is a son' (Bhatnagar and Dube 2005: 1).

Sona and Rupa is a Hindi folktale in which a young prince falls in love with his sisters and intends to marry them. In this folktale, when the sisters reject his proposal and refuse the incestuous relationship a sandalwood tree offers refuge.

> Now, on the bank of the river where they bathed grew a sandalwood tree that the two princesses had watered and tended since they were small. It had grown with them. It was now tall and full-grown.
> On the wedding day, Sona and Rupa climbed the sandalwood tree and hid in its branches.
> (Ramanujan 2009: 16)

In the folktale, when the father and son, representatives of the patriarchal society, stand near the tree and ask the girls to come down, the girls say, 'Higher, higher, O Sandal wood tree' and the tree grew taller and taller. The story ends with these words, 'All at once, clouds gathered. The skies thundered. The tree suddenly split open and took them inside. Before the family's eyes, Sona and Rupa vanished deep within the tree' (Ramanujan 2009: 16). *Sona and Rupa* exemplifies the patriarchal structures that fail to consider women's likes and dislikes. There are three women characters in this story. The mother fails to convince her son. The mother is silenced by the father and the son. The father and the son try to persuade the girls into marriage. The story gives an account of the transition from hierarchic *oikos* to anarchic *oikos*.

Sis-Tie stories celebrate the spirit of sisterhood not just among women, but also among women and trees. A *Narrinai* poem, written during the Sangam age in Tamilnadu, effectively communicates woman–nature relationship. According to the poet, woman and tree share the spirit of sisterhood.

> What Her Girl Friend Said
> to him (on her behalf) when he came by daylight
> Playing with friends one time
> we pressed a ripe seed
> into the white sand
> and forgot about it
> till it sprouted
> and when we nursed it tenderly
> pouring sweet milk with melted butter,
> Mother said,
> 'It qualifies
> as a sister to you, and it's much better
> than you,'
> So,
> We're embarrassed
> To laugh with you here
> (Ramanujan 2006: 33)

The woman–nature relationship in the form of sisterhood reiterates Woody-Woman sensitivity and proximity. The woman's voice in the poem explicates the integrative *oikos* where human beings revere the sacred element of nature. The woman celebrates the spirit of sisterhood with the tree.

Sukhu and Dukhu is an oral tale in which the concept of happiness and sadness are personified as two sisters with contrasting qualities. Dukhu is good-natured, hardworking, sensitive and patient. She maintains an effective relationship with her natural environment and she is rewarded by the Old Mother of the Moon. Dukhu is assisted by the wind in her quest, and on the way, she cleans the place for the cow, relieves a plantain tree from the wild creepers and removes the saddle and bridle for a horse. In contrast, Sukhu shirks her responsibility, refuses to help others, ignores the Old Mother of the Moon's orders and meets with a tragic end. Dukhu's *oikos* is an integrative *oikos*, where animals, plants and human beings live in harmony. 'Dukhu drew water from the well and got herself a broom and washed the cowshed clean as clean could be. . .she tore down all the creepers that were smothering the tree. . .' (Ramanujan 2009: 72). Dukhu embodies eco-sensitivity and eco-consciousness whereas Sukhu is self-centred, who longs for material comforts. Dukhu symbolises contentment. When the Moon Mother asks her to choose a box, she chooses the smallest and a handsome prince rose from it. On the contrary, though Sukhu is also provided with the same kind of opportunities to sustain and survive, her selfishness and craving for luxury and comfort result in an anarchic *oikos*. She chooses the biggest box in the Old Mother of the Moon's court and ends up with a long black snake hissing angrily and finally swallowing her. An ecofeminist reading of the folktale disputes the patriarchal construction of the 'good girl'. According to Mary Daly, there are two types of meaning to the word 'self' in the feminist context: 'a woman's true self and her false self' and 'under patriarchy women have a false self because they are alienated from authentic experience' (Humm 1992: 254). Sukhu and Dukhu may be understood as the two different selves of womanhood within the patriarchal society. Dukhu conforms to the existing system, and thus, emerges a winner. Sukhu symbolises a rebel in the traditional system and pays a heavy price for it. Sukhu is a failure in the patriarchal society as she thinks differently. The folktale *Sukhu and Dukhu* is classified as a *Woody-Woman* story as both women, Sukhu and Dukhu, get an opportunity to care for trees. Dukhu shows her concern to the flora in distress and receives the blessings of nature. Sukhu, on the contrary, does not listen to the voices of nature and suffers defeat.

In *The Child Who Was Poor and Good*, a Greek folktale, a poor woman has four girl children. She was a hardworking woman. But she had money only to feed them. She did not have enough to clothe them. If someone gave them clothes, she gave it to her eldest daughter. The youngest girl went around in a ragged little dress, whether it was summer or winter. The child decided to leave the house. Like Dukhu, the little girl was a kind soul. During her quest, first, she finds a young and featherless bird that had fallen from its nest. 'She took it in her little hands and when she saw a man coming along the road, she asked him to put the bird back in the nest' (Ragan 2000: 60). Then, she meets a spider spinning a web. When she moved along carefully without disturbing the web, the spider thanked her and said, 'Thank you, my good child. What would you have me do for you in return for your kindness to me? Where are you going, all unclad and barefoot?' (Ragan 2000: 60) Finally, she meets a lamb, who gave her some wool to make a fine dress. Nature blesses the girl child for her care and concern for other nonhuman living beings. As she was returning home with the wool in her hands, she came across the bird's nest. The mother bird spoke, 'You dear child!' said the bird's mother. 'How can I thank you? How can I repay your goodness in saving my little one's life?' (Ragan 2000: 61). And with these words, she spun the wool into a long thread. The little girl took the spun thread into a ball and walked towards home. On the way, she met the spider, who took the thread 'and began to weave it, as quick as lightning and as fine as a weaver' (Ragan 2000: 62) and gave the cloth to the little girl. The child took the cloth home and her mother sewed a pretty little dress for her. This tale

FOOD, HOUSEHOLD AND SISTERHOOD

celebrates the theme of sisterhood. The little girl had three sisters at home. But in her quest to find a new dress, she explores the spirit of sisterhood with a little bird, a spider and a lamb, and in return, receives nature's blessings. The distinction between the two types of self – the true self and the false self – of women in a patriarchal society is represented in the oral tales. Hanchi is called the Indian Cinderella tale, which communicates transformation of a different kind. In *Hanchi*, the woman is identified by the food she prepares and not by the glass sandals. Hanchi is described as a clever woman who outwits a lecherous Guruswami. She is an embodiment of *Shakthi* who fights the patriarchal system that tries to treat her as an object. In most of the folktales across the world, the characters do not have names. The name 'Hanchi' symbolises the hidden identity of a woman in an unjust society. The narrator describes,

> The girl in the clay mask wandered from place to place as long as her mother's bundle of bread and rice lasted. Because her mask looked so much like clay tile-hanchu-she changed her name to Hanchi.
>
> (Ramanujan 2009: 343)

These lines reveal the fact that, indeed, the girl had an original identity and an original name, which she had to conceal for the sake of her existence in a patriarchal society. In the Egyptian Cinderella, *Rhodopis,* whose name meant 'rosy-cheeked', was kidnapped by pirates across the Nile River and was sold as a slave. She found herself lonely among the women in the alien land as 'she had pale skin and her cheeks were rosy. Her hair was gold and blew when the wind was windy, and theirs was black and stayed straight. Her eyes were green and theirs are brown.. But she "found friends with the animals". Like her European counterpart Rhodopis also receives a pair of red-rose gold slippers from her master. God Horus came down from the sky in the form of a falcon and took her slipper which looked like "the scrap of the sun" and gave it to the Pharaoh. "Then the pharaoh saw Rhodopis and asked if she would try on the slipper. She did and it fit. Then she became the queen"' (McCarthy 1991: 86).

The Child Who Taught a Lesson to the King is a story narrated by Maariammal from Nambampatti, and underscores the respect for the inherent worth of living beings on earth, which is one of the fundamental principles of Deep Ecology. In this folktale, a child gets lost. The king, disguised as a bangle-seller, finds her and takes her to the palace. When he asks the child about her mother, she says, 'My mother is a very beautiful woman' (Porselvi 2015: 105). The king sent his soldiers to bring all the beautiful women in the town. The child did not find her mother in the group. The next morning, when the mother arrived, the king was shocked to find a woman with 'tattered hair, a plain dull face and lean body' (Porselvi 2015: 105). The king understood the meaning of true beauty, the beauty of mind and heart. The small child had taught a lesson to the king of a country. Mirrors symbolise the patriarchal construction of beauty. There are a number of folktales around the world that have the mirror imagery. In *Snow White and the Seven Dwarfs*, the wicked queen asks the mirror, 'Mirror Mirror on the Wall! Who Is the Fairest of Them All?' The child in *The Child Who Taught a Lesson to the King* mirrors the real beauty of her mother. One of the prerogatives of ecofeminist thought is to respect the sacredness and intrinsic value of life without paying much attention to physical beauty.

In the novella *Unpublished Manuscript* by Ambai, the mirror is an empowering tool. Chentamarai, the protagonist, subverts the theory that surrounds the mirror image. She re-constructs, re-defines the 'self' through imagination by standing in front of the mirror.

> She would raise the mirror half-way, bring it down abruptly, and look fiercely into it – swinging her head sharply to one side. She was the three-eyed one. . . Sometimes, standing a little distance away, she would walk towards the mirror, composing her face in lines of perfect serenity. This was her yogic look. The look that would make people fall at her feet. [. . .] 'Who are you today?' Amma would ask. She had many names. Poets, artists, writers and such. The sex didn't matter. If one day she were Lopamudra, another day she would be Nakkeeran. If one day she were Avvaiyar, another day she would be Paari. Bharathiyar one day. Akka Mahadevi the next [. . .].
>
> (Ambai 2003: 38–39)

The thirteen-year-old girl in *My Mother, Her Crime* is the first-person narrator of that particular story. The author presents an authentic record of the conflict in the little girl's mind through the first-person narration. The biological destiny of the young girl becomes the central conflict of the story. Two issues are addressed in the course of the story. One, that the girl has attained 'puberty', and two, that she is dark. The narrator is an innocent girl who encounters the harsh reality. Talking about 'puberty' is considered a 'taboo'. This meaningless belief leads the young girl into a state of anxiety and anguish. In the beginning of the story, the little girl narrates,

> One evening, as I lie with my head on my mother's lap, some words I had read earlier, come to my mind. 'Amma, what does 'puberty' mean?' Silence. A long silence.
>
> (Ambai 1992: 19–20)

FOOD, HOUSEHOLD AND SISTERHOOD

Later, when her mother is away at a relative's house, the girl attains puberty. The girl-narrator experiences conflict, both physiologically and psychologically. She narrates

> Good God, nothing has happened to me, has it? But even as I ask myself this, I realize that something has happened. Everywhere about me there is the thunderous noise of exploding fireworks. I stand there clutching the flower basket, my breath coming in gasps, lips trembling, shaking all over.
> (Ambai 1992: 22)

She longs for her mother's presence. 'I feel a single desperate need from the depth of my being, like an unquenchable thirst. Amma . . .' (Ambai 1992: 22–23). However, when her mother returns, the girl receives a shock. The bewildered daughter speaks:

> Her words are like a sting. 'And what a time for this wretched business of yours? It's just one more burden for us now'. Whom is she accusing? Noiseless sobs knock at my chest.
> (Ambai 1992: 28)

The narrator is 'silenced'. The mother's words reflect the patriarchal definition of the good and the bad, the beautiful and the ugly, the right and the wrong. In the image of her daughter, the mother visualises the dark girl Radhu rejected, refused by her suitors. At that moment, the mother becomes an agent of 'a social construct' and the child becomes a victim of that social construction. In this case, the laws dictated by patriarchy shatter the loving mother–daughter relationship. The narrator utters the words: 'Endless fears will stay forever in my mind from now on; dark pictures' (Ambai 1992: 29). Women in rural areas discuss their indigenous knowledge with one another. They used to educate the younger generation and raise their level of consciousness through different forms of discourse.

The Goddesses of Beauty and Health in different cultures are: Aphrodite (Greek), Venus (Roman) and so on. Beauty and health are major ecofeminist concerns, related to all the five types of needs mentioned in Maslow's Hierarchy. On the physiological level, girl children and young women, particularly in the third world countries, have a longing for white skin. They become slaves to the commercial market that engulfs them with a range of cosmetics and beauty products. However, when those women fail to acquire the beauty, they lose their self-esteem and also experience a sense of insecurity. They also fail to achieve what they want to achieve. Fairy tales in different cultures promote artificial beauty that is merely physical/superficial. On the contrary, indigenous cultures promote holistic health and beauty that integrates beauty of the mind, body and soul. For example, let us consider the Tamil proverb, '*Ahathin Azhagu Muhathil Theriyum*', and the English translation, 'Face is the index of mind'. The mirror image is of great concern to the feminist writers. In the fairy tale of *Snow White and the Seven Dwarfs*, it is a male voice from the mirror that defines the beautiful and the ugly. Feminists consider the mirror as a symbol of patriarchy. In 'Moments of Being', Virginia Woolf describes:

> There was a small looking-glass in the hall at Talland house. It had, I remember, a ledge with a brush on it. By standing on tiptoe I could see my face in the glass. But I only did this if I was sure that I was alone. I was ashamed of it. A strong feeling of guilt seemed naturally attached to it.
>
> (Warhol and Herndl 1991)

The mirror does not reflect the 'real' self of a woman. In *My Mother, Her Crime*, the father utters a stereotypical comment: 'Here you are, dark girl' (Ambai 1992: 20). The girl narrates, 'Sometimes when my father said that, I would go and look at myself in the mirror hanging in the hall. Then it would seem to me that my mother was whispering to me "You are beautiful"' (Ambai 1992: 21). The mirror symbolises patriarchy and the girl is entrapped inside it.

Women try to re-construct images and symbols to convey their authentic feelings and thought. In women's writing, the female characters are no longer 'angels' and 'monsters'. They no longer symbolise the ideal. They are 'real' human beings experiencing pain and suffering. The woman in the house is no longer 'an angel', but instead, she is a 'caged bird'. The 'caged bird' is not a passive creature. It is forever trying to break the walls of imprisonment. On the contrary, 'an angry goddess' replaces the 'monster' image. She is an independent human being fighting the injustice and hypocrisy of the patriarchal society. Talking about patriarchy, Ambai comments, 'I think that patriarchal society and its hidden values alone have done atrocities against women. I also think that the patriarchal society's heinous crime is the making of woman as one without any hold on her body and the choices associated with it. A woman's body, from sensual feelings to maternity, is not under the control of hers and this lack permits others to define her body according to their own desire' (Ambai 2003: 14).

Nature Woman is a folktale about a king who sets out into the forest for hunting a tiger. When he is seated on top of a tree, he witnesses a huntress giving birth to her child among the bushes. He concludes that giving birth to a child is very simple. He thinks that the queens are throwing a tantrum. When he returns to the palace, he dismisses the court physicians and stops all medical treatment to the pregnant queen. The prime minister of the court understands the situation and finds a solution for it. This story confirms that indeed Nature/Environment empowers women and vice versa. The identification of the *Bhoomi Register* in the study of Paliyar and Pulaiyar tribes contributes to an understanding of the sociocultural factors of those communities that live close to nature. They deem life as sacred, which they term *punitham*. The tribal people live in small groups, which they call *kootam*. They have a joint family setup called *kudumbam*, which is usually matriarchal, with the mother as the head of the family. They worship nature goddesses such as *Bootha Naachi, Palichiamma, Sadachiamma* and *Vadakathiamma*. When a girl attains puberty, the Paliyar people practice *theratti*, where women carry a pot full of fruits and water and place it next to her. The pot is called *arasanipaanai*, which indicates the celebration of womanhood, abundance and life-affirmation. Though these tribal people go out for hunting and kill the animals, they do not have the craving to eat meat and uphold the beliefs of earth-based spirituality.

Though women were considered silent, they have communicated through other forms of discourse that were more powerful and effective in shaping the beliefs, convictions and worldviews of people around them. Folktales abound with a number of examples that exhibit women's wit and humour and subtle messages represented through figurative language. The bonding among women is represented through stories of sisters and sisterhood. The women represent sisterhood not only among women, but also with nonhuman living beings on earth. Women living in rural areas believe in integral health and beauty. These traditional tales exemplify the knowledge and wisdom that is passed down from one generation to another, characterised by environmental, psychological and sociocultural messages, indigenous viewpoint of creation, home, sisterhood, beauty, health and art. They represent tools of consciousness-raising and a binding factor of a group. They not only initiate personal empowerment, but also facilitate the collective strength of a group. In *Psychoanalysis and Feminism*, Juliet Mitchell explains that 'social identity is a gendered identity'. Talking about childhood, Humm verifies, 'Infants become children through socialization in the family. Feminist research has shown how boys and girls are treated differently and socialized in childhood into sex specific gender roles' (Humm 1992: 35). Folktales as Mother Earth Discourse can inspire a gender-sensitive, eco-sensitive form of socialisation to children. Both boys and girls will learn to respect the intrinsic value of one another and understand the spirit of interconnectedness and interdependence. Woman's nature-centred culture promises alternative ways of growth and sustenance to future generations. The following chapter deals with the analysis of folktales that deal with woman's proximity with trees and forests, termed as *Woody-Woman* tales and *Vana-Devi* tales.

5

TREES AND FORESTS

To dwellers in a wood, almost every species of tree has its voice as well as its feature.

— Thomas Hardy

Woody-Woman tales and Vana-Devi tales are characterised by woman's close proximity with trees. The significant aspects of these tales are as follows. In these folktales, the environment is not considered as a mere resource. Human beings are part of the natural environment and nature is also a character in the story. Trees are considered as beings with consciousness, which understand the plight of the suffering. Women and trees nurture people and other nonhuman living beings around them. They represent the qualities of Mother Earth. They epitomise the ecofeminist belief in the sacred. Woody-Woman tales communicate the sturdiness, generosity and selflessness of women and trees.

Woody-Woman tales

What are the different kinds of Woman–Tree association found in folktales from India? How do women and trees care for each other in romantic and realistic contexts? Woody-Woman metaphors find answers to these questions. Woody-Woman tales are characterised by women's identification of their self with the intrinsic value of trees; they find refuge in trees literally, figuratively and spiritually; women consciously seek to protect the trees for various reasons; they empower the trees and the trees, in turn, empower them; the trees are sanctuaries that provide them with comfort and solace when other relationships fail them. However, both trees and women are considered as objects by the materialist consumerist society. The Woody-Woman metaphors are identified in A Flowering Tree, Fulwanti, the Flower Princess, The Pomegranate Queen, Acacia Trees and The Woman Who Was

Loved by a Tree Spirit. The stories that project woman–tree relationship throw light on the ecological movements and activist groups that fight against deforestation and promote afforestation. Stories that deal with the symbiotic relation between plants and women are also considered for study.

Both women and trees are exploited by the patriarchal consumerist society. When women are in trouble, they find refuge in trees. When the trees are in trouble, women form a group and protect them with *Shakthi Consciousness* and *Ahimsa Consciousness*. *Woody-Woman* tales promise a greener planet when read in the context of ecological movements. The trees symbolise an interdependence of life, which is very clearly understood by indigenous women. A metaphor is a figure of speech which involves an implicit comparison and *Woody-Woman* metaphors communicate the symbolic relationship between woman and trees. When an extended metaphor is used in a folktale, it rises to the level of an allegory, a parable or a fable. In *Woody-Woman* stories, nonhuman living beings are identified as central characters in the story. In folklore, women find refuge in trees as a sister, mother or a goddess. Women's association with flora is widely represented in folktales and folk songs which belong to the *Woody-Woman* or *Flora-Fem* type. In *Sangati*, Bama gives an example of a folk song which is sung by women at 'a girl's coming-of-age' (Bama 2005: xx), or in other words, attaining puberty.

> On a Friday morning, at earliest dawn
> She became a *pushpavathi*, so the elders said-
> Her mother was delighted, her father too,
> The uncles arrived, all in a row-
> (chorus of *kulavai*, ululation)
> (Bama 2005: xx)

The term *pushpavathi* signifies 'a flowering woman' and this symbol guides a person to recognise *Flora-Fem* metaphors exemplified in folktales such as *A Flowering Tree*.

In *A Flowering Tree*, the process of woman becoming a tree and the tree becoming a woman exemplifies *stree shakthi* (woman power). In the beginning of the story, the woman guides her sister to be sensitive to nature and also the human being:

> Sister, I'll sit under this tree and meditate. Then you pour the water from this pitcher all over my body. I'll turn into a flowering tree. Then you pluck as many flowers as you want, but do it without breaking a sprout or tearing a leaf. When you're done, pour the water from the other pitcher over me, and I'll become a person

again. The younger sister sat down and thought of the Lord. The older one poured water from the first pitcher all over her sister.

(Ramanujan 1997: 54)

The metaphorical act of woman getting transformed into a tree emphasises the respect for the intrinsic value of all living organisms. Tribal communities worship trees as *Vanadevatai* or goddesses of the forest. They believe that trees are an abode of female goddesses. *A Flowering Tree* is a Kannada folktale narrated by Siddamma and translated into English by A. K. Ramanujan. It is 'a woman's tale', which communicates ecofeminist belief in woman power or *Shakthi*, and the concept of *stree shakthi*, which is *Ahimsa* or nonviolence, and thereby contributes to a peaceful environment. The analysis of the folktale begins with a question: How does the transformation of a woman into a flowering tree communicate the ecofeminist belief in sacredness? The story revolves around a woman who discovers her ability to become a flowering tree to help people around her, particularly her mother, who does 'menial jobs in order to feed and clothe and bring up her children' (Ramanujan 1997: 53). She marries a prince who is enamoured by her beauty and her special powers. Later, she suffers at the hands of her jealous in-laws, exploited as a 'thing'. In a favourable environment, when people show genuine love and concern to her, she finally becomes a human being.

In an article published in 2001 in the ecofem.org e.journal, Martin Delveaux analyses Alice Walker's novels and suggests that these works transcend ecofeminist theory to form 'spiritual ecowomanism'. Delveaux explains, 'Celie identifies herself with a tree which is the only way for her to stand her empty existence and find an 'ally' expressing a symbolic hope for change' (Walker 1982: 2). Similarly, Shug's statement, 'I knew that if I cut a tree, my arm would bleed' (Walker 1982: 167) in the novel communicates Walker's concern for earth-based spirituality. Similarly, the two sisters in the story *A Flowering Tree* represent a relationship of understanding, respect, concern, and above all, sensitivity to life. They represent *Woody-Woman* sensitivity and *Ahimsa Consciousness*.

> At once, her sister changed into a great big tree that seemed to stretch from earth to heaven. The older sister plucked the flowers carefully, without hurting a stalk, or sprout, or leaf. After she had enough to fill a basket or two, she emptied the second pitcher of water over the tree and the tree became a human being again, and the younger sister stood in its place.
>
> (Ramanujan 1997: 54)

The flowering tree that stretches from the earth to the skies signifies woman power, her ability to achieve whatever she wants to achieve. On the contrary, it also reinforces the fact that women are rooted to the ground like the trees, even when they aspire to reach the skies. They are essentially linked to their environment, like Mother Earth.

Transformation is a central theme of *A Flowering Tree*. The woman becomes a tree many times in this story – the first time, spontaneously, for the sake of her mother; the second time, to clear her mother's doubts; the third time, for the prince who intends to marry her; the fourth time, forcefully by her sister-in-law and her friends and ends up as a 'Thing'. The fifth time, the broken branches are set right and 'she became a whole human being again' (Ramanujan 1997: 61). As the narrator tells us,

> She sent for two pitchers of water, uttered chants over them, instructed the girls on how and when to pour the water, and sat down to meditate. The silly girls didn't listen carefully. They poured the water on her indifferently, here and there. She turned into a tree, but only half a tree.
>
> It was already evening and it began to rain, with thunder and lightning. In their greed to get the flowers, they tore up the sprouts and broke the branches. They were in a hurry to get home. So they poured the second pitcher of water at random and ran away. When the princess changed from a tree to a person again, she had no hands and feet. She had only half a body. She was a wounded carcass.
>
> (Ramanujan 1997: 58)

A Flowering Tree can also be read as a parable that challenges the consumerist society, which exploits both women and nature in the name of development. The fourth time, when the woman becomes an incomplete being, half a tree and half a human being, it signifies 'maldevelopment' (Mies and Shiva 2010: 5) – what Vandana Shiva terms 'the death of the feminine principle' (Mies and Shiva 2010: 5).

Maldevelopment is the opposite of sustainable growth. According to Vandana Shiva, 'Maldevelopment is the violation of the integrity of organic, interconnected and interdependent systems, that sets in motion a process of exploitation, inequality, injustice and violence. It is blind to the fact that recognition of nature's harmony and action to maintain it are preconditions for distributive justice' (Mies and Shiva 2010: 5–6). The 'thing' in the folktale *A Flowering Tree* represents the ecofeminist concept of 'maldevelopment', as elucidated by Vandana Shiva. The first time, the transformation of the woman into a flowering tree signifies 'order', whereas the fourth time, it communicates 'discord' and 'chaos'. In the folktale, the first time, the elder sister values the 'spiritual' element in both her younger sister and the flowering tree. As she plucks the flowers gently without touching the plant with her sharp fingernails, she reveals the *Ahimsa* way of life. In contrast, the narrative also gives an account of people who are insensitive to the needs of others in their environment, who crave for material benefits, unmindful of the humanity around them. They harm nature and the human being(s). The woman gets transformed into a flowering tree in her mother's house by choice. This transformation can be understood as integrated *oikos*. The second and the third time, when the mother and her husband command her to change, the woman experiences hierarchic *oikos*; the fourth time, when the sister-in-law forces her to become a tree, the situation is anarchic. The woman becomes complete once again in an integrated *oikos*. When the ecofeminist concerns are analysed in the folktale, the transformation of the woman–tree–woman indicates the 'needs–rights' relationship at various levels. The first time, the woman becomes a flowering tree to fulfil the basic needs of her family, to support her mother. The second time, she gets transformed for safety needs as her mother was worried about the daughter. During the third time, the change is for the sake of love. The fourth time when the security needs are violated, the woman is harmed. The final act of transformation signifies completion and symbolically suggests a moment of self-actualisation. Similar to *A Flowering Tree*, an African folktale retold by Moyra Caldecott titled *The Woman Who Was Turned into a Tree* deals with the transformation of a woman into a tree. According to the storyteller, a man's aggressive nature separates a woman from her nineteen sisters and she is forced to become a tree and wait for the divine intervention to be redeemed from her status of 'disunity, discordance and destruction' (Caldecott 2010: 2). The patriarchal culture seems to promote chaos in contrast to harmony, discordance in the place of peace and destruction in the place of construction.

The Woman–Tree association in the *A Flowering Tree* signifies woman's language of eco-consciousness and eco-sensitivity – in this case, an 'ordinary' villager, Siddamma, recounting the extraordinary power of a woman becoming a tree. It reiterates the understanding of ecofeminist worldviews such as woman power or *Shakthi*, characterised by *Ahimsa* or nonviolence, which paves the way for peaceful and harmonious existence. It inspires the younger generation to revisit the oral tales and appreciate the relevance of such discourses to ascertain gender equity and sustainable development. The word 'grateful' signifies contentment, happiness and peace within. An ecofeminist worldview calls for a way of life where human beings are appreciative of the blessings of Mother Earth and grateful to the fellow living creatures in this planet. When a person is grateful, he or she does not crave for more. 'Enoughness' is a word used by ecofeminists in connection with gratitude. 'The forest also teaches us "enoughness": as the principle of equity, enjoying the gifts of Nature without exploitation and accumulation', says Shiva in her essay *Forests and Freedom* (Shiva 2011a).

Woody-Woman motifs highlight the sensitivity that women have towards trees. The poet and translator A. K. Ramanujan's tryst with the flowering tree motif continues from the folktales to his poetry. His poem *Ecology* published in the collection called *Second Sight* (1986) depicts the effects of a Red Champak tree on the poet persona's mother. During the flowering season, the yellow pollen spreads everywhere and creates migraine in the mother. When the loving son decides to cut down the tree, the mother prevents him from doing so, as she considers the tree a part of the family legacy. The poet describes it thus:

> but Mother, flashing her temper
> ... would not let us cut down
> a flowering tree
> almost as old as her
> (Ramanujan 1991: 40)

The spirituality that is found in *Woody-Woman* relationships in the folktales throw light on the evolution of ecological movements that care for trees. The Chipko Movement evolved out of women's respect and concern for the trees. More than their love and care, the women's belief in the forests as their own life serves as a guiding light to the movement.

As Chandi Prasad Bhatt, founder of the Chipko Movement puts it, 'Our movement goes beyond the erosion of the land, to the erosion of human values. The center of all this is humankind. If we are not in a good relationship with the environment, the environment will be destroyed, and we will lose our ground. But if you halt the erosion of humankind, humankind will halt the erosion of the soil' (Guha 1987: 175). *Woody-Woman* motifs specify the circular principle of nature. In India, women move around the trees in the form of a circle and worship the goddesses of nature. Women and men who worship nature assert that life is a cyclical process, and for this reason, they respect the ancestors and value the unborn. Similarly, they believe that happiness and sadness are part of life, which takes its turn to make a life meaningful. A Garhwali folk song in India effectively communicates the worldviews of indigenous people.

> We offer flowers to you,
> O doorstep of the house, be kind-
> Fill the granary with corn.

It is the festival of flowers-
We offer flowers to you,
O threshold of the house!
May God bless you with an auspicious new year.
May your granary fill till it overflows,
May your crops thrive and wealth grow.
Let these seasons and months come again.
If we survive our times
the Phool Sankranti will return.
                               (Devy 2002: 152)

The song celebrates Creation and life on this earth, fosters a sense of contentment and shows a lifestyle integrated with nature. The words 'fill', 'overflows' and 'grows' suggest a sense of abundance.

The festival of flowers, the *Phool Sankranthi*, the spring season, which is expected to come back, highlights the indigenous belief in the cyclical pattern of life. The worshipping of the 'threshold' indicates a new beginning and the importance of a home or *oikos*. The belief in the cyclical process of life leads on to the trust in transformation. In the folktales from India, one finds that there is no definite beginning, middle and end. Human beings get transformed into animals, birds and trees and vice versa, as represented in A *Flowering Tree*. In these, the narrators and the narrated communicate care and concern for earth as a living being. They are sensitive to their natural environment. They are kind towards plants, birds and animals. Nevertheless, there are certain characters in the stories who are insensitive to the needs of their fellow human beings and their environment. The word 'care' is central to ecofeminist thought. It implies care for one's self and the surrounding environment. Care and nurture are the fundamental qualities of a woman's feminine self. However, a strategic form of ecofeminist thought emphasises the need to be aware of exploitation of women in the name of nature–nurture proposition. And in this way, ecofeminism seeks to counter essentialism. *Woody-Woman* stories reiterate care for Mother Earth.

In certain folktales, the voices of nature are distinctly heard. *Why Trees Whisper* is an Estonian legend retold by Anne Pellowski (2012), which voices out the consciousness of trees cut down for the benefit of man. According to the legend, the trees had a voice in the past. Whenever a man came to cut down a tree, the tree would speak, 'Don't strike me. Can't you see the sticky tears that are already coming out of my body? If you hit me it will bring you bad luck.' A spruce tree would remark, 'Don't cut me down. You will find me of little use for my wood is twisted and knotty.' The narrator informs that God 'took pity on the man' and told him, 'Return to the forest. I will see that hence forth no tree will talk back or contradict you.'

From then on, the storyteller narrates that the trees only whisper softly before they are cut down (http://www.spiritoftrees.org).

This story provides an insight into the voices of nonhuman living beings. In the Indian culture, women believe in the spirituality of trees. The trees symbolise birth, life and afterlife. In *The Golden Age and the Deluge*, the narrator gives an account of *bhoots* who lived on *pipal* trees and guarded the people in the land of Sabarkantha. In the oral tales, the narratives exemplify the folk belief that death is only a transition from life to afterlife. Hence, women and men get transformed into trees, flowers and fruits in their afterlife. In India, trees are worshipped as goddesses termed as *Kalpataru* (wish-fulfilling divine tree), also known as *Kalpavriksha* and *Kalpadruma*. Women in India believe that going round and round the sacred trees, such as the peepal tree, in circles as a form of prayer, brings them all the blessings they ask for. In folktales from India, the recurrent motif of women finding refuge in trees is quite rampant in all languages. In *Acacia Trees*, Putta, the youngest daughter of a village chief, finds refuge in a tree to avoid an incestuous relationship, as in *Sona and Rupa*. Putta sings:

> This mouth calls you Mother
> This mouth calls you Father
> Do you want this mouth to call you
> Mother-in-law and Father-in-law?
> I'll climb, climb, higher, higher, on this acacia tree.
> (Ramanujan 1997: 3)

The tale has elements of the meta narrative in the following line, 'no sooner had she said this than the fruit became a girl, sat in her lap, and told her the whole story' (Ramanujan 1997: 5). However, Putta is not able to survive on the trees, and as a result, she commits suicide and her brother also kills himself. The girl is reborn a fruit tree in her second birth, and once again, a girl, the third time. The story ends with a message that is strongly believed in the Indian tradition. 'The fruit-turned-girl said, "look how things are. My brother did evil (karma), so a spiny bush grows on his burial ground. I kept my virtue (dharma), and a fruit tree grew out of mine. And I'm here"' (Ramanujan 1997: 5). In another version of the tale, the brother and the sister get transformed into fishes and a fruit tree grows out of the girl's fish-bone.

The transformation motif is captured in another *Woody-Woman* tale called *Fulwanti, the Flower Princess*. In this Garasiya Bhil folktale, the protagonist, Fulwanti, gets transformed into a mango tree due to a cruel circumstance before she attains her original form as a complete human being in the end of the story. The heroine, Fulwanti, lives in an integrative *oikos*.

She finds a lover and lives happily until she meets Maya. When Maya takes the form of Fuli and attempts to kill the real Fuli, Fuli experiences anarchic *oikos*. Fulwanti, the fairy princess of flowers, turns into a magic flower, a magic vegetable plant, a golden pumpkin, and finally, into a mango tree. In the end, Fulwanti regains her original form in a safe environment, in the house of old woman Bhalu and a young man Piru, who consider Fulwanti as the daughter of their house, which indicate an integrative *oikos*. *Fulwanti, the Flower Princess* has an identical plot and motif as that of *A Flowering Tree*.

Besides, the mother–daughter relationship is also highlighted. Many folktales selected for study confirm the strong bond between the mother and the daughter. The women's consent is often ignored in a society of gender imbalance and they work together to fight oppression. In *The Pomegranate Queen*, a woman disapproves her father's choice of a bridegroom. As she was considered 'obstinate', the father killed her and buried her in the backyard of their house. In its place, a pomegranate tree sprouted, 'grew tall and green, and it bore a single large flower that opened its petals only at night but at sunrise folded into a bud'. The storyteller narrates, 'The *gowda's* younger daughter lived in it as the Pomegranate Queen; she played tunes on a vina every night' (Ramanujan 1997: 135). The celestial beings are impressed by her beauty and music and Indra's son marries her.

The transformation of the woman into a tree and a tree into woman is a recurrent theme in folktales from India, as identified in *A Flowering Tree*. In the folktale *The Pomegranate Queen*, the description of the mother–daughter meeting is relevant to the understanding of a holistic view of life. Whenever the young woman left the tree, it 'began to wither' (Ramanujan 1997: 137). It came back to life only when the daughter came back to reside in the tree:

> The *gowda's* wife watched the flourishing tree suddenly dry up and die, and she couldn't understand why such things were happening. One day while she was staring at the dry sticks, the Pomegranate Queen came down from heaven with her husband. As soon as she set foot in the yard, the dry sticks came to life, stood up straight, and sprouted green leaves. The *gowda's* wife was amazed. She also noticed that the tree had again put out one large flower. In it, she saw her young daughter . . . Then her daughter and son-in-law saluted her, received her blessings, and went back to their heaven-world. The *gowda's* wife was peaceful and happy from that day on.
> (Ramanujan 1997: 137)

In Indian culture, patriarchal society treats a woman with respect, only based on her relationship with men in her family, community and society.

In the folktales studied under *Woody-Woman* type, a recurrent theme is the relationship between woman and the idea of flowering. In Indian patriarchal society, the concept of a flowering woman is associated with the woman's married life. Without a man, the woman is like a sapless tree, commonly known as *patta maram*, in Tamil. *The Appeal of a Tree*, originally written in Hindi, by folksinger Ghanshyam Sailani, a dedicated Chipko activist, exemplifies the characteristics of the *Woody-Woman* motif.

> I have been standing for ages,
> I wish to live for you.
> Do not chop me, I am yours.
> I wish to give you something in the future.
> (James 2013: 104)

Though the song reflects the angst of the tree quite effectively, a deep ecological reading exposes the anthropocentric worldview exhibited in those lines. The poet believes that the tree lives for the sake of human beings. However, Naess' philosophy of deep ecology reiterates that a tree exists not for the sake of human beings, birds or animals, but because of its own inherent worth.

Ecofeminism inspires a way of life that listens to the voices of women and nature, thereby recognising their inherent worth. In *The Stories Mother Nature Told Her Children* by Jane Andrews, the American story is titled *The Talk of the Trees That Stand in the Village Street*. The author narrates: 'Through the silence there is a little murmur, like a low song. It is the song of the trees: each has its own voice, which may be known from all others by the ear that has learned how to listen' (Andrews 2007: 12). The folktales portray a landscape where women listen to the voices of trees, birds and animals in their environment. During the visit to the tribal areas in Palani Hills, the researcher understood that women and men who live close to nature communicate with plants and trees. Before plucking a flower, a leaf or a fruit, people who believed in the sacredness of the trees got prior permission from them as a sign of reverence. When the native women of Palani Hills were interviewed, they remarked that generally they did not cut down trees for firewood. Instead, they picked twigs that fell down from trees. They called it *chulli* and the *veragu* (firewood) that they carried on their heads, they claimed, were branches of trees. And they never have the intention of cutting down an entire tree.

Seeds are potent symbols of life-affirmation in folktales from India. *The Gift of Truth* is a Tamil folktale narrated by Muniammal, Kolapancheri, Thiruvallur District, and translated by the author, which delineates the individual's responsibility towards the planet. A king invites the children of his town to the palace and puts them to test. He gives some seeds to the children and asks them to grow the plants. After some days, he asks the children to bring the plants. The king believes in identifying the seeds of leadership in small children of his kingdom. Kandan is one of them. He faithfully sows the seeds and waits for the plant to grow. But the seeds do not grow. On a particular day, when the king asks all the children to bring the plants, Kandan takes the empty pot to the palace under the guidance of his mother. The king was happy to see Kandan. He exclaimed, 'It is he! It is he! He is the right person to be the King . . . He speaks the truth. All the seeds that I gave to the children were boiled seeds. How do the boiled seeds grow into plants?' The king announced Kandan as his heir. The story lays emphasis on the importance of tree-planting. It is a parable of universal faith in nature. According to the king, only truth can redeem society.

Seeds are vital in all religions and cultures and there are number of tales about them. In the parable of *The Sower and the Seeds*, we read, 'The seed is the word of God' (Luke 8: 11). Jesus was a conscious thinker who believed in sowing the seeds/words of consciousness in the minds of people. Words are used in both constructive and destructive ways. It is the way we use them that determines whether they are going to bring helpful or harmful results. In the parable of Jesus, the seed symbolises a new beginning, a new dawn, a new life. Jesus was aware of the agricultural fact that a seed can't mature into a fruit without the appropriate conditions for growth. He records the probabilities of seeds falling on the path and devoured by the birds, sown on the rocks that wither away, seeds that fell among the thorns and got choked. He said, 'And some fell into good soil and grew, and yielded a hundredfold' (Luke 8: 8). He was aware of the multifarious dimensions in both nature and human beings. When he said, 'He who has ears to hear, let him hear' (Luke 8: 8), Jesus asserted the importance of conscious listening, which is not just hearing the sounds. Listening is a skill that enhances a deep understanding of life around us.

Another dimension highlighted in the seed tales is the theme of holism. The holistic outlook is reiterated in the parable, *The Tree and Its Fruits*. Jesus said, 'So, every sound tree bears good fruit, but the bad tree bears evil fruit. A sound tree cannot bear evil fruit, nor can a bad tree bear good fruit' (Matthew 7: 17–18). The holistic philosophy of life is similar to the lines from a Purananuru song, *Theethum Nanrum Pirar Thara Vaaraa* (Good or Bad doesn't come from others). The seed holds the core values that are nurtured in a suitable environment to form a flowering tree that later yields fruit. In the present-day world, human beings give importance to superficial aspects. They judge people and situations by the outward appearance. In the parable of *The Mustard Seed*, Jesus elaborates on the significance of the tiny seed. He said, 'it is the smallest of all seeds, but when it has grown it is the greatest of shrubs and becomes a tree, so that the birds of the air come and make nests in its branches' (Matthew 13: 32). These words of Jesus emphasise the theme of interconnectedness and interdependence. One of the fundamental principles of eco-critical praxis is interconnectedness – a belief that all living beings in this planet are connected by a web. One species is dependent on another species amidst flora and fauna. Human beings are also woven into this extraordinary web of existence. Tales about seeds raise pertinent ecofeminist questions such as: What is the significance of seeds in an era of agricultural crisis? What do the boiled seeds signify? Do the seeds offer hope and promise to future generations?

A *Missed Shot* is a story narrated by Paapu from Virudhapatty. It is an *Ahimsa* tale that confirms the intrinsic value of all the nonhuman living beings around us. The story begins in a dense forest, where Prince Mahendra sat on his horse and went for hunting. The prince aimed at the deer and shot the arrow. Quickly, the deer moved away and the arrow struck a mango tree. It was the first time the prince had 'missed his shot'. He bowed down in sadness and returned to the palace. The forest represents an integrated *oikos* before the arrival of the human being, the hunter. At this juncture, the story represents a hierarchic *oikos* where Prince Mahendra thinks that he is superior to the animals. The forest is the home for the mango tree and the parrot. The prince intrudes into the space of the fauna and flora and also attempts to kill a deer. The human beings represent *himsa* behaviour. The mango tree shot by the arrow started withering. The branches started drying up. The birds living in the tree flew away to other trees. But there was one green parrot which was very fond of the mango tree. She didn't want to leave the mango tree. Along with the wilting tree, the parrot was also growing tired and weak. After a few days, a small boy went along to the mango tree. Among the lush green jungle, there was one dried up tree. He heard the sound of a parrot, *'Keech, Keech'*. The boy looked up. The tired parrot was making those sounds. The boy was surprised. He asked the parrot, 'Why are you tired? There are so many healthy trees around. Why are you sitting in the dried up tree?' (Porselvi 2015: 85) The parrot symbolises loyalty and faithfulness, an *Ahimsa* quality of life. The parrot explained, 'I am living in this tree for a very long time. It is this tree which gave me shade. It gave me clean air. It gave me fresh fruits to appease my hunger. Prince Mahendra's arrow missed the shot and killed the tree. The other birds have flown to other trees. But I couldn't. The tree gave me life. How can I leave this tree and be happy' (Porselvi 2015: 85). The boy was overwhelmed. 'Oh parrot, if human beings are thoughtful like you there will not be any conflict. I feel proud of you dear parrot. What do you want me to do? Ask me.' The boy said. The parrot replied softly, 'I don't want anything. Please help the tree to regain its life' (Porselvi 2015: 86). The parrot communicates a higher/deeper level of consciousness compared to man-the-hunter. The boy respects the intrinsic value of the tree and the parrot. He represents an *Ahimsa* person. He brought some water from the nearby brook and poured it near the foot of the tree and blessed it and the tree came back to life. Leaves began to grow. Flowers and fruits appeared. The parrot lived happily in the shade of the tree. Prince Mahendra decided not to hunt anymore. He planted tree saplings all over his country. The people are living happily in the natural environment. In the end of the tale, the forest is restored as integrated *oikos*. The parrot raises the level of consciousness of the human being. In this way, nature becomes a teacher; the prince learns a lesson.

The symbolic and the realistic connections between trees and women are studied using *Woody-Woman* motifs in the Mother Earth Discourse. In the folktales from India, the imaginative relationship between women and trees elucidates the indigenous people's belief in earth-based spirituality. The transformation of a woman into a tree in A *Flowering Tree* suggests the union of woman–nature proximity to celebrate woman power as nature power and vice versa. At the realistic level, the ecofeminist-linguistic framework facilitates the understanding of women's struggle to save trees. The sisters represent *Ahimsa Consciousness* in the story. The transformation of woman into a tree is a predominant motif *in A Flowering Tree, Fulwanti, the Flower Princess, The Pomegranate Queen*. In *The Woman Who Was Loved by a Tree Spirit*, the role is reversed where a young man gets transformed into a tree. In *A Flowering Tree*, the transformation is voluntary. In the other folktales, the transformation is a result of a crisis. Fulwanti's suffering draws attention to the importance of understanding security needs in a patriarchal society. The same ordeal is experienced by Putta in *Acacia Trees*, the two sisters in *Sona and Rupa*, and the daughter in *The Pomegranate Queen*. *Woody-Woman* tales confirm the unique bonding of women and trees in the literal and the figurative level. The significant characteristic identified in these stories is transformation. The inherent worth of the trees is acknowledged by women in these narratives. On the contrary, the trees provide refuge to the suffering women. In relation to the various movements that work for the protection of trees, *Woody-Woman* tales emerge as consciousness-raising tools to make the earth a greener planet. 'The creation of a thousand forests is in one acorn', said Ralph Waldo Emerson. The next section deals with the understanding of *Vana-Devi* motifs that highlight the importance of forests and wilderness.

Mahasweta Devi's *Arjun* is a Bengali story translated into English by Mridula Nath Chakroborty. *Arjun* is an allegory of consciousness-raising. It deals with the collective power of a group of villagers and their fight against deforestation. The story recounts the lives of the Shabars who were exploited by the landlords and politicians such as Bishal Mahato and Ram Haldar. The Arjun tree symbolises the sacred and the divine in the story. 'When the Arjun had been a young tree, the Shabars had offered prayers to it before going on hunting expeditions. Now that it was mature, how grand it was! A shiny bark; the top touching the sky' (Ramakrishnan 2000: 242). When men tried to cut down the Arjun tree, the village people gathered around and invoked the *gram-devata* (village goddess) and created a 'Fear . . . an uncomprehending fear' in the minds of greedy men (Ramakrishnan 2000: 245). In the history of the Chipko Movement, a similar incident happened in March 1973. When 300 ash trees were auctioned to a sports goods manufacturer, the village people of Mandal, beating the drums, protested against them from cutting down the trees.

Vana-Devi tales

Vana-Devi motifs celebrate the forest goddesses in folktales from India. *Vana-Devi* tales are tales about the tree goddesses and their worldview of abundance. *Vana-Devi* motifs represent not only the feminine power and strength, but also the spirit of interconnectedness and interdependence among nonhuman living beings that survive in the forest. *Vana-Devi* motifs interrogate the dominant viewpoint that wilderness is a place of chaos, witches and evil spirits. How do women who live in the rural areas understand the unity of the sacred with nature and culture? Anees Jung, a journalist by profession, in her book *Unveiling India*, provides an intricate record of the cultural aspects of women living close to nature. Her book painstakingly documents the experiences of ordinary women and their testimonies. Anees Jung in *Unveiling India* provides an instance of women giving birth in the forest. She gives an account of a woman called Banadevi who was 'born in a forest and named after it' (Jung 1987: 107). She narrates the following:

> A lone mother gathering firewood in the forest discovered new life sprouting out of her. She separated it from her body with a sickle, brought it home, and found it was a girl. She named her Banadevi, spirit of the forest. . .Today she is among a mass of women in the Himalayan hills, hugging trees, stopping them from being chopped down. . . Her's and other women's non-violent resistance to save "their trees" by hugging them is today hailed as the Chipko movement, a revolutionary weapon in the name of conservation. *Ban jagey, Ban wasi jaagey* is their cry.
>
> (Jung 1987: 107)

Anees Jung describes Gomti, the woman with the river's name, offering a bowl of water to the narrator. According to Jung, 'Gomti walks miles everyday to fetch from a well water that she then cools in large, round jars of red clay'. Women gather around the banyan tree and offer prayers. The women have made clay idols of 'Ishar and Gangaur, the mythical man and wife, who through the ages have remained the embodiment of marital love' (Jung 1987: 18).

In the classic *The Honest Woodcutter and the Fairy* story, there are numerous tales that depict the forest as an abode of tree goddesses and other nature goddesses. *The Magic Bowls* is a Tamil folktale about a poor 'lazy good-for-nothing' man (Ramanujan 2009: 171) and his nagging wife. One day, she gave him a bundle of rice and asked him to go somewhere and earn something for their livelihood. He walked several miles, and at last, found a huge banyan tree that 'lent its shade to weary travellers for many years' (Ramanujan 2009: 172). He fell asleep, 'his head pillowed on the roots of the banyan' (Ramanujan 2009: 172). Mother Nature acts as a surrogate mother to children in need. The banyan tree gave shelter to the tired soul. The banyan tree was an abode for forest/tree goddesses. 'Now there were *vanadevatai* living in the banyan tree' (Ramanujan 2009: 172). The goddesses wished to taste the poor man's bundle of rice and they relished it. When the poor man got up, he was hungry. The *vanadevatai* decided to bless him with four magic bowls that would bring him all the riches. A predominant motif in Indian folktales is 'kindness rewarded'. He went home and lived happily with his wife. A rich jealous man in the village heard this story and wished to get the boons from the *vanadevatai*. He too received the four magic bowls. But 'dozens of big burly men . . . came out of the bowls and went after the host and the hungry guests' (Ramanujan 2009: 175). This simple tale highlights that on the one hand, the importance of goodwill and simplicity results in prosperity, and on the other, envy and jealousy bring forth adversity.

Bonbibi is the forest goddess of the Sundarbans, worshipped by both Hindus and Muslims. People believe that she is the protector of human beings who enter the forest for gathering honey and firewood. She is worshipped as Banadevi by the Hindus. There are number of folktales and folk songs in both the Hindu and Muslim tradition of the Sundarbans. The Muslims believe that *Bonbibi* is the daughter of Ibrahim, a fakir from Mecca. She was raised by a doe in the forest and later became the goddess of the forest. The Hindus believe that *Banadevi* rides a tiger and carries a *trishul* (a weapon with three sharp ends) to protect those who enter the forest. Vandana Shiva interviewed Chamundeyi and Itwari Devi, the local leaders of the Chipko Movement, to 'learn about their hidden strengths' (Mies and Shiva 2010: 247). When Vandana Shiva asked, 'What are the three most important things in life you want to conserve?' Chamundeyi explained, 'Our freedom and forests and food. Without these we are nothing, we are impoverished' (Mies and Shiva 2010: 249). The forest is a central motif in all these stories. Forests have different connotations in the East and West. According to dominant Western thought, the forest symbolises darkness, mystery, confusion, chaos and threat to life. On the contrary, Tagore in his essay *Tapovan* explains that Indian civilisation has been distinctive in locating its source of regeneration, material and intellectual, in the forest, not the city. India's best ideas have come where man was in communion with trees and rivers and lakes, away from the crowds. The peace of the forest has helped the intellectual evolution of man. The culture of the forest has fuelled the culture of Indian society (Tagore 2011). The Mother Earth Discourse praxis is exemplified in the case of Julia Butterfly Hill and her work, *The Legacy of Luna: The Story of a Tree, a Woman, and the Struggle to Save the Redwoods*. As the title indicates, the book is about Julia's environmental campaign to protect the Redwood tree to make the world understand the plight of ancient forests. For 738 days, she lived in the ancient redwood tree called Luna and spread the green message across the globe, communicating the power of woman and nature (http://www.juliabutterfly.com).

Who Is Greater! is a Tamil folktale narrated by Saroja from Nambampatty, which highlights the bond between trees. The story is about maintaining good relationships and respecting one another's space. On the edge of a forest, there was a village. In the forest, a beautiful parrot lived in a hole of a mango tree. Near the mango tree, there was a neem tree. A crow lived comfortably in the neem tree. The parrot and the crow often fought with one another. The parrot said that the mango tree, her home, was the best. The crow contended, 'The neem tree is the best tree in the forest.' One day, the parrot and the crow had a severe fight. 'People enjoy eating the fruits from the mango tree. The breeze that wades across the mango tree is very special. People cannot eat the fruits from the neem tree. They are very bitter. A crow can live only in the bitter neem tree.' The parrot said mockingly at the crow. The crow replied intensely, 'People who eat mangoes fall sick. But the breeze that moves about the neem tree is very special. They have medicinal value. Human beings live longer when they breathe the air from the neem tree' (Porselvi 2015: 81). With the advent of human beings, the forest environment undergoes a radical change. Two men came and stood under the shade of the trees. One man looked up and saw the two birds.

> He told the other man, 'Whatever you say, the parrot is the most beautiful of all birds. Look at the crow, its colour and its voice . . .
> 'The other man said, 'The parrot is beautiful. Yes. But the crows

are known for their unity. When a crow dies, thousands of crows gather around. When a crow gets food s/he shares it with many crows. Who else has this quality?' The two men started fighting with one another. After some time they started beating one another.

(Porselvi 2015: 81)

Using the *oikos* theory, one is able to comprehend that human beings exemplify anarchic *oikos*, the birds signify hierarchic *oikos* and the trees communicate integrated *oikos* as they are firmly rooted to the ground. This story allegorically confirms the fact that the intrusion of selfish, greedy insensitive human beings into the forests disturbs the order and harmony in Mother Nature. 'Trees are living symbols of peace and hope. A tree has roots in the soil yet reaches to the sky. It tells us that in order to aspire we need to be grounded and that no matter how high we go it is from our roots that we draw sustenance', said Wangari Maathai in the epilogue of her memoir, *Unbowed* (Maathai 2006). The forest represents peace and harmony. The intrusion of man into the forest with his anthropocentric viewpoint creates chaos in the environment. In this tale, we find three different forms of living beings belonging to flora, fauna and human species. This tale highlights the theme of equality among nature and human beings. There was a discussion among the neem tree and the mango tree, a crow who lived under the neem tree and the parrot who lived in the mango tree and two human beings who sat under the two trees. The difference in perspective is an enlightening theme of the story. The trees never fight with one another. They respect their differences. The birds have a loud discussion. But they do not fight. Only the human beings fight with one another when they do not respect the intrinsic value of others. This tale projects the level of consciousness of living beings in this planet. All living beings have consciousness with which they connect with one another. This parable exemplifies the superior level of consciousness found in the trees and other nonhuman living beings. Human beings use their reason to dominate others, whereas flora and fauna are endowed with a consciousness that embraces other beings with care and concern.

Elephant and the Hunter is a story narrated by Kee Raa. A hunter set out into the forest for hunting and gets lost in the jungle. There, he finds a huge elephant who rescues him and treats him as a guest. When the hunter returns to the city, he goes to a dolls shop. When the man asked what those dolls were made of, the shopkeeper said that the dolls were made of ivory from the elephant tusk and he promised to pay a lot of money for the tusk. When the hunter heard this, he became greedy, and without any second thought, he decided to get the tusks from the elephant he knew. Immediately, he rushed to the forest and reached the cave where the elephant lived. When he told the elephant, 'They are giving a good price for tusks. Let me have yours. The elephant heard this, he became furious. The angry elephant tossed the hunter in the air and taught him a lesson' (Porselvi 2015: 31). The hunter's greed led to his downfall. The story highlights the exploitation of nature's abundance in a materialist society. The elephant represents the integrated *oikos* and the hunter stands for the hierarchic *oikos* that further leads to anarchic *oikos*. As Mahatma Gandhi said, 'What we are doing to the forests of the world is but a mirror reflection of what we are doing to ourselves and to one another.' This story highlights man's consumerist materialist ideals that motivate him to exploit nature. In this tale, the elephant represents the worldview of abundance and the hunter represents the worldview of scarcity.

Vana-Devi motifs are identified in the folktale *The Wood Maiden* from Czechoslovakia. *Woody-Woman* concerns are defined by the respect for the inherent worth and the belief in interdependence of trees and human beings. In *The Wood Maiden*, the protagonist Betushka is a little girl, the daughter of a poor widow who 'pastured the goats in the birch wood' (Ragan 2000: 54). Betushka lived in close proximity with nature. Every day, she went into the forest, sat under a tree and converted the flax into thread using a spindle. Betushka was the child of Mother Nature. She danced and sang 'until the woods echoed' (Ragan 2000: 54) and hunted wild berries and fruits from the forest. The storyteller remarks, 'The little goats, resting on the grass thought: "What a merry little shepherdess we have!" (Ragan 2000: 54). The wood maiden is the goddess of the forest with long golden hair and 'a wreath of woodland flowers' (Ragan 2000: 54). The wood maiden taught Betushka to dance. The two women danced throughout the day and forgot the mundane activities. Betushka returns home without spinning the flax yarn.

The woman–nature proximity is characterised by the complementary principles epitomised by the Yin-Yang principles. They are: real and magical; nature and culture; day and night; life and death; black and white; good and evil; active and passive; sun and moon; emotion and reason; young and old; individual and communal; radical and conformist; and so on. A comparative study of the tales lends itself to the following dimensions. Betushka is expected to spin a yarn using flax. In *The Wood Maiden*, the mother represents the physical reality and the wood maiden represents a spiritual reality. The mother is realistic, the wood maiden is magical. When Betushka returns home with her work incomplete, the mother is unhappy. In this tale, the wood maiden represents nature and the mother represents culture. The wood maiden signifies freedom and confidence that women inherit from nature. She represents *Shakthi Consciousness*. *The Wood Maiden* deals with the theme of quest. Betushka sets out into the forest for a purpose. Their quest is a quest for self-discovery. Betushka's name rhymes with Betula, the scientific name for the birch trees. In *The Wood Maiden*, the predominant colour is white. The wood fairy is dressed in silky white gown. It highlights the Eurocentric viewpoint that white symbolises purity, beauty and chastity. In a patriarchal society, women have a true self and a false self, according to feminist thought. The women's narratives are designed in a circular fashion, which denotes their belief in the cyclical pattern of life. By identifying the complicated net of ecological, sociological, economic and cultural chaos created by the existing dominant systems that suffocate nature and human beings alike, these folktales as Mother Earth Discourse recognise the scope of indigenous women's simple stories that offer hope to mend the systems and knit a web of harmony and peace. The recognition of *Vana-Devi* metaphors underscore woman–tree relationships, perceived both in imagination and reality. As a chief prerogative to the welfare of Mother Earth and all her children, *Vana-Devi* motifs in folktales reinforce the importance of protecting and safeguarding trees on the face of planet earth. The transformation of a woman into a tree and vice versa indicates the proximity of two identical living species on earth that care for people around them.

Vana-Devi concerns are defined by respect for the inherent worth and belief in interdependence of trees and human beings. *Vana-Devi* sensitivity connects these eco-conscious motifs in folktales with environmental movements such as the Chipko Movement, Silent Valley Movement and the Green Belt Movement. By recreating 'nature-culture', can women achieve self-realisation and self-discovery and achieve what they wanted to achieve by flowering forth in the need for self-actualisation? *Woody-Woman* metaphors help one to understand the benefits of planting trees, conservation of the woods and underscore the harmful effects of deforestation. 'A nation that destroys its soils destroys itself. Forests are the lungs of our land, purifying the air and giving fresh strength to our people', said Franklin D. Roosevelt. Forests and soil are inextricably connected to one another. The next chapter deals with the identification of *Tellus-Ma* and *Aqua-Stree* motifs related to land, soil and water in folktales from India.

6

LAND AND WATER

> *We love this earth as a newborn loves its mother's heartbeat. So, if we sell you our land, love it as we have loved it. Care for it, as we have cared for it. Hold in your mind the memory of the land as it is when you receive it. Preserve the land for all children, and love it, as God loves us. As we are part of the land, you too are part of the land. This earth is precious to us. It is also precious to you.*
>
> — Chief Seattle

Mother Earth or *Bhoomi* is our origin and the end. *Tellus-Ma* motifs throw light on the ecological concerns related to land and soil. Environmentalists believe that the ecological problems have an answer in the maintenance of good soil. Is the soil healthy? In the first place, is there is any scope in rejuvenating the soil? How does the consumerist society look at land and soil? How do the indigenous people view the terrain? These are some of the questions raised by *Tellus-Ma* motifs in folktales from India and across the world. Linguistically, the motif is titled *Tellus-Ma* as 'tell us ma' as a humble dutiful human being asking for the Mother's guidance for a better living. The predominant features of *Aqua-Stree* tales are as follows: women identify their 'self' in a society in close proximity with the flowing river amidst lot of hurdles and pitfalls; the river is also a symbol of the empowered self an independent woman; rain is often considered a male symbol, providing nourishment to Mother Earth; like water, women nurture life wherever they are present; water does not have any differences or bias just as a mother has care and concern for all her children. But both women and water bodies are restricted, dammed, manipulated, polluted, misused and exploited by the dominant systems all over the world.

LAND AND WATER

Tellus-Ma tales

The Chipko women were sensitive to the needs of the environment. Their consciousness was in union with the consciousness of trees, which helped them to embrace trees as their very life. Bachni Devi, who hails from Adwani village, protested against the cutting down of trees in the forests when the village headman, her own husband, got a contract to fell trees. The women joined together and raised their voices singing, 'What do the forests bear? /Soil, water and pure air/Soil, water and pure air/Sustain the earth and all she bears' (Shiva 2010: 77). In an interview, when Itwari Devi, a local leader of Chipko Movement, was asked about her source of strength (Shakti) and the strength of the Chipko Movement, she replied, 'Shakti comes to us from these forests and grasslands, we watch them grow, year in and year out through their internal shakti and we derive our strength from it. . . Our power is nature's power' (Mies and Shiva 2010: 251).

The Weeds in the Grain is a parable of Jesus that has lot of relevance in the mechanised, reductionist and consumerist society. He compared the kingdom of heaven to a man who sowed good seed in his field. When his men were sleeping, his enemy came and sowed weeds among the wheat, and went away. So, when the plants grew up and bore grain, the weeds also appeared. When the servants came and said to him, 'Sir, did you not sow good seed in your field? How then has it weeds?' He said to them, 'An enemy has done this.' The servants said to him, 'Then do you want us to go and gather them?' But he said, 'No; lest in gathering the weeds you root up the wheat along with them. Let both grow together until the harvest; and at harvest time I will tell the reapers, Gather the weeds first and bind them in bundles to be burned, but gather the wheat into my barn' (Matthew 13: 24–30). This parable reiterates the spirit of tolerance associated with *Bhoomi*/Mother Earth. In an era of insensitivity and intolerance, human beings wish to destroy anything that is not useful to them. In olden days, farmers had quite a different attitude towards weeds. They thought that weeds can be removed at the appropriate time without disturbing the crops. They allowed the weeds to grow, but made sure they did not disturb the crops. But today, the people have zero tolerance to weeds. They do not want the weeds to grow. Hence, they use pesticides and chemical fertilisers that not only kill the weeds, but also affect the crops and the soil in which they grow. Jesus was aware of the agricultural fact that a seed can't mature into a fruit without the appropriate conditions for growth. He records the probabilities of seeds falling on the path and devoured by the birds, sown on the rocks that wither away, seeds that fell among the thorns and got choked.

Tellus-Ma motifs represent the sacredness of land, soil and the terrain in folktales from around the world. According to several Creation tales, human beings were formed from soil and they return to soil. Earth was the womb that held life in the beginning. 'Fashioned from clay, we carry the memory of the earth. Ancient, forgotten things stir within our hearts, memories from the time before the mind was born' (O'Donohue 2004). The porous nature of soil and the malleable texture of clay signify the spirit of interconnectedness and interdependence of life on Earth. Indigenous people revere the soil as mother. *Tellus* or *Terra Mater* is worshipped as *Bhoomi Thaai* or *Bhooma Devi* in India. However, the most exploited resource in India is soil. The materialistic society has rung the death knell to numerous species of flora and fauna because of their insensitive behaviour towards the land. In an era when human beings aspire to reach other planets, there is an urgent need to reconsider the worldviews that dominate the land as a mere dead resource. Reconnecting with the land and soil is an important prerogative of ecofeminist thought. Reassessing the value systems that commodify land and soil is the need of the hour. Jules Pretty in *The Earth Only Endures: On Reconnecting with Nature and Our Place in It* explicates the importance of stories that promise change.

> In these predominantly oral cultures, the values of stories and relations with the land are important ... They do not see the world as inanimate, with natural resources to be exploited, gathered, shot and eaten. These things are done, but only in certain ways, and the world is respected and treated with care. Indigenous people believe that if they cause harm to nature, then they will themselves come to harm, whether it is speaking without respect of certain animals, or whether it is overfishing a lake or hunting out a certain type of animal.
>
> (Pretty 2007: 159)

The study of folktales from India using the ecofeminist-linguistic frame motivates a process of 'reconnecting' with Mother Earth. The oral tales represent a culture that provides a space for all the subjects (not objects) in nature. As Chief Seattle asserts,

> Even the rocks that seem to lie dumb as they swelter in the sun along the silent seashore in solemn grandeur thrill with memories of past events connected with the fate of my people, and the very dust under your feet responds more lovingly to our footsteps than to yours, because it is the ashes of our ancestors, and our bare feet

are conscious of the sympathetic touch, for the soil is rich with the life of our kindred.

(Creation Stories of the World 44)

On the pedagogical level, folktales emerge as effective tools in ecological literacy as they reiterate the intrinsic value of human and nonhuman beings on this earth. According to the indigenous worldviews, land and soil have consciousness, the rocks and stones have consciousness, the river and the sea have consciousness.

The Greedy Man is a story is narrated by Anjalai from Chorancheri, classified as a *Tellus-Ma* tale. Govindan was always selfish and greedy to acquire more and more property. He metaphorically represents the dominant consumerist society that rules the globalised world. His principles are contradictory forces to peaceful, simple living. He had a craving to buy whatever he saw in front of him. On the way, he saw a guava orchard and he wanted to buy the orchard for himself. He went directly to the owner of the orchard and asked him. The owner of the orchard puts Govindan to a test in which the greedy man loses all that he wanted to possess. Land is one of the most exploited resources in the modern urbanised mechanised society. We can interpret this tale as a modern-day parable of materialism. People are carried away by the glitz and glamour of the thousands of products in the market and become slaves to those commodities. People buy for the sake of buying. On the one hand, there is surplus food supply. On the other, people die of hunger and malnutrition. It is not only Govindan who learns a lesson at the end of the story, but also the millions of people who run the rat race of consumerism. Aldo Leopold claims, 'Land, then is not merely soil; it is a fountain of energy flowing through a circuit of soils, plants and animals' (1949). This deep understanding of land is necessary to understand the dynamics of Mother Earth and alters the perspective of viewing her as a mere commodity. The land provides sustenance and space to life on this planet. The Native Americans believed, 'Treat the earth well: it was not given to you by your parents, it was loaned to you by your children. We do not inherit the Earth from our ancestors we borrow it from our children' and 'One does not sell the earth upon which the people walk' (Lewis and Clark 2005). The indigenous tribes across the world revere land and soil as Mother. These worldviews challenge the human beings mindless craving to acquire land as a property and a commercial enterprise.

Ecofeminists believe that the future of Mother Earth is in the hands of women and that it is time for women to 'mother' the Earth. Discussing the role of women in agriculture and sustainable development, Vandana Shiva (2011b) in her article 'Who Will Feed the World' in the *Resurgence* online magazine, explains, 'Agriculture has been evolved by women. Most of the world's farmers are women, and most girls are future farmers' (Shiva 2011b). Women are involved directly with food security. Research reveals that 80 per cent of the food needs are managed by women in the household. The chain of biodiversity is interlinked, as Vandana Shiva put it, 'From field to kitchen, from seed to food, women's strength is diversity, and their capacities are eroded when this diversity is eroded' (Shiva 2011b). Revisiting the indigenous knowledge systems of women provides new sights for reshaping a non-hierarchical-pluralistic paradigm in our community, society and the world at large.

Krishnammal and her husband, Jagannathan, are social activists with Gandhian principles from Tamilnadu who are working in Tamilnadu to protect the rights of landless Dalits in the Tanjore District. For their tireless work, they received the alternative Nobel in 2008. Krishnammal Jagannathan (90 years) was awarded Right Livelihood for Realising 'Gandhian Vision of Social Justice and Sustainable Human Development'. Early in life, she met Gandhi and Vinoba Bhave and got inspired by their belief in *Ahimsa* and *Satyagraha*. In an interview to Amy Goodman, Krishnammal describes the angst of the Dalit labourers:

> Dalits are the native people, are native of South India, Dravidians. But because of their work, physical labour, they are considered to be low-caste people . . .
> You see, because they are mixing their brain and intelligence and the physical labour on the land, working on the land, cultivating the land and the dirt. Their hands and their body, everything is dirty because of the soil. And they are considered to be untouchables . . . These people are working on the land, so their looks are dirty. So the word has come: "untouchable."
>
> (Goodman 2008)

LAFTI (Land for Tillers' Freedom), based on the Gandhian idea of equitable land distribution as a basis for rural economic development, was started by the Gandhian couple in 1981. Ecofeminism acknowledges the needs and rights of the subaltern men and women in relation to their environment. Krishnammal Jagannathan and her works are examples of authentic ecofeminist experiences, characterised by *Shakthi-Ahimsa-Shanthi* Consciousness. The Mother Earth Discourse challenges the shallow ecological understanding of the materialist community and also promotes a deep ecological understanding of the land consciousness and the human consciousness that work together for the well-being of the planet.

Leaders Are Sown is a Tamil folktale narrated by Dhanalakshmi from Kavarapatti. The story is about a country ruled by a dictator, an *oikos* characterised by hierarchy. In the same country, there lived a mango tree in a forest which signified an integrated *oikos*. A mango which hung on that tree, for a long time, wished to move around freely. 'If the wind blows, I'll happily run away. But even when the wind is strong I am not falling down, "Che . . . What a life? The mango felt sad until something happened"' (Porselvi 2015: 23). One day, Velu, who lived in a nearby hilly town, walked down the road and saw the mango tree. When he saw the mangoes, his mouth watered. Immediately, he took a stone and aimed at the mango. With the help of Velu, the mango finds freedom in his life.

> The mango felt happy to reach the ground and started rolling down. Velu did not find the mango. Suddenly it started raining heavily. The mango gasped for breath. The rain water pulled the mango into a pit. The soil covered the pit. The mango which was lying under the soil for a long time sprouted into a tiny plant. And a new mango tree began to grow.
> (Porselvi 2015: 23)

At the same time, Velu and his friends protested against the dictator, and one day, he became the king. He worked for the welfare of his people, and as a democratic leader, he tried to recreate the integrated *oikos*. One day Velu, the leader, went into the forest, and his eyes fell on a mango tree full of mangoes. When he went near the mango tree, he heard the below:

> Do you recognize me? Oh King! When you were young, you threw a stone at me. I ran. I ran and fell into a pit. The soil covered me. I surfaced out of the soil and has grown into a huge tree. At the same time, you have grown up and become a king. You have defeated the dictatorship in your kingdom. I patiently waited in the soil. I have grown up into a big tree. I produce abundant breeze. You stood rooted on the ground . . . Both of us were patient and believed in our ambition and we have won.
> (Porselvi 2015: 23)

What is the role of the soil or land in this story? In this simple tale, the mango's quest for freedom is similar to Velu's pursuit for leadership. At the same time, when the mango is sown, Velu is sworn as a leader of the country. The soil is the platform that allows human beings and nature to aspire to great heights. Both Velu and the mango tree epitomise patience, a quality associated with *Tellus Mater*, the goddess of land. This tale highlights the *Shakthi Consciousness* or the inherent power of nature and human beings where they attain what they want to attain in their quest for self-actualisation. The mango seed is a symbol of hope. Velu has the seeds of a democratic leader within him in the beginning of the story. The human–nature relationship in the tale highlights the indigenous people's belief in interconnectedness. The supreme values of patience, tolerance and trust are reiterated in this oral tale. The folktale *Leaders Are Sown* can be read as a parable that connects land and democracy. 'Earth Democracy' is a new movement started by Dr Vandana Shiva's 'Navdanya' (2012). According to Vandana Shiva, 'Earth Democracy'

> provides an alternative worldview in which humans are embedded in the Earth Family, we are connected to each other through love, compassion, not hatred and violence and ecological responsibility and economic justice replaces greed, consumerism and competition as objectives of human life.
> (http://www.navdanya.org/earth-democracy)

In her book *Soil Not Oil*, Vandana Shiva contemplates on the crucial fact the 'there is no alternative to fertile soil to sustain life on Earth. Soil is a metaphor for decentralised and deep democracy' (Shiva 2009). The earthworm and the other living organisms are equally important as human beings in Earth Democracy.

Earthworms are the main contributors that enrich and improve the quality of the soil for plants, animals and even human beings. Earthworms are friends of Mother Earth. They are called ecosystem engineers who break down the organic matter in a process called decomposition for maintaining healthy soil. Charles Darwin called them 'nature's ploughs', who are responsible for mixing layers of soil and integrating the organic matter into the soil to make it fertile. Women who are involved in farming know the value of such living organisms. Earthworms create tunnels by burrowing into the soil, which aerates the soil to allow air, water and nutrients to reach deep down into the soil. They eat organic matter such as decaying foliage or leaves in the soil. Since the plants cannot use this organic matter directly, Mother Nature facilitates a process called casting, where the earthworm digests organic matter and releases waste from their bodies. Castings contain many important nutrients that are useful to the plants and crops. In organic farming, people consciously use earthworm castings as garden fertiliser.

Landscape is metaphorically related to the mindscape of the woman narrator. As early as in 1905, Rokeya Sakhawat Hossain's wrote *Sultana's Dream*, a pioneering effort in literature which best illustrates woman–nature–language relationships to confirm the philosophy of cultural ecofeminism in India. This feminist utopia is nothing but a rediscovery of 'Ladyland, free from sin and harm' (Chaudhuri 2004: 104). In the consciousness-raising dialogue between 'Sister Sara' and 'Sultana', the readers find the stark difference between the social systems that exist in India and in the 'ladyland'. The women appreciate the natural environment in the dream world, that is, the women's exclusive skills, such as embroidery, knitting and needlework and the pleasure of maintaining a vegetable garden as a part of the ecofeminist Utopia. In a simple storytelling mode, Rokeya Hossain has described the significance of women's education and its impact on the invention of alternative methods of energy consumption for sustainable development as early as in the twentieth century. As a visionary woman, Hossain, through the words of 'Sister Sara', elaborates:

> While the women were engaged in scientific researches, the men of this country were busy increasing their military power. When they came to know that the female universities were able to draw water from the atmosphere and collect heat from the sun, they only laughed at the members of the universities and called the whole thing 'a sentimental nightmare'!
> (Chaudhuri 2004: 107–08)

A century later, when human beings had exhausted most of the natural resources on Planet Earth, at last, they are looking up to the Sun for solar energy and to the clouds for rainwater harvesting. Hossain prophetically describes this in her work, 'One of these invented a wonderful balloon, to which they attached a number of pipes. By means of this captive balloon, which they managed to keep afloat above the cloudland, they could draw as much water from the atmosphere as they pleased' (Chaudhuri 2004: 107–108).

Some of the popular *Tellus-Ma* proverbs are: The earth is a beehive; we all enter by the same door but live in different cells (Bantu). Treat the earth well: it was not given to you by your parents; it was loaned to you by your children. We do not inherit the Earth from our Ancestors; we borrow it from our Children (Native American). *Tellus-Ma* tales confirm the fundamental belief that all living beings on this earth are equal and each has intrinsic value of its own. As conscious spiritual beings, human beings have the unique responsibility of communicating this belief among fellow living beings for peaceful coexistence.

Aqua-Stree *tales*

Aqua-Stree narratives hint at woman's relationship with water. They provide references for both realistic and romantic connections between woman and water. Hence, this dimension of study raises ecofeminist questions such as: How are women related to water bodies in their environment? What is the symbolic significance of rivers as goddesses? What are the ways in which women care for water? *Aqua-Stree* tales concentrate on the relationship between woman and water bodies in the natural environment, rain, river or sea. *Stree* refers to a woman who relates with aqua or water in various forms in her day-to-day life. In folklore, the rain and the sea are personified as male gods, whereas the river is always personified a woman, such as Ganga, Kaveri and Narmada.

The intrinsic value of a river and the people who live on the banks of the river are comprehended from the Narmada River Valley Movement. The role of women in safeguarding the rights of the environment is obvious in this context. Medha Patkar is an activist leader of the environmental movement which works against the construction of the dam across the Narmada River. In an interview, she explained the spirit of womanhood or *Shakthi* behind the campaign. 'The concept of womanhood, of mata, (mother) has automatically got connected with this whole movement, although the concept of Narmada as mata is very much part of (it). So if the feminine tone is given, both to the leadership and the participants-then (it all) comes together' (Mies and Shiva 2010: 5). Narmada Bachao Andolan is a people's movement which unites nature rights with human rights.

In Hindu mythology, River Ganga is supposed to have descended from heaven. Quite paradoxically, the reverence for the intrinsic value of water bodies is of major concern to the ecofeminists. Water has been misused and exploited by human beings in the consumerist world. It is imperative to understand the value of water at this moment of climate change and environmental crisis. In rural areas, women travel several miles to fetch water from a river or a pond. Water crisis sends an alarming signal to the existence of life, which includes plant life, animal life and human life. Innasiamma, a farmer from A. Vellodu, explains that she used to walk five miles to fetch water from a pond. Women farmers who were interviewed in the course of the study believe that the Western scientific advancements and technological growth have contributed very little to the traditional form of agriculture and biodiversity.

In *Staying Alive*, Vandana Shiva terms water as 'the disappearing source' (Shiva 2010: 179). Vandana Shiva quotes a folk song by Daya Pawar that represents the voice of a rural Dalit woman from Maharashtra, which deals with the effect of building dams. These women work hard to provide food for their entire family. They are always driven by a quest to fulfil the basic needs of people around. She forgets her 'self' and works for the survival of life around her, which is reflected in the following lines:

> *I collect yesterday's husk for today's meal*
> *The sun rises*

And my spirit sinks.
Hiding my baby under a basket
And hiding my tears
I go to build the dam
            (Shiva 2010: 184)

The song reflects the lives of millions of people who are displaced in the name of construction of dams. The woman presents the success of building a dam, on the one hand, and the failure of humanism, on the other. She has worked hard, but without any wage. The basic needs of food and water are unfulfilled. The sugarcane fields are 'lush and juicy', ready for industrial growth, whereas the woman walks

miles through forests
In search of a drop of drinking water
I water the vegetation with drops of my sweat
As dry leaves fall and fill my parched yard.
            (Shiva 2010: 184)

The irony of the situation narrated by Daya's song is a challenge to future generations. The morning indicated by the phrases 'the dawn breaks' and 'the sun rises' offers hope to the privileged. On the contrary, the woman labourer has to bury her life in tears. The poem outlines the importance of understanding the woman–nature relationship in the context of water resources. Daya's song exposes the harsh reality of women's suffering in the villages and suburbs of India and exemplifies the Mother Earth Discourse.

Women in India are named after the rivers flowing in their region. Anees Jung gives an account of a woman named Gomti 'with the river's name' (Jung 1987: 18), who walked several miles every day to fetch well-water for drinking. She narrates that Gomti greeted her with a bowl of water, as it was customary to honour a stranger in that way. This episode clearly underscores the woman–water connection that bridges the gap between imagination and reality. *Aqua-Stree* patterns are significant motifs in Indian oral tales such as *How the Mahi River Married the Sea*, *The Goddess of Mahi River*, *The Rain God's Bride*, *The Rain King's Wife* and *The Rain Prince's Bride*. These tales communicate the close affinity between women and nature.

In *How the Mahi River Married the Sea*, the central image is the Mahi River. The narrator attempts to challenge the stereotypes by describing Mahi as an 'independent, strong-willed' (Adhikary 2003: 1) and a 'confident' woman. She is neither an 'angel' nor a 'monster'. The folktale is a subversion of the conventional fairy tale plot, where a young man goes in search of the princess and marries her. Mahi leaves the father's house, faces a number of hurdles in life, but ultimately achieves what she wanted to achieve. The story *How the Mahi River married the Sea* challenges the patriarchal definitions of beauty. Mahi's friends called her 'little Kali'. In a footnote, the author Qiron Adhikary explains that River Mahi was 'dark in colour', often called 'Satpura's dark-skinned daughter' (Adhikary 2003: 1). The patriarchal consumerist culture, in the form of cosmetics industry, promotes 'fair' complexion as 'ideal beauty'; as a result, the girls who are dark suffer with a sense of low self-esteem right from their childhood days. The suffering and pain a 'dark' girl child undergoes in Indian society is a bane to womanhood and her *Shakthi*. Ambai's short story entitled *My Mother, Her Crime* exposes the conflicts a 'dark' child undergoes in Indian society, particularly when she attains puberty. The little girl in Ambai's story in her first-person narration communicates her mother's anguish in the following manner. 'Her words are like a sting. "And what a time for this wretched business of yours? It's just one more burden for us now" whom is she accusing? Noiseless sobs knock at my chest' (Ambai 1992: 28). In this story, the mother becomes a patriarchal 'construct' and the daughter becomes a victim. In contrast to this, Mahi is proud of her beauty and her dark colour. In the 'Mahi River' stories, the ending is quite significant in communicating the strength and power of womanhood. 'Seeing Mahi confidently looking forward to battle, the frightened Sea surrendered unconditionally. Mahi took him by the hand and married him, and her army of stones was laid to rest in her riverbed forever' (Adhikary 2003: 3).

In another version of the story *The Goddess of the Mahi River*, the central woman character is elevated to the level of a mighty goddess. In the introduction to the tale, the writer explains that 'Mahi's military style reminds one of the popular Hindu deities, Durga and Kali' (Adhikary 2003: 5). However, in the end of the story, she is tamed by her lover, the Sea. The two different versions of the Mahi River story demonstrate the concerns, worldviews and consciousness of the storyteller. Qiron Adhikary's feminist rendering of the story challenges the patriarchal systems, such as father Satpura's house, the rough path Mahi decides to venture out into and her final victory over the Sea God, much more effectively than Beck's version. The Mahi River stories exemplify Mother Earth Spirituality and Mother Earth Proximity. The woman and the river share analogous qualities with one another in the story. The river rises from a source or origin, which symbolises the parental home for a woman. The woman goes through trials and tribulations before achieving her goal in life. A close reading of the two folktales suggests the difference in terms of narrative presentation. In the feminist version, the title *How the Mahi River Married the Sea* signifies constructive action and dynamic process. Whereas in Brenda Beck's edition, the title *The Goddess of Mahi River* suggests the stereotyping of women as goddesses worshipped on a pedestal, which amounts to transcendental form of spirituality. Ecofeminism believes in earth-based spirituality and goddesses are part of nature, representing Mother Earth. An earth-centred worldview informs that human beings are only a speck in the canvas of the entire universe. When Mother Earth remains silent and peaceful, human beings underestimate nature power. When there is an earthquake or a tsunami, the people are threatened by nature's magnitude and supremacy. However, Mother Nature continues to be generous in transferring her positive energy to all her children in an unbiased manner. Women in folktales from India gain *Shakthi* or power from nature and communicate it to the fellow creatures around her.

Since ancient times, women have been placed in the margins. She is either venerated as a goddess, or treated as an inanimate thing. Ecofeminism calls for an affirmation of woman power, the acknowledgement of the power within. Realising the inherent worth of a woman and treating her as a complete human being, with thoughts, emotions, words and consciousness, will pave the way for a new society, characterised by love, care, concern and peace. The process of empowerment is both individualistic and collective. On the one hand, a woman's quest from self to self-actualisation is considered an essential progress; on the other, the necessity to understand the collective power of a group is vital in bringing about emancipation. Self-realisation is, therefore, not just the discovery of one's individual self, but the realisation of the inherent worth of others. Respecting the spiritual element of fellow beings is sure to bring about social change. By integrating the ideals of deep ecology with ecofeminist principles, one ends up in understanding ecofeminist spirituality that values life on this earth. Mahi's quest is a symbolic quest to attain self-actualisation where a woman strives to achieve her ambition in life. Going up the ladder of Maslow's hierarchy of needs, she moves towards the third level, the need to belong and to love. Though her self-esteem is hurt, she does not lose her strength. In the folktales, the importance given to spirituality forms the first key feature of woman–nature relationships, identified in this research. According to Deep Ecologist Arne Naess, there are two types of 'self'. The difference between 'self' and 'Self' is that the former signifies the individualistic self whereas the latter denotes the expanded self or 'atman', as perceived by the Eastern traditions. The union of Mahi with the Sea indicates the woman's longing to be a part of nature, to unite her 'self' with the eternal 'Self'. There are three important concerns which come to the fore in this folktale. They are woman's need for belonging, self-esteem and self-actualisation.

The folktales, according to Propp's narrative structure, begin with 'absentation' where a member of the family, who is usually a man, leaves the house, an 'interdiction' when the hero is warned 'not to go' and a 'violation of interdiction', when the hero leaves the house. In 'Mahi tales' considered for study, it is the woman who leaves the house. Thus, women who were enclosed within the four walls of the house attempted an imaginative escape, which had a cathartic effect on the narrator and the listeners. The last function, according to Propp, is the wedding where the hero marries the heroine, whereas in *How the Mahi River Married the Sea*, there is a reversal of roles, where the heroine marries the hero. This *Aqua-Stree* tale is a subversion of the traditional patriarchal fairy tales.

An ecofeminist approach to the folktales suggests that woman and nature suffer a great deal in the patriarchal society. Women are silenced, oppressed and exploited, along with trees, water bodies, birds and animals. The folktales abound with the sacred, nature, culture relationship that indicates the integrative *oikos*. However, an oikofeminist reading of the stories reveals that women and nature suffer a great deal in the hierarchic and anarchic *oikos*. However, some stories emphasise the transition of human beings from anarchic or hierarchic *oikos* to integrative *oikos*. An *oikos* reading of the Mahi River stories implies two different types of environment in which a woman lives. The father's house as a patriarchal setup indicates hierarchic *oikos*. Father Satpura does not want his daughter Mahi to leave the house. Mahi's tryst with nature during the journey suggests an integrative *oikos*. Nevertheless, in the end, when Mahi marries the Sea, the tale *How the Mahi River Married the Sea* indicates an integrative *oikos* whereas *The Goddess of Mahi River* indicates a possibility of hierarchic *oikos*, as revealed in the following lines.

> Mahi took him by the hand and married him, and her army of stones was laid to rest in her riverbed forever.
>
> (Adhikary 2003: 3)

> He married her, and her army of stones was laid to rest in the bed of the river, forever.
>
> (Beck et al. 1987: 7)

The study of woman–river motifs underlines the characteristics of nature, such as free-flowing dynamism and perseverance in moments of trouble. *Aqua-Stree* proximity is highlighted by the study of *oikos* in the Mahi River stories. To comprehend ecofeminist issues in the folktales from India, the oikopoetic tool suggested by Dr Nirmal Selvamony is employed. Integrative *oikos* is the *oikos* of ecofeminist thought, which unites sacred, nature, culture and the humans into a meaningful whole. Communities with anthropocentric, androcentric worldviews promote hierarchic political *oikos*.

Human beings show their domination and power over nature in this type of *oikos*. For example, hunting is considered as a privilege of human beings. Maria Mies explains that 'man-the-hunter' myth entails the different levels of violence in man's relationship with the natural environment. She explains that a hunter's tools are not only used against animals, but exploited as 'means of coercion against fellow human beings' (Mies, Bennholdt-Thomsen and von Werlhof 1988: 50). *Aqua-Stree* motifs reinstate the sensitivity of women towards nature. Feminist re-reading of history and anthropology reveals the fact that hunting was believed a 'whole-group activity' and it 'did not mean fighting' (Miles 1989: 31). Men 'appropriated' not only plants and animals but also women for their benefit. The objective relationship between man and nature has severed nature and culture.

River Woman is a central metaphor in Mamang Dai's poetry. Mamang Dai is a notable writer of Arunachal Pradesh who celebrates nature in her poetry. She has written poems on rivers, clouds, rain and mountains. Some of her famous works are *River Poems, Arunachal Pradesh: The Hidden Land* and *Legends of Pensam*. Mamang Dai's works are in tune with the tribal folklore where nature is interlaced with people's consciousness. In her article 'The Nature of Faith and Worship among the Adis', Dai explains, 'the great forest, the mountains and the environment shaped the consciousness of the Adi people' (Vohra 2013: 45). According to Bipin Patsani, Dai's poetry has a 'rare passion and flow, fresh and full like the Siang River that meanders through her valley' (Dai 2013: 1). In her poem 'Small Towns and the River', Dai writes, 'The river has a soul./In the summer it cuts through the land/like a torrent of grief. Sometimes./sometimes, I think it holds its breath/seeking the land of fish and stars' (Dai 2004). According to Dai, the river is a living being with a spirit or essence of its own. The eternity of the river is juxtaposed with the mortality of human beings in the lines, 'life and death, life and death' (Dai 2004) and 'the river knows the immortality of water' (Dai 2004). The poem highlights the tribal people's belief in the cyclical pattern of life. On the one hand, the river reminds her of the happy memories of childhood. On the other hand, she remembers the 'dreadful silence' of people witnessing death.

On a similar note, Dai, in her introduction to 'The Legends of Pensam', describes Arunachal Pradesh as one of the 'greenest' (Dai 2006: xi) states in India, 'criss-crossed by rivers and high mountain ranges running north-south that divide into five river valleys' (Dai 2006: xi). Tribal women and men believe in a culture close to nature. According to Dai, the river knows the past, governs the present and promises a ray of hope to the 'future generations'. In 'An Obscure Place', the river becomes an epitome of history, culture and civilisation. 'The history of our race/begins with the place of stories./We do not know if the language we speak/belongs to a written past. . . . We slept by the river./But do not speak of victory yet' (Dai 2006). When the Adi people 'slept by the river', Mother Earth comforted them. The river woman calms the people's mind and provides strength to all living beings. History is always equated with the written word. The stories belong to the oral tradition, which is the forte of women. It provides an impetus to revisit the past in search of 'her stories'.

Ecofeminists defy this reductionist worldview by highlighting the power of Mother Nature. In her poem 'The Sorrow of Women', Mamang Dai writes, 'They are talking about a place/Where rice flows on the streets/ About a place where there is gold /in the leaves of trees,/They are talking about displacement, . . . And they are talking about escape,/about liberty, men and guns, /Ah! The urgency for survival./But what will they do/Not knowing the sorrow of women' (Dai 2006). The poem deals with the conflict of the indigenous way of life and the mechanical life of the globalised world. The tribal people worship nature and revere the spiritual element in all living beings. The words 'displacement' and 'survival' in the poem raise serious issues about the indigenous people's right to existence in the modern world. According to Dai, the tribal people live in an in-between space called 'Pensam'. 'The Missing Link' raises the existential questions of tribal people in the age of transition. The poem begins with the creation myth of Arunachal Pradesh. 'I will remember then/the great river that turned, turning/with the fire of the first sun,/away from the old land of red robed men/and poisonous ritual,/when the seven brothers fled south/disturbing the hornbills in their summer nests' (Dai 2006). The earth is created with the blessings of the 'great river' and the 'first sun'. Arunachal Pradesh is one of the seven states called the 'Seven Sisters'. The other states are Assam, Meghalaya, Manipur, Mizoram, Nagaland and Tripura. From an ecofeminist standpoint, one identifies that the seven sisters are representatives of nature-culture. Whereas the seven brothers are identified as men who moved away from nature and created an anthropocentric society. They trouble 'the hornbills' (the state bird) 'in their summer nests'. They disturb the harmony in nature.

The tribal people believe that all living beings are relatives who live in the circle of life together, acknowledging coexistence and interdependence. Similarly, Julekha Begum, a peasant woman from Gaibhandha, Bangladesh, says, 'Life is a whole, it is a circle. That which destroys the circle should be stopped' (Mitra and Basu 2009: 4). In 'The Missing Link', Dai writes, 'The River was the green and white vein of our lives'. The title suggests that life on earth is perceived by the tribal people in the form of a circle and the rampant exploitation of natural resources breaks the chains of harmony. Women's understanding of the nonhuman world finds representations in

Mamang Dai's poetry. In 'Birthplace', she writes, 'We are the children of the rain/Of the cloud woman' (Dai 2009). Like the river woman, the cloud woman is an *Aqua-Stree* motif that affirms the strength of women as *Shakthi*. Rain symbolises hope to the indigenous people who suffer from the heat of controversies that affect their livelihood. Nature offers solace to the human beings in misery. 'Now when it rains/I equate the white magnolia with perfect joy/Spring clouds, stroke of sunlight/The brushstrokes of my transformed heart' (Dai 2009). The alternative worldviews reiterate that Mother Earth, the woman, was created first. The first man was the son of Mother Earth. As Mamang Dai, in her poem 'Birthplace' writes, 'The first drop of water/gave birth to man' (Dai 2009). The water bodies in nature symbolise life, hope and strength to humankind. The construction of the numerous dams across the various rivers in the country signifies the greed of the consumerist society. In an interview, Mamang Dai explains that the numerous hydel projects imposed on the state pose a threat to both people and nature. 'In Siang side there has been little public agitation. People are just beginning to organize themselves. And we don't need them, neither for our own energy requirement even if we export to the rest of the country we can try with one project and see how well it works' (Sarah 2012). An ecofeminist consideration of Mamang Dai's poetry lends itself to the identification of themes that indicate a culture close to nature. The various tenets of ecofeminist thought, such as interconnectedness of life forms, the interdependence of human and non human living beings and the respect for the intrinsic value of life, are represented in Mamang Dai's poetry. The *Aqua-Stree* motifs affirm the spiritual relationship between women and water. At the same time, ecofeminism intends to wake up people from a romantic reverie. It exposes the man-made hierarchical systems that oppress women and environment.

In the age of global warming, tremors, melting of glaciers and the rising of the sea level indicate that our planet is moving towards anarchic *oikos*. Anarchic *oikos* is an *oikos* of confusion and chaos. Materialism, consumerism and exploitation go hand in hand to create an anarchic *oikos* in a patriarchal consumerist, materialistic society. When the intrinsic value of the living creatures is not recognised, it results in an anarchic *oikos*. Anarchic *oikos* is also characterised by extreme importance given to reasoning and rationality and a complete negation of intuition and imagination. Folktales project the consciousness of women and men who wish to recreate the integrated *oikos*. The Mother Earth Discourse is a way of identifying woman–environment issues that prevail in the contemporary society. It seeks to highlight worldviews of indigenous people that emphasise life-sustenance of Mother Earth and her children and the accountability of human beings towards living and nonliving beings existing on this planet. Feminisation is considered the need of the hour and it begins with the acknowledgement of Mother Earth as a living being.

Aqua-Stree patterns are motifs that describe women and their link with water bodies such as rivers, ponds and rain. These motifs are identified in stories such as *The Rain God's Bride*, *The Rain King's Wife* and *The Rain Prince's Bride*. Among the folktales from India, stories of the Rain Gods and Goddesses are quite popular. Rain is a sign of hope, which promises fertility, growth and change. Mother Earth is getting heated up day by day due to global warming and climate change and rain offers consolation to the plant and the animal kingdom. The three folktales that deal with rain are *The Rain God's Bride*, *The Rain King's Wife* and *The Rain Prince's Bride*. *The Rain God's Bride* and *The Rain Prince's Bride* are two different versions of the same story – a tale of love between the Rain God and a poor girl, the daughter of a farmer. On the contrary, *The Rain King's Wife* deals with the love story of the Rain King and a princess. Rain is a supreme example of equality and reinforces the concept of earth democracy. It does not show partiality to rich or poor, black or white, man or woman. In all the three versions, the Rain God showers His blessings on the earth and the heroines show their gratitude by marrying him. In the first two versions, the poor girl gets transformed into Maya or the goddess of lightning. In the third version, the princess suffers at the hands of the jealous wives of the Rain King.

In *The Rain God's Bride*, Maya, the only daughter of a family, represents the 'first farmer'. According to the narrator, 'they ate roots and berries and the bark of trees, and fruit when they could find any, and they boiled the leaves of plants they found' (Adhikary 2003: 9). Woman–nature sensitivity is a characteristic feature in *The Rain God's Bride*. Maya, the heroine, is sensitive not only to the needs of her parents, but also to the environment. Maya learns the art of cultivating plants from an old farmer couple. When there is no rain and the crops suffer, she prays to the Rain God and promises to marry Him. The storyteller narrates, 'I will always love you' and 'I will always guide you', said Maya (Adhikary 2003: 11) and she gets transformed into the goddess of lightning for the sake of her family and her environment. The titles indicate the patriarchal social system existing from ancient times in which the woman is supposed to be dependent on man all her life, as prescribed by Manusmriti. The woman is termed either a 'bride' or a 'wife' to the Rain King. In *The Rain God's Bride*, Maya becomes the goddess of lightning at the end of the tale, only to follow her husband wherever he goes. In the feminist version of this origin-story of thunder, lightning and rain, Maya leads the Rain God in her journey of life.

What the Cloud and the Stars Wished For is a story narrated by Loganayagi from Arunachalanagar. In the tale, one day, God met each and every creature to find out what they wished for. First, he met a cloud and asked him what he wished for. The cloud replied that he wished to touch the earth. 'God granted him to become rain and it touched the earth. Then one day God asked the cloud, whether he was happy. The cloud looked sad. God asked him, why he is unhappy. The cloud replied that when he lived above he was clean. But when he reached the earth he becomes dirty' (Porselvi 2015: 43). Another day, God asked the stars what they wished for. The stars replied that they would like to go down to the earth. God granted them to become tiny fireflies and they reached the earth. The next day, God asked them whether their wish had come true. But the stars looked sad. God asked them why they were unhappy. The stars replied that they flew around happily. But the people caught them and crushed them. Then, God explained calmly, 'It is always good to exist in the place where we belong to. The place we belong to is the place of happiness' (Porselvi 2015: 43). There are several folktales about the cloud and the rain in many cultures across the world. The clouds symbolise purity, wealth, blessing and goodness. In the tale selected for study, the origin of rain from the clouds affirms the blessings of nature. At the same time, the story also communicates the importance of understanding a particular space or an environment. The clouds are comfortable when they live above. When they reach the ground, they become dirty. In the same way, the stars are also not comfortable when they reach the terrain as sparkling fireflies. They are treated cruelly by the human beings. The clouds and the stars signify the aspirations of an individual.

Folklore as discourse can be considered as a social, cultural and literary phenomenon. Discourse, according to Von Dijk, 'is not a simple enterprise. In its full richness it involves all the levels and methods of analysis of language, cognition, interaction, society and culture' (Jaworski and Coupland 1999: 1–2). In the context of *Aqua-Stree* patterns, one is able to celebrate the woman–water relationship in the romantic context in the folktales from India. Nevertheless, in reality, women suffer a great deal in the context of water crisis. Hence, the ecofeminist-linguistic framework provides space to integrate the romantic and the realistic understanding of woman–water relationships through *Aqua-Stree* motifs. The *Aqua-Stree* patterns throw light on the environmental issues related to water. If human beings understand the intrinsic value of a river, they would not pollute it. In Chennai, for example, the Cooum River runs through the city in distress. Had people realised the inherent worth of the river, it would have remained a perennial river, sustaining life around. The *Aqua-Stree* patterns identified in the folktales from India reaffirm the spiritual relationship between women and rivers in the character of Mahi in the tale *How the Mahi River Married the Sea* and women and rain in the character of Maya in *The Rain God's Bride*. The closeness of the life of women and the rivers indicate *Aqua-Stree* proximity. Both Mahi and Maya are dynamic women who believe in a practical approach to life, which suggests ecofeminist belief in practicality.

Aqua-Stree concerns underscore the freedom of thought, expression and mobility of women restrained by patriarchal constructions, which are akin to the huge dams that lay constraints on the mighty rivers. The needs and rights of water bodies to be free from pollution are denied in the modern times. At this juncture, the irresponsibility of human beings towards water raises the consciousness of the readers to the diminishing water resources on the face of the earth on the one hand, and the melting of glaciers and the rising of the sea level, on the other. Both Mahi and Maya exhibit *Shakthi Consciousness* as they represent the self-motivated power of womanhood. They overcome the hurdles in their life and achieve what they wanted to achieve through nonviolent methods or the *Ahimsa* way of life. They are epitomes of woman–nature power reinforcing *Aqua-Stree* worldviews such as interdependence and a holistic approach to life. The symbolism of rain reiterates the cyclical pattern of life.

Aqua-Stree patterns connect women with water resources. Women's association with rivers and rain is recognised as life-affirming motifs in the folktales from India. Mother Earth spirituality not only celebrates women as goddesses of nature, but also venerates all living creatures as beings endowed with sacredness. As a result, ecofeminism attempts to defend the rights of women and rights of nature and guard the rights of all the marginalised, oppressed groups too. In the folktales from India, one finds that ecofeminist spirituality is earth-based spirituality, as found in the veneration of the rivers as goddesses. Hence, the ill-treatment of rivers, misuse of water and the impact on the suffering women are understood in the course of the study. The difference between the ideal and the real relationship of *Aqua-Stree* relationships contributes to a sociological understanding of the water crisis and poverty in India.

The reverence shown to rivers as goddesses is understood from the two versions of Mahi stories, *How the Mahi River Married the Sea* and *The Goddess of Mahi River*. Mahi symbolises woman power, who achieved what she wanted to achieve, and she also symbolises the bond between woman power and nature's power. She is an embodiment of *Shakthi Consciousness*. The dark-coloured river-woman Mahi is a symbol of motivation to women and girls who consider themselves dark and ugly. The Rain stories such as *The Rain God's Bride*, *The Rain King's Wife* and *The Rain Prince's Bride* indicate the dependency of life on water. Maya, the goddess of lightning, promises to guide the Rain God in *The Rain God's Bride*, which confirms an ecofeminist stance. *Aqua-Stree* narratives inspire ways of realising the intrinsic value of water bodies. With the principle of *Ahimsa*, the living beings in these oral tales celebrate rivers and rain that nourish the planet.

It motivates human beings to be responsible in the relationship with water bodies. It stresses upon the folk beliefs that venerate the life-giving water as gods and goddesses. A comparison between the folktales selected for study and the Dalit woman's voice in Daya Pawar's song on the building of dams offers the difference between the worldview of women in nature-culture, which is one of abundance, and the worldview of men in patriarchal culture, which is one of insufficiency. Mamang Dai's poetry also re-affirms the belief in respecting the water bodies around us. *Aqua-Stree* patterns in the Mother Earth Discourse model unravel the importance of respecting water and acknowledging the woman–water connection in folk discourse from India. The water bodies in a pristine natural environment are symbolic representations of earth's dynamism and energy that nourish the trees, plants, animals, human beings and grass without partiality. However, the advent of industries, importance given to machineries and construction of dams have affected the course of the water bodies. For example, Pallikaranai is a marshland, 20 km from Chennai, considered as a reserve forest area. Environmentalists fear that it is one of the last few natural ecosystems that are fast diminishing due to the advent of factories and real estate. The rich marshland houses nearly 106 species of birds and a variety of animals and fishes, which are threatened by man's greed. In the following chapter, the bird-woman, *Aves-Eve* motifs and animal–woman, *Fauna-Fem* motifs are identified in folktales from India.

7
BIRDS AND ANIMALS

> *The animals of the world exist for their own reasons. They were not made for humans any more than black people were made for white, or women created for men.*
>
> — Alice Walker

Another major concern of the ecofeminist thinkers is the responsibility of the human beings towards nonhuman living beings on Planet Earth. The animals are identified as living subjects who communicate their inherent worth in the folktales from India. In studying the relationship between women and the animals, ecofeminists such as Josephine Donovan acknowledged the importance of identifying 'the absent referent', which refers to 'the real or material entity signified by the linguistic symbol, the word, which is termed the signifier' (Gaard and Murphy 1998: 75), as represented in her essay *Ecofeminist Literary Criticism: Reading the Orange*. Another ecofeminist thinker, Carol Adams, a champion of animal rights, explains that in the expression 'meat-eating', 'meat' is the signifier and 'animal' is the absent referent.

In Mother Earth Discourse approach to folktales from India, there is an effort to identify the 'absent referent' as a living being endowed with a spiritual element. In this way, the proposed paradigm offers a critique on the logic of dominations prevalent in the contemporary society. This 'revalidation of narrative' and the 'restoring of the absent referent' (Gaard and Murphy 1998: 76) can be experimented in a classroom as a productive form of ecofeminist pedagogy. In his article 'The Animal Manifesto' in the *Resurgence*, online magazine, Marc Bekoff lists six reasons to respect the consciousness of animals: '1. All animals share the Earth, and we must coexist. 2. Animals think and feel. 3. Animals have and deserve compassion. 4. Connection breeds caring; alienation breeds disrespect. 5. Our world is not compassionate to animals. 6. Acting compassionately helps all beings and our world' (Bekoff 2012). Folktales emerge as authentic representations of indigenous people's worldviews, who naturally believe in the principles mentioned in the Animal Manifesto.

The images that draw a link between woman and birds are called *Aves-Eve* kind, which forms the fifth kind of motif. The significant features of bird–woman tales are as follows: women communicate with birds in both the literal and metaphorical sense; they consider the birds as their own relation, for example, brother, sister or mother; the birds become surrogate parents to women and men in distress; women nurture the birds and the birds, in turn, nurture the human beings; birds signify power and independence and offer hope to women who are enslaved by the patriarchal systems. *Fauna-Fem* symbols highlight the relationship between woman and animals with the following features: women share a unique bond with animals; they protect the animals in distress and they are, in turn, saved by the animals; they symbolise the inherent power of nature that is found in both animals and human beings; the women relate to the animals by understanding their consciousness; the animals represent the benign qualities of Mother Nature in folktales from India.

Aves-Eve tales

Rachel Carson is one of the early spokespersons of ecological thought, who communicated her concern for the birds and environment in her book *Silent Spring*, published on 27 September 1962 by Houghton Mifflin, and considered as an inspiration to various environmental movements all over the world. According to Carson, 'the "control of nature" is a phrase conceived in arrogance, born of the Neanderthal age of biology and philosophy, when it was supposed that nature exists for the convenience of man' (257). Carson investigated the excessive use of chemical fertilisers and their harmful effects on the environment. In *Silent Spring*, Carson (2000) highlights the death of several species of birds. The title denotes that the birds do not chirp even in the season of spring. After the publication of the book, the US government banned DDT and also made changes in environmental laws to protect air, land and water. All these movements reinforce the value of life and reiterate the importance of feminine power and collective strength to bring about change on earth.

The images of the feathered friends of women are identified in the following tales: *The Girl Who Understood Birds, The Boy Who Could Speak with Birds, Bopoluchi, The Kite's Daughter, Heron Boy, Those Clever Crows, Sanykisar the Crow-Girl* and *The Pigeon's Bride*. A tribal tale of the *Pulaiyar* tribe is also studied under this category. In folktales, the birds are found in close proximity with the woman character. Women understand the language of birds. Some stories portray bird as a surrogate mother while others present the bird as a child to a childless woman. Birds serve as a link between women and the natural world. Folktales do not portray images of 'the caged bird' and 'bird with the broken wing', as found in literary texts.

> The metaphor of the caged bird can be extended to include the 'cages' which block women off from public life. In this sense, the walls of a house may be a cage; the rules and regulations regarding 'feminine' behaviour may be a cage.
>
> (Goodman 1996: 25)

The caged bird symbolises a woman entrapped within the patriarchal setup called the house. 'The caged bird' is another face of 'the angel' in women's writing. Women experience conflict between domesticity and creativity, between silences and speech, between the harsh stifling reality and free imaginary space. Some women find self-expression only through imagination. Ambai's short story called 'Wings' was originally entitled *Siragugal Muriyum* in Tamil, which means 'wings get broken'. Chaya, the 'protagonist', symbolises the bird caught in the cage of domestic trial. Chaya is unable to express her real feelings. She feels suffocated. 'Wings' symbolise 'the power to transcend the mundane world' (Cooper 2012: 193). The author narrates, 'She needed to spread her wings. She had to beat her wings in the wide steadfast silence of the skies. That was life' (A Purple Sea 1992: 48). These lines indicate that the woman was merely 'surviving' and not actually 'living'. This idea raises the feminist issue of woman's identity of the self. However, in the folk narratives, the birds are strong and untamed. They live freely in the natural habitat. At times, these birds become victims at the hands of selfish human beings. *Aves-Eve* tales provide answers to the questions: How do women show their sensitivity to birds in folktales from India? What is the significance of studying bird–woman stories?

Women are very courageous in their thoughts and deeds, with a deep understanding of their environment. They are witty women with a quick presence of mind, as exemplified in their popular storytelling activity. *Aves-Eve* spirituality confirms the inherent worth of birds and their relationship with women. This story asserts not only the interdependency of human beings and nature, but also the indigenous belief in woman power. Women worship nature as goddesses such as *Mariamman*, the goddess of rain, and *Palichiamman* (goddess of the *Paliyar* tribe). They revere Valli, wife of Lord Murugan, as a woman of their community (*Palanimalai Pazhangudigal-Paliyarum Pulaiyarum*). At this moment, it is necessary to understand the significance of bird–woman relationships, which are identified through *Aves-Eve* images through the Mother Earth Discourse. The deep ecological understanding of the intrinsic value of birds is reiterated by Adrienne Rich's description of the Great Blue Heron. In the essay *Woman and Bird*, she provides an insight into the relationship of women and birds.

> Wandered inadvertently or purposefully inland, maybe drought-driven, to a back yard habitat, it is a bird, *Ardea herodias*, whose form, dimensions, and habits have been described by ornithologists, yet whose intangible ways of being and knowing remain beyond my—or anyone's—reach . . . The tall, foot-poised creature had a life . . . a place of its own in the universe. Its place, and mine, I believe, are equal and interdependent.
>
> (Rich 2003: 7)

The inherent worth of the birds as living subjects and their relationship with women are explored through *Aves-Eve* motifs in folktales from India. Adrienne Rich's description juxtaposes the anthropomorphic worldview that defines the bird in scientific terms and the deep ecological worldview that respects the inherent worth of the bird. The passage illustrates the bird–woman communication that emerges from the need to acknowledge the intrinsic value of life.

The Girl Who Understood the Birds can be read as a modern-day parable of the environmental crisis that people are facing in today's world. The 'clever daughter' of a farmer attempts to communicate her sensitivity and consciousness towards the natural environment. Indigenous women are believed to have traditional wisdom and knowledge of agriculture and farming. For example, when the researcher interviewed Jayanthi, a woman who has been selling greens for the past fifteen years in Chennai, she explained the traditional methods of farming, which includes the use of natural manure. The girl in the folktale serves as a medium between the world of nature and world of human beings. She understands the language of birds and indicates changes in weather and hazards in the environment to the people around her, according to the bird's warning. The author narrates,

> The farmer would often send his daughter for water, and the girl would take her time wandering through the jungle. There she made friends with the birds and soon came to understand their language. The birds often talked about how wicked humans were and how they mistreated the animals of the jungle. But mostly the birds talked about the weather. The girl was very pleased that she understood the birds so well, because the birds seemed to be experts at predicting the weather.
>
> (Adhikary 2003: 37)

In this folktale, a little girl appreciates the 'language' of the birds, but quite ironically, the father fails to understand his daughter. 'But father,' said the girl, 'it's true. I heard the birds say so, and the birds are my friends. They never lie, either.' The girl's father became angry with her. 'Understand the birds, indeed! You lazy girl,' he cried, 'all you want to do is hang out in the jungle all day so you can shirk the farm work. . .' (Adhikary 2003: 37). The father, who represents the patriarchal society, 'simply ignored' his daughter's words. But 'The mother, of course, had always believed in her daughter, and was convinced that she spoke the truth' (Adhikary 2003: 39). The tale focuses on the twin themes of speech and silence. The story highlights the need for woman's expression. On many occasions, women are silenced for being irrational, when in reality, they are intuitive and communicate a deeper level of eco-sensitivity. Woman's relationship with the natural environment is considered as absurd. The father uses violence against the birds and towards his daughter. The mother is also silenced. The father kills the birds and forces the daughter to eat the soup. 'Eat the soup or we will beat you severely', said the little girl's father. In the end of the story, the little girl becomes insane and is 'silenced' forever. 'Her eyes became dull and clouded. Soon, the little girl could not understand the birds anymore; she became dull. . .' (Adhikary 2003: 40). The girl's insanity and the 'terrible famine' (Adhikary 2003: 41) symbolise a threat to women and the environment. The famine implies a paradox to the fertility of the Earth Goddess. In the end, the girl's father feels 'terribly guilty' for his act. However, men and women who exploit Mother Earth in various ways do not realise their mistake. The total 'chaos' in the folktale *The Girl Who Understood the Birds* would have been reduced to a great extent if the mother and daughter had used their collective strength, the language of *Ahimsa* and the language of *Shakthi* to raise the consciousness of the father and other people in the neighbourhood. An *oikos* reading of the folktale *The Girl Who Understood the Birds* would suggest that the story begins with an integrative *oikos*, moves on to hierarchic *oikos*, and finally, ends with an anarchic *oikos*. In the integrative *oikos*, the girl lives in harmony with nature and understands the language of birds. The girl's house exemplifies hierarchic *oikos* in the order of the father, mother and the little girl. The end suggests an anarchic *oikos*.

The Girl Who Understood the Birds raises some significant questions: 'What is the significance of women's language of the environment? What is the significance "of" women's language "for" the environment?' In the Indian folk discourse, do women remain silent always? Who are those silenced women? What are the ways in which they are silenced? How are they silenced? When are they silenced? Why are they silenced? What is the significance of women's language of the environment (language of *Ahimsa*)?

What is the significance of women's language for the environment (language of Shakthi)? *The Boy Who Could Speak with Birds* is a folktale with the same plot of *The Girl Who Understood Birds*. The title suggests the difference between a boy and a girl and its power over speech in a patriarchal society. In the feminist folktale, the title suggests the importance given to understanding, and in the alternative version, the title highlights the boy's capability to 'speak' with the birds. In both the narratives, the mother has a strong intuition and belief in the child's eco-sensitivity and indigenous knowledge. On the contrary, the father dismisses the child's words 'as a form of madness' (Adhikary 2003: 64). The woman communicating with the birds appears as a recurring motif in many folktales.

Aves-Eve motifs, as identified in folktales from India, reinforce the inherent worth of birds and their relationship with women. The girl 'who understood the birds' in the Nagaland folktale and the boy 'who could speak with birds' in the forest represent the spirit of sensitivity towards the nonhuman living beings in their environment. However, the father figure in both the stories stands for the rationalist male-dominated society who punishes the child for being 'irrational'. The communication between the birds and the eco-sensitive human beings portrayed in folktales indicates the lacunae in the minds of people in the civilised society. In *Bopoluchi*, a Punjabi folktale, a thief deceives the pretty village woman Bopoluchi, disguised as her uncle from a distant place. When he attempts to take her along, a crow in a tree croaked, a peacock screamed, a jackal howled the same song:

> Bopoluchi, beware!
> Smell the danger in the air!
> It's no uncle that relieves you
> But a robber who deceives you!
> (Ramanujan 2009: 8)

Bopoluchi is a brave young woman who fights for herself using her wit and courage with the help of Mother Nature. Like the Pulaiyar tale, *Bopoluchi* also reiterates the interdependence of human and nonhuman living beings represented in folktales from India.

The Kite's Daughter is an Assamese folktale, which begins with a description of the family where a woman bore only daughters and not sons. 'A rich potter had no sons. His wife bore him only daughters. When his wife became pregnant again he told her, "You'd better not give birth to a daughter this time. If you do, I'll sell you to the Gypsies"' (Ramanujan 2009: 124). In this interesting tale, a kite wanted to bring up the baby. She carries the child to her nest in the banyan tree and takes great care of her. The child grows into a young woman like a princess. The bird teaches a song to the young woman,

> O wind
> That shakes the leaves
> Of this banyan tree,
> Bring me my mother,
> Bring me my mother, my kite!
> (Ramanujan 2009: 125)

The young woman marries a rich merchant who already had seven wives. Whenever the co-wives ill-treated her, the kite helps her daughter from trouble. As a result, the jealous co-wives plotted against the bird and finally killed it. The kite's daughter lives in a safe environment in her mother's house, in the kite's nest, which signifies an integrative *oikos*. The kite's daughter is transported into a hierarchic *oikos* when she enters her in-law's house. She also happened to experience anarchic *oikos* due to the jealousy of other women in her family. However, the innocent girl who did not have any contempt or anger against anyone in this world was blessed by the laws of nature and her song brought her back to the integrative *oikos*.

> My mother was a potter's wife.
>   She let me drift along the river
> My mother was a kite who brought me up.
>   A merchant prince was my husband then,
> And my seven co-wives sold me to a fisherman.
>   Here I sit, a guardian now of drying fish
> (Ramanujan 2009: 130)

According to A. K. Ramanujan, the Assamese tale *The Kite's Daughter* belongs to the storytelling tradition of 'an abandoned girl raised by a bird', also common in Kannada, Konkani, Tamil and Telugu languages. At times, the narratives have the bird's role replaced by animals and the co-wives substituted by sisters-in-law. *The Kite's Daughter* throws light on the preference of the boy child over the girl child in many parts of India. Female infanticide is quite common in the country even today.

In *Sanykisar, the Crow-Girl*, the central character flees from a stifling reality and nature comforts her. Sanykisar is a popular folk figure in Kashmir. In order to escape an incestuous relationship, the girl finds refuge in a tree. 'Sanykisar sowed the seeds as directed, and lo, seven tall and strong trees shot up. She climbed one and rested on the top' (Beck 1987: 51). When people tried to cut down the trees, Mother Moon comforts her. When she is once again in trouble, a 'crow-father' helps her to finally become a Queen. *Heron Boy* suggests a reversal of the parent–child relationship, in comparison with *The Kite's Daughter*. In *Heron Boy*, a woman gives birth to a heron. The heron-boy builds a palace for his parents. The kind-hearted parents welcome an old woman and treat her with cucumbers from their garden, and to their surprise, the heron falls down dead and 'as the bird stopped breathing, an eighteen-year-old boy appeared in its place and stood in front' of them (Ramanujan 2009: 162). Stories such as *The Kite's Daughter* and *Heron Boy* indicate an alternative form of procreation. Nature acts as a surrogate mother and a substitute child in these stories, which have a therapeutic value on the audience, as they console the minds of childless mothers and comfort the hearts of orphaned children.

Those Clever Crows is a Dungri Garasiya adivasi folktale, which portrays the interdependence of human beings and nature. This story can be read as a modern-day parable of food crisis rampant in the globalised, liberalised, privatised world. The tale recounts a terrible famine in the land of King Garu and Queen Fulmani. On one side, the famine affects each and every living creature in the country, including the birds and animals. On the other, the kings and queens, the rich are not affected by famine. Hence, the story raises a significant ecofeminist question: how do Queen Fulmani and Mother Nature work together to solve the food crisis in their country? The woman is an embodiment of eco-consciousness, eco-sensitivity and sacrifice by which she is able to transcend the material reality and identify the spiritual self in all living creatures in the story. She had the ability to understand the bird's language and comprehend the plight of the birds. 'There's not a morsel I can bring for our young ones,' cried mother-crow, 'this is the third day they have to stay hungry. What are we to do?' (Sres 2007: 72) When the king does not help her, Queen Fulmani decides to give her life for the sake of the bird's family. The king finally realised his mistake and said, 'This is something I just cannot permit! My queen, stop this, and I will have the state granaries opened, and food will be available to crows, other birds, and all animals and people in the land!' (Sres 2007: 74). People with the worldview of abundance believe that Mother Earth can fulfil each and every living creature's need if there is no greed, as remarked by Gandhi. Human beings who are greedy exhibit a worldview of scarcity. *Those Clever Crows* depicts the conflict between the worldview of abundance and worldview of scarcity. The communication process that happens between Queen Fulmani and the crows symbolically suggests the dynamics of consciousness-raising. The folktale *Those Clever Crows* begins with anarchic *oikos* in the land of Garasiya Bhils. The relationship between Queen Fulmani and the crows paves the way for an integrative *oikos*. As Queen Fulmani recognises the sacred in nonhuman living creatures around her, she reverses the patriarchal beliefs and recreates a society characteristic of nature culture.

According to Vandana Shiva and Maria Mies, in the third world countries such as India, women in the rural areas promote the importance of 'subsistence perspective'. The word 'subsistence' implies survival or life. 'Sustainability' is another term closely associated with 'subsistence'. The subsistence perspective challenges commodity production and consumerist culture. It provides a platform for the unpaid work of housewives, peasants and workers of the informal sector. Subsistence standpoint has a direct bearing on sustainability for the following reasons. The production and consumption are viewed as a sacred act. In the name of development, the surplus is wasted on one side, and there is a demand on the other side. *Those Clever Crows* reiterate the importance of sustainability and subsistence perspective.

There are a number of folktales about house sparrows in India. The disappearance of sparrows is of grave concern to the environmentalists. They believe that the electromagnetic radiations from the mobile phones have destroyed them. The house sparrows were once closely associated with human beings, and hence, appear in a great number of folktales from India. 'The sparrows feel comfortable on a thorny bush' is an Indian proverb, with the ironic message that thorny bushes protect the little feathered creatures from all kinds of danger, including fauna and human race. The fate of the disappearing sparrows throws light on the insensitive behaviour of the human race. A *Golden Sparrow* is a South Indian folktale that portrays the indigenous belief in the cyclical pattern of life, where suffering and poverty are followed by riches when one is sincere in his/her work. A poor old woman becomes rich when a magical sparrow appears in her wounded hand and lays golden eggs. The narrator informs, 'it chirped and hopped all over the house, laying golden eggs wherever it perched. The old woman was delighted' (Ramanujan 1997: 72). On the other side, a jealous neighbour voluntarily creates a wound in the hand to witness the magical sparrow. But to her dismay, she loses her hand due to selfishness and careless behaviour. The story also gives an account of the Indian tradition of smearing cow dung in the entrance of the house.

> One morning, a poor old woman was washing the small yard in front of her door so that she could draw a rangoli design on it. While she was smearing the floor with cow dung paste to prepare the ground for the design, a thorn entered her palm.
> (Ramanujan 1997: 71–72)

The story raises two significant issues: What are the benefits of following the tradition? What are the harmful effects of following such practices? In villages, even today, cow dung is smeared on the walls and floors as it is considered as an insect repellent. Cow dung is used as a manure and bio fuel in rural areas to substitute the harmful pesticides and insecticides that are unsafe to human beings, animals, birds, plants, soil and water in the environment. But how does a woman safeguard herself from the negative effects of those practices? Do they get immediate medical attention? Some women survive several decades of their life with chronic illnesses due to sheer ignorance or fear.

Where Do the Sparrows Live! can be read as a modern parable of environmental concern. The sparrows are in jeopardy in the world of environmental chaos. In the story *Where Do the Sparrows Live!*, the sparrows don't find a safe and secure environment to live, to lay eggs and to nurture the young ones. First, the sparrows build the nest among the crops in the farm.

> When the sparrows flew away to fetch food, the children who took care of the cattle took the little ones to play with. The sparrows returned to the nest. The young ones were missing. The mother sparrow started weeping. The father sparrow comforted the mother sparrow and said, 'Next time we will go to the bamboo forest and you can lay the eggs there. There we will be safe.' The children steal the young ones.
>
> (Porselvi 2015: 97)

Second, the sparrows build their nest in the bamboo trees. The bamboo trees catch fire and burn the nest. 'When the sparrows flew away to fetch food, the wind blew heavily. The bamboo trees rubbed one another and caught fire' (Porselvi 2015: 97). Finally, the sparrows request the Sea King to protect their little ones. The king of the sea was surprised to see the tiny sparrows taking refuge in him. But he also decided to play a trick with them. When the sparrows flew away to fetch food, the king hid the little ones.

> The father sparrow flew to the land and called all his friends and relatives. All the sparrows decided to support him. Hearing this, the peacock, the cock, the swan, the crow and the parrot prayed to their favourite gods and goddesses and went towards the sea. The animals and the insects also saw this and joined the army. Together they took all the water from the sea and poured it on the land. The sea became dry . . . The King of the sea pleaded, 'Give me my water.' All the living creatures prayed to the gods and goddesses for the sake of the sea.
>
> (Porselvi 2015: 97)

In Act V scene ii of Hamlet by Shakespeare, Hamlet remarks, 'There's a special providence in the fall of a sparrow', which reflects the biblical verse, 'Are not two sparrows sold for a farthing? And one of them shall not fall on the ground without your Father' (Matthew 10: 29). Sparrows are little creatures that inspire human beings to be caring and sensitive towards nature. They signify the sacredness of life on this planet. They challenge the human beings to become conscious of their spirituality for a better living.

The Princess and the Parrots is a tale narrated by Chellammal from Kottaikaranpatty. The story highlights the theme of acceptance of the girl child in our society, which is a concern of ecofeminist thought. Hence, it is tale of Shakthi Consciousness. Once upon a time, in a certain town, there lived a king and queen. The queen was expecting her child. Before he left for hunting, the king told his wife, if a girl child is born, she is destined to die. 'Kill her and save the blood in a container. If a boy child is born deck him with gold jewels and lay him in a casket.' He ordered that only if the child is a boy, he can live. If the child is a girl, she should be killed. A Bengali folk song reads thus:

> Ten months and ten days
> The mother dreams on ever
> I'll have a son I'll see him grow
> Now she's a daughter's mother.
> (Tharu and Lalita 2011: 134)

In the beginning of the folk song, the mother mourns the birth of a girl child for the following reasons: when she grows up, she must go to an alien home; her presence in the maternal home is like a dream; even if parents have seven sons, they can live with their seven wives in their homes, but a daughter cannot live with her parents. The final stanza of the folk lyric describes the moment a daughter is leaving her home.

> Mother weeps and father weeps,
> So does the bride's brother;
> For she goes away this very day
> And breaks the heart of her mother.
> (Tharu and Lalita 2011: 134)

Since ancient times, the patriarchal society has conditioned the minds of women and men to be vindictive towards the birth and upbringing of a girl child. The Princess and the Parrots juxtaposes the constructive, procreative and protective role of the woman, the mother and the destructive role of the man-the-hunter. The queen delivered a girl child, but did not have the

BIRDS AND ANIMALS

heart to kill the child. She decked the child with gold jewels, laid her in a basket and set it afloat in a river. The girl child is saved by the seven green parrots that lived on a huge banyan tree on the banks of the river.

> On the banks of the river there was a huge banyan tree. On the tree there lived seven green parrots. One parrot said, 'I am feeling thirsty. I will go drink some water from the river.' She flew down to the river and saw the casket floating by. She flew down and stood on the casket and drank the water from the river. Suddenly she had a child crying. The parrot flew back to the tree and called her brother, '*Killianna Killianna*, I hear a small child crying in the casket!' They took the child to their nest and nurtured her.
>
> (Porselvi 2015: 53)

In this tale, the parrots symbolise collective strength and represent care and nurture of Mother Earth. They act as surrogate parents. In the end of the tale, the king realises his mistake. He makes up his mind to treat both the boy child and the girl child alike in future. Together, the king and the queen go to the banyan tree in the riverbank and request the parrots for their child. The parrots were happy to give the girl child to them. They thank the parrots and return home with the girl child.

In order to comprehend the indigenous ecofeminist discourse, the author studied an oral tale from Tamilnadu, *The Brother Bird*. In Palani Hills, the people of the Pulaiyar tribe narrate a story.

> Once upon a time in the Pulaiyar tribe a woman got married to a man in a distant place. The woman did not like her husband's house for some reasons.
>
> She started walking towards her mother's house at night time. It was a fearsome dense forest. And the thieves were around. At dawn a group of robbers saw the woman travelling alone and they stopped her. Knowing that she was alone they came close to her.
>
> At that moment the *kaana solai kuruvi* whistled in an out of the ordinary manner. The woman immediately called out in the direction of the bird's voice, "My Brother, Brother are you there, come soon". And the bird responded to her cry like a human being.
>
> The thieves in fear of the people around quickly disappeared. The woman thanked the bird and reached home safely.
>
> (Society for Integrated Development of Tribals 2002)

The predominant motif in the story is the Aves-Eve image, which signifies the relationship between woman and a bird in the tale. The tribal tale from

Palani Hills confirms the indigenous people's belief in interdependence of life forms, as signified in the communication of *kaana solai kuruvi* or a wild sparrow to the woman in distress. The Pulaiyar tribe believes in a worldview of abundance and respect for Mother Nature. They live in the jungles and communicate with birds and animals. Themes of interconnectedness and interdependence are highlighted by this Aves-Eve story. Tribal communities such as the Paliyar and the Pulaiyar believe in the interconnectedness of life. For example, when men go into the forests to collect fruits, they do not collect all the fruits from the trees. They consciously leave some of the fruits behind in the trees for the birds and animals and some for the wandering travellers. When a man gets a jackfruit or honey, he shares it with his entire community. The worldview of tribal people is the worldview of abundance. Both men and women inherit and reciprocate the spirit of abundance from Mother Nature.

The Pigeon's Bride from Yugoslavia is a story with bird–woman motifs. A talented princess was interested in doing embroidery. She turned into a bird everyday and flew to the tall tower. There, she sat and did her embroidery without any interruption and worked 'to her heart's content' (Ragan 2000: 64). One day, she saw a pigeon that sat in the window of the tower. She fell in love with the pigeon at first sight. Every day, the pigeon came to the windowsill and the princess offered a bowl of milk to him. The princess ignored her embroidery work and waited for the pigeon. One day, 'the bird's feathers opened like a shirt and out of the feather shirt stepped a handsome youth' (Ragan 2000: 65). The Pigeon Lover met her every day. When the king and the queen wished to get their daughter married, the princess disclosed the story of her Pigeon Lover. She forgot her lover's advice to 'not to communicate'. As a result, the Pigeon Lover stopped coming to the palace tower. After several hardships, the princess met her Pigeon Lover and redeemed him from the curse.

This tale subverts the conventional fairy-tale ending, where it is usually the prince who comes to the rescue of the princess. The princess is a dynamic woman who excels in her talent, caring towards other living creatures and also bold enough to solve her problems through her communication skills. She knows what to talk, when to talk, whom to talk, where to talk, why to talk and how to talk. Though the prince had warned her to be silent, she believes in expressing herself. This folktale highlights the woman's sensitivity to nature, her belief in the sacredness of life, her productive and practical outlook at life. Besides, she represents the *Shakthi Consciousness* of women gaining power from nature. In the end, she emerges as a victorious heroine who defines her life through her action. She asserts that the secret of her beauty is nothing but 'Happiness!' (Ragan 2000: 71) She regained a happy life since she remained true to herself.

Aves-Eve images reinforce the ecosensitivity of women towards other living organisms in this planet. The feminist images are revisited and compared to the ecofeminist images characterised by Shakthi. *Aves-Eve* images identify the strength that women and birds derive from wild nature. Undeniably, these oral tales provide an account of woman–bird communication in the oral discourse in India. The closeness of woman with nature is identified in *The Girl Who Understood Birds* and in the tribal tale *The Brother Bird*. The analysis of these folktales confirms that women who live close to nature are sensitive to the needs of nature and all living beings in her environment. These women understand the language of birds, animals and plants. They communicate with nonhuman living beings and their culture is shaped by respect, care and concern for them. In folktales such as *Bopoluchi, The Kite's Daughter, Heron Boy, Sanykisar, The Crow Girl* and *Those Clever Crows*, Mother Earth, in the form of animals, birds, trees and flowers in her environment, comforts the suffering woman. In times of food crisis, women and birds get together and find a solution, as in *Those Clever Crows*.

Nature and women are not passive in the folktales from India. Women's thoughts, words and deeds emerge from alternative worldviews. The worldviews of the narrator and the narrated in the folktales from India represent a counter-system to androcentric, anthropocentric worldviews that consider women and nature as objects or consumerist products. With the fundamental belief in the spiritual element of all living creatures, Mother Earth Worldviews offer hope to the dismal scenario in our society, culture and environment. In folktales such as *The Kite's Daughter, Sanykisar, The crow-girl* and *Heron Boy*, nature in the form of birds recognises the sacredness of life and provides comfort to the suffering human beings. *Aves-Eve* stories enlighten the close relationship between birds and women. The bird–woman communication, a common motif in a number of folktales across the world, reinforces women's sensitivity towards her environment. The creation of birds as surrogate mothers and foster fathers in these oral tales renders a cathartic effect to the suffering. Similarly, animals also share a close proximity with women in folktales from India. The following section deals with *Fauna-Fem* motifs.

Fauna-Fem tales

Some stories reinforce the power of woman as in the tale *The Tiger Woman*. Stories such as *Nonviolence, Nagarani (Serpent Queen), The Serpent Mother, The Tiger Woman* and *The Porcupine Daughter* are filled with FaunaFem symbols. *Soni's Story* by Anita Rampal is a modern-day fable that critiques the superstitious beliefs of rural people. *A Man Is . . .* is an oral tale narrated by a rural woman about man's greed and nature's goodness. Folk narratives abound with animals as important symbols helping the suffering woman. 'An important part of any culture is its system of symbolic representation of reality – the attribution of meaning to perception. Symbolism is an instrument of knowledge and the most ancient and fundamental method of expression, one which reveals aspects of reality which escapes other modes of expression' (Cooper 2012: 7). *Fauna-Fem* stories can be read as parables, fables or allegory, with animal characters representing the worldviews and consciousness of the native storytellers. In the folktales from India, the *Fauna-Fem* motif highlights the importance of respecting the language of animals in nature. In his article, 'Lost in a Forest of Symbols: Can Some Animal, Bird, Tree or Djinn Help Us Understand Myth and Folklore?', Alok Bhalla quotes an extract from Italo Calvino's *Italian Folktales*:

> His father looked at him in amazement.
> 'How would you know what the sparrows are saying? You're not a soothsayer, are you?'
> 'No, but my teacher taught me the languages of various animals.'
> 'Don't tell me where the money went!' said the father.
> 'What was the teacher thinking of? I meant him to teach you the languages of men, not of dumb beasts.'
>
> (Bhalla 2010: 1–2)

Transcending the anthropomorphic interpretation of fables and parables, this approach facilitates the understanding of the inherent worth of fauna. In her essay *Animal Rights and Feminist Theory*, Josephine Donovan explains that 'out of a woman's relational culture of caring and attentive love . . . emerges the basis for a feminist ethic for the treatment of animals . . . If we listen, we can hear them' (Gaard and Murphy 1998: 185). In the folktales chosen for analysis, women show love and care towards animals and the animals reciprocate their affection.

Article 4 of Mother Earth Rights states that 'Every animal has the right to live free from torture, cruel treatment or punishment by human beings'. The woman–animal association is studied under this category called *Fauna-Fem* symbols. This research raises certain vital ecofeminist questions: How does woman–animal relationship in the folktales promote the concept of *Shakthi*? How does woman–animal relationship in the folktales promote the concept of *Ahimsa*? How do the animal characters in select folktales from India reverse the anthropocentric worldviews? The union of the *Shakthi Consciousness* of the living creatures with the *Shakthi Consciousness* of the *Prakriti* is exemplified in a story called *The Tiger*. It is a parable that puts forth the understanding of consciousness in day-to-day life. A master and his disciples come across a tiger in the jungle. The disciples run away in fright. But the teacher remains calm.

> The master turned his gaze fearlessly towards the tiger, emptied his mind from all thoughts, and entered a kind of trance. In his consciousness he embraced everything in the universe including the tiger. In this deep meditation the consciousness of the teacher became one with consciousness of the tiger.
>
> (Sasson 2010)

Later, when the tiger lowered its head and left the place quietly, the disciples asked for the reason. When human beings have clarity in their thoughts and make attempts to understand the consciousness of other living beings, they are united with the universe on a 'spiritual' level. At that moment of consciousness-raising, the environment and the universe at large are filled with peace and harmony. Though folktales tend to be anthropomorphic, on closer reading, these oral tales try to capture the consciousness of non-human living organisms and speak for the well-being of the natural environment. Josephine Donovan, in her essay *Reading the Orange*, quotes Gary Kowalski's 'interspecies meditation', which reads

> Look into the eyes of an animal. It might be your dog or cat...
> Pay attention to what you see: the years of living present within those eyes...
> Contemplate their shape. Notice the angles and curves of individuality that make the face of this creature a unique work of art, crafted by time and desire.
> And as you look into this being's eyes, pay attention also to what you cannot see, the inwardness, the selfhood, the 'I' that is as singular as its outward expression.
> What you look upon is a living spirit. Greet it and respect it. Appreciate it for what it is...
>
> (Gaard and Murphy 1998: 88)

Respect for the inherent worth of a living creature is a common belief in Deep Ecology and Ecofeminism. In the Mother Earth Discourse, the animals are 'subjects' and not 'objects'. According to Donovan, 'such a reconception will restore the absent referent as a "thou" to the text' (Gaard and Murphy 1998: 74). *Fauna-Fem* symbols reiterate the 'I-Thou' relationship between woman and animals in her environment.

In *The Porcupine Daughter*, a little girl gets transformed into a porcupine in order to teach her greedy father a lesson. The daughter expresses her anguish, 'Dear father, you cheated our mother, the earth, and she cursed me and turned me into a porcupine' (Adhikary 2003: 91). The little girl considers the earth as her Mother and accepts the chastisement. The story also suggests the way farmers treat porcupines in Gujarat.

> The kunabi began to weep. 'Oh, poor child, my greed brought you to this pass. Henceforth let no kunabi injure or kill you or any of your kind. Let all porcupines be welcome to anything they like in our fields.'
> That is why, in Gujarat, porcupines are never hunted or killed, and they are allowed to eat whatever they like from the farmer's fields; and the porcupine's cry sounds like the weeping of a human child.
>
> (Adhikary 2003: 92)

According to Edward B Tylor, an English anthropologist, primitive people attributed to the elements, the animals, the plants, and the rocks the personalities and souls, and this becomes the crust of folklore. He believed in the concept of animism, which recognises the presence of a spiritual element or the soul in all living creatures. Folktales with animal characters have been read as allegories since ancient times. The transformation of the little girl into a porcupine confirms the indigenous belief in the consciousness of nonhuman living beings on this earth.

Snakes are important characters in folktales from India. A snake symbolises evil in the Eurocentric system of beliefs. In India, snakes are worshipped as a god or a goddess. Snakes are worshipped as gods and goddesses in different aboriginal cultures across the world. Wadjet, also known as 'The Green One' in the Egyptian mythology, is the goddess of the city of Dep. In India, snakes are worshipped as a goddess in the name of Manasa, the queen of snakes in the villages of Sundarbans, West Bengal. Janguli and Tara are Tibetan goddesses who have power over snakes. In *The Serpent Mother*, a pregnant woman shares her favourite 'khir' with a pregnant serpent. When the young woman finds out that someone had eaten the 'khir', she gives a blessing. She narrates, 'I craved to eat khir. I had some crusts here, but when I went for my bath, someone ate them up. Well, she must be someone unhappy like myself and may have been hungry. I'm glad that someone was made happy by my khir' (Ramanujan 2009: 256). When the woman tells the serpent that she did not have her parents, the serpent with a sense of gratitude replies, 'Daughter, do not worry. From today on, just think of me and my kin as your parental relatives' (Ramanujan 2009: 256). The serpent gets transformed into a noblewoman, Rajput in appearance and visits the young woman's house to celebrate the first pregnancy and also takes her home to deliver the child. The story also gives an account of the next generation, where the children are blessed by the relationship of the woman and the serpent mother. The tale ends with these words, 'May the Serpent Mother be good to us all as she was good to her!' (Ramanujan 2009: 262).

In another story, *The Youngest Daughter-in-Law and Her Snake Brothers*, the protagonist is sensitive to the needs of animals and receives blessings from Mother Nature. Maya, the protagonist of the story, was a clever and beautiful, but a poor girl. She fell in love with the youngest son of a rich merchant and married him. The in-laws disliked Maya because she was poor. On a rainy day, Maya went to the pond to get some fish. When she returned home and took out the fish, she found that they had turned into snakes. Maya did not kill the snakes as she knew they were 'sacred to Manasa' (Adhikary 2003: 43). Manasa, the snake goddess, recognised Maya's kindness. The snake goddess took the form of a wealthy lady and visited Maya's house. The goddess took Maya in her chariot and blessed her with gifts. Manasa proclaimed that Maya was no longer an orphan, but she will be known as her own daughter, who had eight snake-brothers. These *Fauna-Fem* folktales animals are a source of comfort to women, particularly for those who are poor or orphaned. Snakes play the role of a surrogate mother, sister or brother to the suffering woman. The Serpent God, in the name of Manasa, is worshipped in the villages of Kerala, Tamilnadu, Bengal and Karnataka. The relationship between Mother Earth and the snake goddess is captured in the following folk song.

> Thou pretty Serpent Maiden
> The serpents at eight directions
> Awake and arrive to the earth.
> Thou noblest and worshipful family god.
> Thou Mother Goddess Earth
> Reigning supreme over the universe
> Attired in river Ganges
> Stars garlanding thy neck
> The planets lighting you
> Sun and Moon thy holy lamps.
> We bow at your ornamented feet
> Graced with anklets
> Thou noblest and worshipful family god.
>   (Muthukumaraswamy 2008: 119)

In Kerala, women worship serpent gods by drawing designs and patterns called 'Kalams'. Suresh Kumar, in his article 'Serpent God Worship Ritual in Kerala', explains that 'laying colour floor drawings or "Kalams" with minute specifications and in elaborate picturesque designs is one method to express piety among rural folk and it reveals great diversity of cultural discourse' (Muthukumaraswamy 2008: 104–05). He asserts that more than fear or dread, people worshipped snake gods out of love and admiration. *Nonviolence* is a parable narrated by Shri Ramakrishna to emphasise the importance of *Ahimsa Consciousness*. *Nonviolence* is a story of consciousness-raising. In this tale, with the blessings of a sadhu, a snake happens to lead a life of nonviolence. However, the human beings in the environment are cruel towards him. Though the story does not have a woman character, it highlights the ecofeminist belief in the sacredness of life, the intrinsic value of living creatures. The story ends with the holy man's words, 'I asked you not to bite anyone. But I didn't ask you not to hiss!' An ecofeminist approach to life suggests the importance of expressing oneself through nonviolent forms of communication.

The eco-sensitivity towards life is reinforced by the indigenous people in their day-to-day life. Iris Murdoch, in her work *Metaphysics as a Guide to Morals*, explicates 'reverence for life and being, for otherness, is something which can be taught or suggested very early. Don't kill the poor spider, put him out in the garden' (Murdoch 1994: 337). The native people of the Palani Hills communicate the concern for nonhuman living beings in the same way. For example, when they offer food to animals, they place it on a large leaf which they pluck out of a climber near their hut and serve. And while plucking the leaf, they make sure that the nails do not hurt the plant. *Soni's Story* by Anita Rampal is an example of a consciousness-raising Mother Earth Discourse with a snake motif of a different kind. The story is about a schoolgirl's effort to create awareness among the village people to solve the crisis of 'the curse of the *naagdevta* (serpent-god)'. Soni belongs to a small town called Dhar in Madhya Pradesh. When Soni and her friends, with the help of the science teacher, found that the 'affliction' of leaves was not because of any supernatural element, 'they succeeded in exposing the tiny culprit, less than a millimetre in size, embedded within the leaf' (Khullar 2005: 292). The students solved the problem of the villagers through their collective strength. They used their education as a tool for liberation, a weapon against the superstitions and false beliefs. The girl students who live close to nature identify the issue with critical consciousness and raise the consciousness of the village people. According to Paulo Freire, education is the 'praxis of liberation' (Freire 2006: vii). By communicating the critical consciousness of Soni and her friends, Anita Rampal's Discourse confirms the power of consciousness-raising discourse. *Soni's Story* is chosen for analysis to highlight the difference between beliefs and superstitious beliefs prevalent among rural people in India.

BIRDS AND ANIMALS

The Tiger Woman is a feminist folktale that can be read at multiple levels using ecofeminist thought and interpretation. The transformation of a woman into a tiger and back into a woman suggests the innate strength of woman in essence. However, the metaphor of cannibalism does not fit into the paradigm of *Shakthi–Ahimsa–Shanthi* consciousness. The woman is advised not to drink water from the enchanted pool for fear of getting transformed into a beast. Like the archetypal Adam and Eve myth, where human beings were not allowed to eat the fruit of a particular tree, in this Manipuri tale, the man knows and the woman does not know the fact that people who drink water from the enchanted pool will turn into a tiger. In the end of the story, the woman is chased out of the house by her husband and forced to go into the forest. The tiger woman might symbolise a rebel who does not conform to the patriarchal system. The story might also suggest the status of bold and courageous women in a society and in the world at large.

The folktale *Respect for Life* is narrated by Kee Raa. The story revolves around the life of a fisherman and his wife. Every day, he went to the pond, caught some fish and sold them, and with that money, they bought food grains, made some porridge and ate it. Whenever he caught fish, the husband and wife wanted to prepare *meen kuzhambu* (fish gravy) and eat. One day, he got two *Viraal* fish. He took them home and gave them to his wife and asked her to make *meen kuzhambu*. When she was about to cut the fish, the fishes started crying like human beings. The woman was surprised and asked why they were crying. The fishes replied that they were husband and wife . . . newly married. They said that there were pearls in their stomach. Then she exclaimed, 'f we leave you back in the pond somebody will catch you. How will you give us the pearls? The fishes replied, "Allow us to be there in your house tank till full moon. Then we will give the pearl. You take the pearl and leave us back in the pond, we will survive", they suggested' (Porselvi 2015: 109). She agreed to the plan. The fisherman's wife was sensitive to the needs of her environment and respected nature. She poured water into the tank and left the fishes inside. Then, she went into the backyard and took some mushroom and prepared a dish with it. When her husband came back after a bath, she served him food. He asked, 'I told you to make *meen kuzhambu* and why did you prepare mushroom?' She narrated the whole story to her husband. It was the full moon night. As the fishes had instructed, the fisherman and his wife placed the water tank in the full moon light. The fishes brought out two huge pearls from their mouth. The couple could not control their happiness. They kept the pearl safe inside their house. They left the fishes back in the pond.

The story illustrates the kind-heartedness of women and men living close to nature. A month later, the king had a wound in his leg. He tried every medicine. He tried all the astrological solutions. But he did not find a cure. The village physician visited him and said that the only cure is to powder a fully developed pearl and tie it around the wound. The king sent the minister into the town to find out if anyone has a fully developed pearl. The couple came to know this. They said, 'When we were about to cut the fish to make the curry, we found these two pearls'. They gave the pearls to the king. The king applied the ground pearl on his wound. Within a few days, the wound got healed. The king was very happy. The king called the couple and thanked them and gave them *pinjai* (dry land), *nanjai* (wetland, suitable for cultivation) and *thophu* (a grove) cattle and a house. The fisherman and his wife lived happily, and at times, they went to the pond and gave food to the fishes.

A Man Is . . . is a folktale narrated by Anjalaiammal from Pidarithangal, Thiruvallur district, Tamilnadu. *A Man Is . . .* is a very powerful fable that communicates the need to respect the intrinsic value of life around us. There are three important characters in the tale: the man, the tiger and the bear. The tiger's attempt to feed on the man is the characteristic nature of wild animals. The bear represents the benign qualities of Mother Earth. He stands for the integrated *oikos*. Quite ironically, the man's selfish thoughts convey his wish to push the bear down indicate hierarchic *oikos*. In this tale, the animal world represents the *Ahimsa* way of life, in contrast to violence in the mind of a man. The bear epitomises the *Ahimsa* way of life. The human being is selfish and confirms his *himsa* behaviour in the tale.

The Monkey and the Woodcutter is a tale narrated by Kee Raa. In the edge of a forest, there lived a woodcutter. The woodcutter and his wife were greedy. One day, the woodcutter was chopping wood in the forest. A monkey came running towards him. The monkey told the woodcutter, 'If you take care of me I will do you good.' The woodcutter took the monkey to his house. The monkey was affectionate towards them. He carried out all the tasks. He would carry lunch for the woodcutter every day. At times, he guarded the house. One day, the monkey went to the king's palace. When he saw the gold coins in the treasury, he took some of it for his master. The woodcutter and his wife felt very happy. They showered their love for the monkey (Porselvi 2015: 93). The human beings exploit the monkey to fulfil their greed. In the end of the tale, the monkey becomes conscious of the exploitation and returns to the forest, the integrated *oikos*. The woodcutter rushed to the banks of the pond and found the monkey. 'Alas! I thought this monkey would bring me more riches, gold coins and jewels. But now it is all gone. This horrible creature has died so soon.' His wife said, 'Thank God! He did not die in our house. Let him become one with the soil. Let us go.' The monkey heard this and understood the truth. Will he go in the direction of the woodcutter's house? He said to himself, 'the forest is better than these ungrateful people.' The monkey ran towards the forest. The human beings stand for *himsa* ideals whereas the monkey stands for the *Ahimsa* ideals in nature (Porselvi 2015: 93).

Do Good unto Your Enemies was narrated by Dhanalakshmi from Anaikattucheri. The story is about a long-tailed monkey who is unique and proactive. When the mother monkeys went to work every day to bring food for their children, the little ones played around throughout the day. The other monkeys made fun of the little monkey who had a very long tail. One day, when the other monkeys were playing around, suddenly, they heard the sound of a large vehicle that came to catch the monkeys. Several men rushed towards the monkeys, caught them one by one and put them in their truck. The long-tailed monkey understood the situation, climbed down the tree and took the key from the engine of the truck. In the meantime, the mother monkeys had returned from work. They ran towards the vehicle and saved all their little ones. The little monkeys realised their mistake and apologised to the long-tailed monkey. They all started playing together happily. The long-tailed monkey represents *Ahimsa* consciousness in the story. He not only forgives the other monkeys who teased him, but also saves them from danger. Ecofeminism believes in the proactive understanding of one's self and the environment. A person with *Ahimsa* consciousness understands and respects the needs and the space of people around him. This simple tale justifies the *Ahimsa* philosophy of life.

Little Red Cap is classified as a *woody-woman* tale as the central character is a little girl who loved the woods. There are different versions of 'The Little Red Riding Hood' story. The most popular ones are 'Little Red Riding Hood' by Charles Perrault, 'Little Red Cap' by Jacob and Wilhelm Grimm, 'Little Red Hood' by Lower Lusatia, 'Little Red Hat' popular in Italy/Austria and 'The Grandmother' popular in France. In the 'Little Red Cap', the grandmother lives in the forest. She understands her environment and represents nature. Little Red Cap is a child of culture in the beginning of the story. Little Red Cap is supposed to deliver cake and wine for her ailing grandmother. The women's worldview emphasises nurture, nourishment and life. On the contrary, the wolf and the hunter are representatives of the patriarchal society and they symbolise death in the story. *Little Red Cap* discovers herself and her environment when she collects flowers in the forest. They no longer follow the path designated by the patriarchal society. In both the tales, the mothers are agents of patriarchy. The girls are punished by the patriarchal system for their exploration of their free will. According to history, these folktales originated at a time when female independence was considered a dangerous thing. The Little Red Cap does not have a name of her own. Her identity is defined by the red cap prepared by her grandmother. In Anne Sexton's poem *Red Riding Hood*,

> there was just little Red Riding Hood,
> so called because her grandmother
> made her a red cape and she was never without it.
> . . .
> she loved her grandmother who lived
> far from the city in the big wood.
> (Sexton 2014)

Historically speaking, in the 1600s France, when this version of the story was quite popular, clothing codes were very stringent. Red was a colour of rebellion and nonconformist ideals.

Little Red Riding Hood stories were cautionary tales to small children. In a fairy tale called 'The Red Shoes' by Hans Christian Andersen, a little girl is punished for dancing with her red shoes. Dr Clarissa Pinkola Estes, a psychologist, in her book *Women Who Run with the Wolves*, gives an account of myths, fairy tales, and stories that help women reconnect with nature. In those tales, women's belief in group identity is often compared to the unity found among a pack of wolves.

> Wolves and women are relational by nature, inquiring, possessed of great endurance and strength. They are deeply intuitive, intensely concerned with their young, their mates, and their pack. They are experienced in adapting to constantly changing circumstances; they are fiercely stalwart and very brave. Yet both have been hounded harassed, and falsely imputed to be devouring, overly aggressive, of less value than those who are their detractors.
> (Estes 1995: 2)

The identity of the lonely grandmother in *Little Red Cap* poses an ecofeminist concern. Old women are considered wicked. Many versions of the Little Red Riding Hood story present the grandmother as a lonely person living in the forest, and also the creator of the red cloak or the red cap for the little girl. In many societies, older women were considered as a burden or a threat to society. They were targeted as witches and eventually killed. 'The Red Shoes' by Hans Christian Andersen also portrays the old woman as a witch who gives the shoes to the little girl. The Little Red Cap's grandmother in the forest symbolises the Wild Woman archetypes. Little Red Cap undergoes a quest, discovers herself, and finally, returns home after self-realisation.

BIRDS AND ANIMALS

A Deep Ecological reading of the story *Little Red Cap* interrogates the portrayal of the wolf as a 'wicked' and 'cruel' character. From an anthropocentric viewpoint, animals such s the wolf, fox and snake are considered evil. 'Through deep experience, deep questioning and deep commitment emerges deep ecology', says Stephan Harding. According to Deep Ecology, 'All life has value in itself, independent of its usefulness to humans' (www.schumachercollege.org.uk). In his article, 'What Is Deep Ecology?' Stephan Harding discusses Aldo Leopold's 'deep experience' with the wolves. One morning, Leopold was out with some friends on a walk in the mountains. Being hunters, they carried their rifles with them, in case they got a chance to kill some wolves. Eventually, an old wolf was down by the side of the river, and Leopold rushed down to gloat at her death. What met him was a fierce green fire dying in the wolf's eyes. He writes in a chapter titled 'Thinking like a Mountain' that: 'there was something new to me in those eyes, something known only to her and to the mountain. I thought that because fewer wolves meant more deer, that no wolves would mean hunter's paradise. But after seeing the green fire die, I sensed that neither the wolf nor the mountain agreed with such a view' (www.schumachercollege.org.uk).

On the contrary, St. Francis of Assisi tamed a wolf with his love by calling it 'Brother Wolf'. It is said that the wolf lived for two years among the townspeople, going from door to door for food. It hurt no one and no one hurt it. The wolf led a peaceful life and epitomised *Ahimsa Consciousness* and *Shanti Consciousness*. This anecdote from St. Francis of Assisi's life reiterates ecofeminist spirituality as earth-based spirituality.

The depiction of snakes in stories such as *The Serpent Mother* and *Nonviolence* as responsible beings reverses the element of evil attached to serpents in dominant archetypal myths. It confirms the belief that as children of Mother Earth, animals do not hurt other creatures out of selfishness, craving or accumulation. According to nature's design, animals fulfil their basic needs by chasing their prey, which does amount to and differs from the hunting strategies employed by men to satiate their greed. At a different level, *Soni's Story* cautions people to be aware of systems that make use of indigenous beliefs as a tool of oppression against uneducated rural mass. *The Porcupine Daughter* and *The Tiger Woman* provide an account of transformation, a common technique used by narrators of folklore. The fishes in *Respect for Life*, the bear in *A Man Is*, the elephant in *Elephant and the Hunter*, and the monkey in *The Monkey and the Woodcutter*, and *Do Good unto Your Enemies* represent the spirit of interconnectedness, interdependence and intrinsic value of life.

Mother Earth Discourse attempts to study the connection between women and animals through *Fauna-Fem* narratives from India. These stories reiterate the interdependence of human–nonhuman life on this planet. The recognition of all living organisms as subjects fulfils the ecofeminist belief in egalitarianism. *Fauna-Fem* symbols communicate the principle of *Ahimsa* that pervades the entire universe and reinforce the discipline and order in the nonhuman natural world, as indicated in the story *Nonviolence*. In the *Fauna-Fem* stories, animals do not hurt other living beings, apart from their natural prey. The snakes share an affectionate relationship with women in the folktales such as *Nagarani (Serpent Queen)*, *The Serpent Mother* and *The Youngest Daughter-in-Law and Her Snake Brothers*. *The Tiger Woman* communicates woman power that is controlled by patriarchal norms. *The Porcupine Daughter* is another folktale that reiterates the importance of respecting the inherent worth of all living beings on this earth. *Fauna-Fem* tales challenge the stereotyped images of animals in the conventional fables and literary texts. The world of fauna is characterised by the principle of *Ahimsa*. The relationship between women and animals is one of care and concern. *Fauna-Fem* narratives reinforce the intrinsic value of animals and their interdependence with other species on earth.

Animal–woman relationships or *Fauna-Fem* motifs recognised in folktales from India are a revelation to people who grow up in a society with anthropocentric values. The folktales considered for study affirm the need to view the world from the point of view of fauna. The conversion indicates an alternative space created by women as a form of escape from the constraints of patriarchal society. The stories facilitate the need to be sensitive to animals and recognise their inherent worth in an era of exploitation and ill-treatment. This chapter dealt with the analysis of woman–nature motifs *Aves-Eve* and *Fauna-Fem* in folktales from India and also from around the world. The following chapter includes the summing up, findings and recommendations, suggestions for future research and the conclusion.

Conclusion
REVISITING FOLKTALES

Ecofeminist thought has initiated an alternative form of looking at the folk discourse for a constructive approach to life. The folktales from India, in this book, represent motifs that communicate woman–nature proximity, care for Mother Earth and respect for the intrinsic value of life and acknowledge interdependence and interconnectedness. At the beginning of the study, certain issues have been raised regarding ecofeminism and linguistics. In order to analyse folktales from India, an ecofeminist-linguistic framework is evolved for the understanding of woman–nature–language relationships. This chapter gives an account of the findings and conclusions arrived at in this study. This study has provided insights into nature-culture as a way of life. Mother Earth Discourse as a pragmatic folklore theory celebrates women's nature-culture on one side, and upholds woman-nature needs and rights, on the other. It highlights the importance of viewing the world from a holistic perspective through the eyes of women and nature. It is believed that a constructive consciousness can be realised only with the collective power of groups in the entire web of life. The ecofeminist-linguistic framework emphasises the importance of studying woman–nature–silences and woman–nature–language relationships.

The objectives of ecofeminist-linguistic approach – the search for the voices of the silenced, the unexpressed and the unheard – have been guided by the ecofeminist and the sociolinguistic praxis in this research. The purpose of ecofeminist-linguistic framework is to revisit folktales and oral tales and reconstruct new meanings in women–nature–culture that communicate alternative worldviews for the sustainability of Mother Earth. The ecofeminist-linguistic structure has evolved from the synthesis of ecofeminist movements, literary theories, experiences and pedagogies to form a meaningful tool of consciousness-raising. The folktales from India are analysed using the ecofeminist-linguistic framework to provide 'a consistent linguistic basis for content analysis' (Llamas, Mullany and Stockwell 2007: 46). This systematic approach to the folktales from India outlines six stages in the dynamics of discourse analysis and synthesis. The ecofeminist-linguistic framework in the form of the beehive model is characterised by Mother Earth Motifs, Mother Earth Relationships, Mother Earth Concerns, Mother Earth Worldviews, Mother Earth Consciousness and Mother Earth Lingua Franca. The beehive model symbolises a system with which folktales from India are revisited, reread and reconstructed within ecofeminist thought processes. In this process of revisiting the folktales, the motifs, the relationships, the concerns, the worldviews and the consciousness are identified and understood from an ecofeminist-linguistic perspective.

Rediscovering green paths

Ecofeminist Literary Criticism is an emerging trend in the field of literature and the ecofeminist-linguistic framework exemplifies an Indian approach to study folktales from India. Folktales are classified into twelve types, based on the nature–woman motifs. They are related to woman's association with her home and her environment. *Akam* Woman – The Creator and the Created: *Isis Panthea, Amma-I-Appan*; Silence and Speech: *Her-Meta, Athena's Wit*; Food, Household and Sisterhood; *Annamangai, Sis-Tie* and *Puram*; Woman–Trees and Forests: *Woody-Woman, Vana-Devi*; Land and Water: *Tellus-Ma, Aqua-Stree*; Birds and Animals: *Aves-Eve* and *Fauna-Fem*. The analysis of Mother Earth motifs provides ample evidence of indigenous worldviews that promote reverence to life on this planet. The motifs are symbolised by a floral design that signifies woman–nature–culture.

The Mother Earth Discourse can be explored in folklore across the world. From the analysis and synthesis of folktales from India, we identify the following green values in women and men who live close to nature. As an extension of *Shakthi Consciousness*, we find the different ecofeminist concerns such as *sathyam* (truth), *annadhaanam* (sharing, alms), *porumai* (patience), *stree shakthi* of women, *shakthi* of a girl child, *uzhaippu* (hard work), *nunnarivu* (sensitivity) and *karunai* (compassion). In relation to *Ahimsa Consciousness*, *jeeva karunyam* (nonviolence), *samayosidha bhudhi* (proactive thinking), *irakkam* (compassion), *visuvasam* (loyalty), *nambakathanmai* (trustworthiness), *naermai* (honesty), *aka azhagu* (beauty of the mind) and *nanri kadan* (gratitude) are identified. In relation to *Shanthi Consciousness*, *elimai* (simplicity), *idam, porul arithal* (prudence), *thannai arithal* (knowing oneself), *mana niraivu* (satisfaction), *niraivu* (contentment), *thannalamatra ennam* (selflessness), *adakkam* (humility) and *nal ennam* (good will) have been recognised.

In general, the analysis of folktales as woman–nature narratives has highlighted the following aspects. The women's narratives are designed in a circular fashion, which denotes their belief in the cyclical pattern of life.

CONCLUSION

The faith in life before birth and after death inspires them to respect the unborn as well as the dead equally. In terms of both content and structure, woman's tales reinforce the importance of circular designs over squares and triangles that restrict the modern 'out-of-the box' thinking. Women's cultural practices such as drawing rangoli, kolam, weaving and embroidery promote spherical shapes and designs drawn from nature. Similarly, folktales as Mother Earth Discourse communicate the thought processes of indigenous people, which are circular in nature.

The woman–nature association represented in the folktales from India, challenges the social construction of womanhood in a patriarchal society. The alternative worldviews of tribal people reiterate the innate strength of women acquired from the natural environment. They challenge the social issues of women. They throw light on women's concerns such as puberty, menstruation, childbirth, abortion and other issues related to her body, which affect her environment and vice versa. Women's role and responsibility towards their home (*akam*) and the Home (*puram*), the world at large, is effectively presented in folktales in India. These try to answer questions about essentialism in ecofeminist theory. In folktales as Mother Earth Discourse, both *akam* and *puram* are important to a woman. Women empower *akam* and *puram*, and in turn, both *akam* and *puram* empower women.

The folktales also elucidate the social problems such as female infanticide, incest, sexual harassment and ill-treatment of widows in our society. Tribal worldviews offer an alternative form of social system that treats women in a better way as human beings with a 'spiritual' element in them. Ten significant facets of Mother Earth worldviews have been identified in the course of this research. They include care for Mother Earth, concern for a holistic outlook, respect for inherent worth, appreciation of nature's abundance, acknowledgement of interdependence, emphasis on circular principles, recognition of nature power, affirmation of woman power, assertion of pluralism and belief in synergising knowledge. Folk literature provides ample evidence of human beings caring for trees, rivers, birds and animals. The Earth Mother's care for her children and the lives of indigenous people reinforces the responsibility of human beings to reciprocate care and concern to our planet. The cultures of women who live close to nature are shaped by the idea of interdependence. The rites and rituals that women follow in their day-to-day life are understood as an extension of their relationship with nature. The alternative myths that challenge the man-the-hunter myth are identified to recreate a world characterised by *Shakthi, Ahimsa* and *Shanthi.*

Ecofeminist belief in the sacredness of life, guiding human beings to respect the inherent worth of all creation, is reinforced by woman–nature motifs in folktales from India. A close look at tribal living provides evidence

CONCLUSION

of people who revere the soil, the water bodies in their environment, the trees and also the tiny insects and reptiles. They venerate life as a gift from the Creator and celebrate the interconnectedness through songs and stories. The worldview of indigenous people is the worldview of abundance, where Mother Nature provides food, shelter and security for all. Human beings who live close to nature believe that they have a major role in leading a responsible life. By sharing nature's abundance with the nonhuman living beings, these people feel a sense of contentment, which contributes to peaceful living.

The Mother Earth Discourse denotes the subsistence perspective of women. Ecofeminism does not subscribe to material production, growth of consumerist culture or the development of industries that pollute the environment and disturb the peace of fauna and flora on the face of the earth. The materialist tendencies are reversed in this viewpoint. Ecofeminists believe that humankind is only a thread in the entire web of life. The thoughts and actions of human beings affect the network of interdependence positively or negatively. The man-made environmental disasters such as deforestation, chemical catastrophes, nuclear wars and pollution have created a number of wounds on the face of the earth. A belief in the collective strength of human beings to heal these wounds would facilitate *Gaia* to recuperate from her sickness. The folktales from India provide ways to recognise nature power. The inherent power of each and every living and nonliving creature on this planet is said to emanate nature power at various degrees. When the supremacy of nature is acknowledged by human beings, they gain more power from Mother Earth. The affirmation of woman power does not stop with the deification of women as goddesses. It involves the empowerment of women in the day-to-day reality. Storytelling is recognised as a tool of consciousness-raising. The select tales studied in this research process reiterate the alternative worldviews and consciousness of indigenous people that provide solutions for the problems created by the patriarchal consumerist society.

As indigenous people assert the necessity for pluralism, for genuine growth and development, the analysis of folktales has facilitated the identification of multiple voices, multifarious viewpoints, diverse holistic theories and different schools of nonviolence and peace under one canopy. With the belief in synergising knowledge, the hierarchical systems are quashed within the Mother Earth Discourse structure. The philosophy of those simple women can be emulated by women, children and men, living in the other parts of the country and across the globe. Mother Earth Discourse enables earth-centreed knowledge systems that help one to reconnect with culture and tradition to bring about transformation. Each and every living creature is respected for its intrinsic value. At the pedagogical level, the

CONCLUSION

learners are respected for their inherent worth and the teacher as a facilitator and a 'cultural worker' realises the responsibility of synthesising the indigenous 'knowledge-systems' into a meaningful whole.

As a future direction to ecofeminist ethnography or ethnolinguistics (the relationship between culture and language), Mother Earth Discourse approach to folklore is perceived as a means by which the rich source of native language and culture of women and marginalised groups can be studied using sociolinguistic methods. The *Terra Mater Lexis* can be incorporated in nature-writing to bring about social change. Words that indicate Mother Earth and terms that contribute to the well-being of the planet can be collected through research, which can result in Mother Earth/ Ecofeminist lexicography. This is possible because the folktales are not stories based on fantasy, but they rely on imagination that is closely related to reality. As ecofeminist thinkers believe in praxis, which necessarily includes practice with theory, Mother Earth Discourse seeks to realise the importance of practicality. At this juncture, the word 'discourse' acquires a special significance that indicates the possibility of word-into-action. Through the symbolic tales narrated by women, one can infer women's in-depth understanding of their environment, their practical approach to life and the pro-active measures they take for life sustenance, and this contributes to the concept of Mother Earth Practicality. The case studies exemplify ecofeminist experiences and communicate the epistemology of indigenous women who have the original knowledge of agriculture and farming. Moreover, these women share a number of common traits, which reinforce ecofeminist ideology and thought processes. They show care and concern for Mother Earth and people around them.

Mother Earth Discourse lends itself to the identification of Mother Earth or *Terra Mater Lexis* that foster positive energy and dynamics in an environment. Spivak's challenging question 'Can the Subaltern Speak?' raises the issues that surround the 'silent' and 'silenced' people. Mother Earth Discourse is envisioned to be a subaltern tool, which could be used to identify the voices of people living in rural areas and tribal regions in India. A subaltern reading of the folktales promises new avenues towards an egalitarian society. The simple stories of rural and tribal men and women in villages contribute to the well-being of nature. This research has clearly outlined the fact that subaltern people speak in an alternative form of discourse, which is either not heard, or listened to, by people in the mainstream culture. Mother Earth Discourse challenges hierarchies in social systems and recreate a space of equality and collective efficiency.

As a sociocultural tool, the ecofeminist-linguistic framework attempts to bring about social change in terms of gender equity and sustainable progress. The ecofeminist-sociolinguist has a major role in exploring the ethnography of women, children and oppressed men in the context of nature-culture. Mother Earth Discourse is a linguistic instrument which studies the issues of women's silence and speech and the environmental factors that affect them. The ecofeminist-language teacher plays a major role in facilitating a culture of expression, whereby the silenced groups regain a voice in the English language with confidence and self-esteem. Storytelling is identified as a method in ecofeminist pedagogy where the learners get a chance to narrate tales that reflect their worldviews and consciousness, unlike the traditional system, where only the teacher has a voice over the silenced set of students. Mother Earth Discourse reveals the world of women, their experiences, and their view of life, the relationship between their society, culture and nature. It does not generalise woman's experience. Rather, it attempts to study different kinds of women and their knowledge of environment. The holistic approach to life is highlighted in all the dimensions of their day-to-day activities. The significance of domestic cultures and their influence on the society, environment and world at large are studied using the proposed paradigm.

Redefining new roads

This study underscores a pertinent idea that folktales are not just a medium of entertainment, but a vital instrument to understand the worldviews and consciousness of the apparently silent people. The recommendations and the suggestions for future study are as follows. An ecofeminist interpretation of folktales from different parts of the world would definitely provide an insight into the motifs, relationships, concerns, worldviews and consciousness of indigenous people and they can be studied either in the native language or in translation. Folk songs, folktales and folk drama can be translated from regional and vernacular languages into English and studied as the Mother Earth Discourse.

The ecofeminist-translator has a significant task of transferring the Mother Earth Discourse from local languages to English and vice versa. The translation of the tale of the *Pulaiyar* tribe provides an opportunity to appreciate the worldviews of that community. Ecofeminist translation is also visualised as a new area of study, which can be explored further in future. The lingua franca of native tribes can be studied using the proposed paradigm and words that form a part of *Bhoomi Register* can be documented and studied, contributing to Mother Earth lexicography. Using the ecofeminist-linguistic framework, *Terra Mater Lexis* can be identified in the novels and short stories of Rajam Krishnan, Bama, Ambai and Mahasweta Devi as all the four writers provide an authentic record of women in their nature-culture.

CONCLUSION

A *Deep Ecological* reading of the folktales from India and around the world would throw light on the principles proposed by Arne Naess on respecting the intrinsic value of all living beings on this earth. A combination of *Deep Ecological* theories and ecofeminist principles together would definitely offer a holistic method of recognising gender equity. An oikofeminist reading of the folktales can also be carried out by integrating Dr Selvamony's *oikos* theory with ecofeminist theories to study the cosmos in which women live, to comprehend their environment and read the significance of the integrative *oikos* over hierarchic and anarchic *oikos*. A study of proverbs, folk songs and riddles and folk art forms using *Isis Panthea, Amma-I-Appan, Her-Meta, Athena's Wit, Woody-Woman, Vana-Devi, Tellus-Ma, Aqua-Stree, Aves-Eve and Fauna-Fem* motifs can be carried out using the ecofeminist-linguistic framework. This research has provided evidence of folk songs that communicate care and concern to Mother Earth and her children. Each motif in the proposed framework can be studied in detail to unravel new meanings in folklore as Mother Earth Discourse. This will enable the understanding of women–nature relationships that care for Mother Earth, respect the intrinsic value of all living creatures and acknowledge interconnectedness of life.

By understanding the folk discourse in various forms, it is possible to create environmental awareness among the students using the proposed paradigm. It helps them to be critically aware of things happening around them. It facilitates them to understand the living and nonliving beings in their environment. They learn to respect nature and fellow human beings in a better way. It helps them to identify a path towards gender equity and ecologically sustainable development. Mother Earth Discourse fits in as a suitable instrument to study the narratives of women and other marginalised groups. Hence, it is recognised as an educational medium of promoting alternative worldviews that are conducive to the well-being of the planet.

Reweaving nature-culture

A resurgence of attention to the folk narratives in women's nature-culture would definitely revive the strong roots of wisdom that explicate intrinsic power of an individual and the collective power of a group, inspire nonviolent ways of leading the day-to-day lives and sow seeds of peaceful coexistence. This recovery will facilitate the younger generation to grow up as responsible human beings at home, in the community, in the society and world at large. The folktales from India try to capture women's imagination and thought processes in a much more authentic fashion than literary works. The motifs and symbols are not just simple metaphors. A deeper understanding of women's discourse reveals the life-affirming worldviews

CONCLUSION

that can provide a way out of the existing chaos in our society, culture and environment.

Within the ecofeminist-linguistic framework, Mother Earth Discourse integrates comparative methods, anthropological motifs and patterns, national folklore perspectives, psychoanalytical dimensions and structural approaches within its ambit. This study has described the feminine tradition of storytelling as an educational process that begins at home. Mother Earth is the personification of tolerance, compassion and magnanimity. An ecofeminist is a woman, man or a child who cares for Mother Earth and respects the spiritual element in all living creatures. Thus, ecofeminism envisions praxis of *Shakthi* (power), *Ahimsa* (nonviolence) and *Shanthi* (peace) consciousness. These alternative forms of discourse reiterate a holistic approach to life and facilitate an 'ecological conversion', in the words of Pope Francis in his encyclical letter titled 'Laudato Si' (Praise be to you) 'on care for our common Home' (Pope Francis 2015: 167). Revisiting the tribal worldviews enables new paths towards sustainable development and peaceful coexistence.

The understanding of nature-culture through the Mother Earth Discourse paves way for a better natural environment and a healthy society for women, children and other marginalised groups. In the ecofeminist outlook of life, each and every living creature is revered as a special element that contributes to the harmony of the planet. Thinking beyond the dominant man-made languages, Mother Earth Discourse provides a background to value the discourse of nonhuman living and nonliving beings that communicate concern and love for the well-being of the planet. The communication of animals, birds, trees, mountains, rivers, breeze and rain are revered as important forms of the Mother Earth Discourse.

Mother Earth Discourse confirms the fact that human beings are only a part of the web and their knowledge and understanding is limited to their consciousness and understanding of their environment; the other nonhuman inhabitants of this planet also have consciousnesses that shape and mould their existence and dynamics in life. Human beings who live close to nature have the indigenous knowledge to understand the needs and rights of earth, water, trees, plants, animals, birds, insects and also the fellow human beings.

The ecofeminist-linguistic framework has offered a novel approach to folktales from India that takes into its purview the identification and understanding of women–nature motifs, relationships, concerns, worldviews, consciousness and consciousness-raising expressions. The ecofeminist-linguistic approach has explored the seeds of silence and discovered a new language revealing new meanings. The evolution of the Mother Earth

CONCLUSION

Discourse from folktales from India contributes to social and linguistic empowerment of women, which is termed as a process of conscientisation or *conscienticazao*. In an age of environmental crisis, the alternative worldviews represented in the folktales promise hope for the well-being of Mother Earth and all Her children and a better society for future generations.

GLOSSARY

Aippasi (Tamil)   month that occurs around October 18 to November 18
adakkam (Tamil)   humility
aka azhagu (Tamil)   beauty of mind
Ahimsa (Sanskrit)   nonviolence, opposite of *himsa* or violence
akam (Tamil)   home, interior space and also heart and soul in *Sangam* poetry
Amma (Tamil)   mother; term of endearment used to address a woman with respect
annadhaanam (Tamil)   sharing, distributing food as a form of charity
Ardhanarishvara (Sanskrit)   the image of God as half-male and half-female, Siva and Shakthi
Ayya (Tamil)   father; term of endearment used to address a man with respect
Bhoomi (Tamil/Sanskrit)   Mother Earth
Bonbibi (Bengali)   forest goddess of the Sundarbans worshipped by Muslims
cholam (Tamil)   maize or corn grown as a food crop
chulli (Tamil)   twigs that fall down from the tree, used as a fuel
conscientizacao (Portuguese)   conscientisation/consciousness-raising process
ellu punnaaku (Tamil)   sesame oil cake used as fodder for cattle and manure for plants
Gaia (Greek)   goddess of Earth, equivalent to Bhoomi/Mother Earth
gram-devata (Sanskrit)   village goddess who protects the people and other living beings
irakkam (Tamil)   compassion
Jagam (Sanskrit)   universe
jeeva karunyam (Tamil/Sanskrit)   nonviolence; compassion to living beings
Kadabu (Kannada)   sweet puffs, a traditional snack
kadalai punnaaku (Tamil)   groundnut-oil cake used as fodder for cattle and manure for crops

GLOSSARY

Kalam (Malayalam)   traditional flower arrangement done on auspicious occasions
Kalpataru (Sanskrit)   wish-fulfilling tree
kambu/keppai (Tamil)   ragi, finger millet used as a food grain
Karthigai (Tamil)   month that occurs around November 18 to December 18
karunai (Tamil)   compassion
Killianna (Tamil)   *Killi* – parrot, *Anna* – brother
kolam (Tamil)   the traditional drawing usually done near the entrance of the house
kozhukattai (Tamil)   a steamed snack made of rice flour, coconut and jaggery
kurinji (Tamil)   mountainous region represented in Sangam poetry
Mandala (Sanskrit)   a form of drawing used for prayer and meditation
manathakkali keerai (Tamil)   a type of green that is used to detoxify the body
marudham (Tamil)   agricultural area represented in Sangam poetry
meen kuzhambu (Tamil)   fish curry/gravy
moolikai (Tamil)   medicinal herbs and plants
mullai (Tamil)   forest region represented in Sangam poetry
naermai (Tamil)   honesty
nambakathanmai (Tamil)   trustworthiness
nanjai (Tamil)   also called *nansai*, meaning wet, cultivable land
nal ennam (Tamil)   sense of good will
niraivu (Tamil)   contentment
neythal (Tamil)   coastal area represented in Sangam poetry
nunnarivu (Tamil)   sensitivity
oikos (Greek)   home, Planet Earth
oppari (Tamil)   dirge, sung to mourn the dead
padayatra (Sanskrit/Tamil)   devotees walking to the temple as a form of prayer, pilgrimage
palai (Tamil)   arid land represented in Sangam poetry
Parashakti (Tamil/Sanskrit)   omnipotent feminine principle
pinjai (Tamil)   also called *punsai*, meaning dryland
ponnanganni keerai (Tamil)   a type of green, which is good for improving eyesight
porumai (Tamil)   patience
Prakriti (Sanskrit)   the all-pervading feminine principle that governs the cosmos
puram (Tamil)   the exterior world, complementary to *akam* in Sangam poetry
Purusha (Sanskrit)   the complementary masculine principle to Prakriti
rangoli (Hindi)   a colourful floor art/drawing done on auspicious occasions

GLOSSARY

Roraattu/Thalattu (Tamil)   lullaby sung by mother to put the child to sleep
samayosidha bhudhi (Sanskrit/Tamil)   proactive thinking
Sangam literature   ancient Tamil literature, written from 300 BCE to 300 CE
Satyagraha (Sanskrit)   nonviolent form of protest
sathyam (Tamil/Sanskrit)   truth
Shakthi (Tamil/Sanskrit)   power and energy associated with women
Shanthi (Tamil/Sanskrit)   peace and harmony
thinai (Tamil)   the five types of landscapes represented in Sangam poetry; moral rectitude
thophu (Tamil)   grove or orchard
uzhaippu (Tamil)   hard work
vallarai keerai (Tamil)   greens that boosts the memory power
Vanadevatai (Tamil)   forest goddess; *Banadevi* (Bengali); *Vanadevata* (Hindi)
venthaya keerai (Tamil)   fenugreek leaves that balance the blood sugar levels
veragu (Tamil)   firewood
Viraal (Tamil)   a type of fish, murrel in English
visuvasam (Tamil)   loyalty, fidelity, faith

BIBLIOGRAPHY

Works Cited

Primary Sources

Adhikary, Qiran. 2003. *Feminist Folktales from India*. Oakland: Masalai Press.
Beck, Brenda, Peter J. Claus and Jawaharlal Handoo. (Eds.). 1987. *Folktales of India*. London: The University of Chicago Press Ltd.
Porselvi, Mary Vidya. 2015. *Bhoomi Tales*. Chennai: CSWR Publication.
Ragan, Kathleen. 2000. *Fearless Girls, Wise Women and Beloved Sisters – Heroines in Folktales from Around the World*. London: W.W. Norton and Company Inc.
Ramanujan, A. K. 1997. *A Flowering Tree and Other Oral Tales from India*. New Delhi: Penguin Books.
———. 2009. *Folktales from India – A Selection of Oral Tales from Twenty-Two Languages*. New Delhi: Penguin Books Ltd.
Sres, Marija. 2007. *First There Was Woman and Other Stories: Folktales of the Dungri Garasiya Bhils*. New Delhi: Zubaan Books.

Secondary Sources

Adams, Carol. (Ed.). 1993. *Ecofeminism and the Sacred*. New York: The Continuum Publishing Company.
Allaby, Michael. 2005. *Oxford Dictionary of Ecology*. Oxford: Oxford University Press.
Ambai. 1992. *A Purple Sea*. Madras: East-West Books Pvt Ltd.
———. 2003. *Two Novellas and a Story*. New Delhi: Katha Publications.
Andrews, Jane. 2007. *The Stories Mother Nature Told Her Children*. Chapel Hill, NC: Yesterday's Classics.
Bama. 2005. *Sangati*. New Delhi: Oxford University Press.
Basu, Amrita. (Ed.). 1995. *The Challenge of Local Feminisms: Women's Movements in Global Perspective*. Colorado: Westview Press Inc.

BIBLIOGRAPHY

Bhatnagar, Rashmi Dube and Reena Dube. 2005. *Female Infanticide in India: A Feminist Cultural History*. New York: State University of New York Press.

Buzan, Tony and Barry Buzan. 2010. *The Mind Map Book: Unlock Your Creativity, Boost Your Memory, Change Your Life*. Essex: Pearson Publishers.

Cameron, Deborah. (Ed.). 1998. *The Feminist Critique of Language*. London: Routledge.

Carson, Rachel. 2000. *Silent Spring*. London: Penguin Books Ltd.

Casey, Dawn and Anne Wilson. 2009. *The Barefoot Book of Earth Tales*. Cambridge: Barefoot Books.

Chaudhuri, Maitrayee. (Ed.). 2004. *Feminism in India*. New Delhi: Kali for Women.

Cooper J. C. (Ed.). 2012. *An Illustrated Encyclopaedia of Traditional Symbols*. London: Thames and Hudson Ltd.

Dai, Mamang. 2006. *The Legends of Pensam*. New Delhi: Penguin Books.

Desai, Neera. 2006. *Feminism as Experience – Thoughts and Narratives*. Mumbai: Sparrow Publications.

Devy, G. N. (Ed.). 2002. *Painted Words – An Anthology of Tribal Literature*. New Delhi: Penguin Books Ltd.

Dharwadker. 2004. *The Collected Essays of A.K. Ramanujan*. Oxford: Oxford University Press.

Diamond, Irene and Gloria Feman Orenstein. (Eds.). 1990. *Reweaving the World: The Emergence of Ecofeminism*. San Francisco: Sierra Club Books.

Estes, Clarissa Pinkola. 1995. *Women Who Run with the Wolves*. New York: The Random House Publishing Group Inc.

Fairclough, N. 2003. *Analysing Discourse: Textual Analysis for Social Research*. London: Routledge.

Francis, Pope. 2015. *Encyclical Letter Laudato Si 'Praise Be to You'*. Trivandrum: Carmel International Publishing House.

Freire, Paulo. 2006. *Pedagogy of the Oppressed*. London: Continuum.

Gaard, Greta. (Ed.). 1993. *Ecofeminism – Women, Animals, Nature*. Philadelphia: Temple University Press.

Gaard, Greta and Patrick D. Murphy. (Ed.). 1998. *Ecofeminist Literary Criticism – Theory, Interpretation, Pedagogy*. Chicago: University of Illinois Press.

George, Grey. 1956. *Polynesian Mythology* (Ed. by William W. Bird). Christchurch: Whitcombe and Tombs Ltd.

Glotfelty, Cheryll. (Ed.). 1996. *The Ecocriticism Reader*. Georgia: University of Georgia Press.

Goldberg, Ellen. 2002. *Lord Who Is Half Woman: Ardhanarisvara in Indian and Feminist Perspective*. New York: State University of New York Press.

Goodman, Lizbeth. (Ed.). 1996. *Literature and Gender*. London: Routledge.

Gottlieb, S. Roger. 2004. *This Sacred Earth: Religion, Nature, Environment*. New York: Routledge.

Guha, Ranajit. (Ed.). 1987. *Subaltern Studies V*. New Delhi: Oxford University Press.

Harish, Ranjana and Bharathi Harishankar. (Ed.). 2003. *Shakthi: Multidisciplinary Perspectives on Women's Empowerment in India*. New Delhi: Rawat Publications.

BIBLIOGRAPHY

Hart, George. 2002. *The Four Hundred Songs of War & Wisdom – An Anthology of Poems from Classical Tamil – The Purananuru* (Translations from the Asian Classics). Columbia: Columbia University Press.

Hooks, Bell. 2000. *Feminist Theory: Margin to Center*. Cambridge: South End Press.

Hudson, R. A. 1996. *Sociolinguistics (Second Edition)*. Cambridge: Cambridge University Press.

Humm, Maggie. 1992. *Feminisms: A Reader*. London: Longman Publishing Group.

James, George. 1999. *Ethical Perspectives on Environmental Issues in India*. New Delhi: A.P.H. Publishing Corporation.

———. 2013. *Ecology Is Permanent Economy*. New York: State University of New York Press.

Jaworski, A. and N. Coupland. (Ed.). 1999. *The Discourse Reader*. London: Routledge.

Johnstone, Barbara. 2000. *Qualitative Methods in Sociolinguistics*. Oxford: Oxford University Press.

Jung, Anees. 1987. *Unveiling India*. New Delhi: Penguin Books Ltd.

Kamala, N. (Ed.). 2009. *Translating Women: Indian Interventions*. New Delhi: Zubaan Books.

Kheel, Marti. 2008. *Nature Ethics*. New York: Rowman and Littlefield Publishers Inc.

Khullar, Mala. 2005. *Writing the Woman's Movement*. New Delhi: Zubaan Books.

Krishnan, Rajam. 2002. *When the Kurinji Blooms*. New Delhi: Orient Longman Pvt Ltd.

Letherby, Gayle. 2003. *Feminist Research in Theory and Practice*. Buckingham: Open University Press.

Llamas, Carmen, Louise Mullany and Peter Stockwell. (Eds.). 2007. *The Routledge Companion to Sociolinguistics*. London: Routledge.

Lovelock, James. 2006. *The Revenge of Gaia: Why the Earth Is Fighting Back – and How We Can Still Save Humanity*. Santa Barbara, CA: Allen Lane.

———. 2009. *The Vanishing Face of Gaia: A Final Warning: Enjoy It While You Can*. Santa Barbara, CA: Allen Lane.

Maathai, Wangari. 2006. *Unbowed – One Woman's Story*. London: William Heinemann.

Macdonald, Margaret Read. 2005. *Earth Care: World Folktales to Talk About*. Arkansas: August House Publishers Inc.

McCarthy, Tara. 1991. *Multicultural Fables and Fairy Tales*. New York: Scholastic Professional Books.

McConnell-Ginet, Sally and Penelope Eckert. 2003. *Language and Gender*. Cambridge: Cambridge University Press.

Meyerhoff, Miriam. 2006. *Introducing Sociolinguistics*. London: Routledge.

Mies, Maria and Vandana Shiva. 2010. *Ecofeminism*. Jaipur: Rawat Publications.

Mies, Maria, Veronika Bennholdt-Thomsen and Claudia von Werlhof. 1988. *Women: The Last Colony*. New Delhi: Kali for Women.

Miles, Rosalind. 1989. *The Women's History of the World*. London: HarperCollins Publisher.

Mitra, Debamitra and Kasturi Basu. (Eds.). 2009. *Ecofeminism – An Overview*. Agartala: ICFAI University Press.
Monteith, Moira. (Ed.). 1986. *Women's Writing: A Challenge to Theory*. Sussex: The Harvester Press Ltd.
Murdoch, Iris. 1994. *Metaphysics as a Guide to Morals*. London: Penguin Books.
Muthukumaraswamy, M. D. (Ed.). 2006. *Folklore as Discourse*. Chennai: National Folklore Support Centre.
O'Donohue, John. 2004. *Beauty: The Invisible Embrace*. New York: Harper Collins Publisher.
Philippi, Donald L. (Trans.). 1962. *The Masks of God: Oriental Mythology*. New York: Viking Press.
Plant, Judith. (Ed.). 1989. *Healing the Wounds: The Promise of Ecofeminism*. Philadelphia: New Society.
Pretty, Jules. 2007. *The Earth Only Endures: On Reconnecting with Nature and Our Place in It*. London: Earthscan.
Raheja, Gloria Goodwin. (Ed.). 2003. *Gendered Dialogues and Cultural Critique*. New Delhi: Kali for Women.
Ramakrishnan, E. V. (Ed.). 2000. *Indian Short Stories 1900–2000*. New Delhi: Sahitya Akademi.
Ramanujan, A. K. (Trans. and Ed.). 2006. *Poems of Love and War*. Oxford: Oxford University Press.
Ramazanoglu, Caroline and Janet Holland. 2002. *Feminist Methodology – Challenges and Choices*. London: Sage Publications.
Rich, Adrienne. 2003. *What Is Found There – Notebook on Poetry and Politics*. London: Norton and Company.
Rose, Deborah Lee. 2001. *The People Who Hugged the Trees*. Lanham: Roberts Rinehart Publication.
Ruether, Rosemary Radford. 1975. *New Woman/New Earth*. New York: Seabury Press.
Sankofa aka Anderson, David A. 1991. *The Origin of Life on Earth: An African Creation Myth*. Mt. Airy: Maryland Sights Productions.
Scheub, Harold. 2002. *The Poem in the Story*. London: The University of Wisconsin Press.
Sebastian, Joseph. 1995. *God as Feminine*. Tiruchirapalli: St. Paul's Seminary Publications.
Selvamony, Nirmal. 1998. *Persona in Tolkaappiyam*. Chennai: International Institute of Tamil Studies.
Selvamony, Nirmal, Nirmaldasan and Rayson K. Alex. (Eds.). 2007. *Essays in Ecocriticism*. New Delhi: Sarup and Sons and Osle-India.
Sessions, George. (Ed.). 1995. *Deep Ecology for the 21st Century: Readings on the Philosophy and Practice of the New Environmentalism*. Boston: Shambhala.
Sharma, Subash. 2009. *Why People Protest – An Analysis of Ecological Movements*. New Delhi: Ministry of Information and Broadcasting Government of India-Publication Division.
Sherman, Josepha. 2009. *World Folklore for Storytellers*. London: Routledge.

Shiva, Vandana. 2000. *Stolen Harvest: The Hijacking of the Global Food Supply*. Cambridge: South End Press.

———. 2010. *Staying Alive – Women, Ecology and Development*. New York: South End Press.

Smith, Ramsay W. 2003. *Myths and Legends of the Australian Aborigines*. New York: Dover Publications Inc.

Society for Integrated Development of Tribals. 2002. *Palanimalai Pazhangudigal – Paliyarum Pulaiyarum*. Madurai: SIDT.

Starhawk. 1999. *The Spiral Dance*. New York: Harper Collins.

Stein, Jane. 1997. *Empowerment and Women's Health – Theory, Methods and Practice*. London: Zed Books Ltd.

Stratton, Peter and Nicky Hayes. 1989. *A Student's Dictionary of Psychology*. New Delhi: Universal Book Stall.

Sturgeon, Noel. 1997. *Ecofeminist Natures*. London: Routledge.

Sutton, W. Philip. 2007. *The Environment – A Sociological Introduction*. Cambridge: Polity Press.

Tharu, Susie and K. Lalita. (Eds.). 2011. *Women Writing in India – 600 B.C. to the Present*. New Delhi: Oxford University Press. Walker, Alice. 1982. *The Color Purple*. New York: Pocket Books.

———. 2005. *Anything We Love Can Be Saved*. London: Phoenix Press.

Walls, Jan and Yvonne Walls. (Trans. and Eds.). 1984. *Classical Chinese Myths*. Hong Kong: Joint Publishing Company.

Wardhaugh, Ronald. 1992. *An Introduction to Sociolinguistics*. Oxford: Blackwell Publishers.

Warhol, R. Robyn and Diane Price Herndl. (Eds.). 1991. *Feminisms – An Anthology of Literary Theory and Criticism*. New Jersey: Rutgers University Press.

Warren, J. Karen. (Ed.). 1997. *Ecofeminism – Women, Culture, Nature*. Bloomington, IN: Indiana University Press.

Waugh, Patricia. 1984. *Metafiction: The Theory and Practice of Self-Conscious Fiction*. New York: Routledge.

Yule, George. 2014. *The Study of Language (Fifth Edition)*. Cambridge: Cambridge University Press.

Zvelebil, Kamil. 1986. *Literary Conventions in Akam Poetry*. Madras: Institute of Asian Studies.

Journals

Myers, Fred. (Ed.). 1995. Cultural Anthropology. *Journal of the Society for Cultural Anthropology*. Vol. 10. No. 4. Arlington: American Anthropological Association. Web: 24 October 2013.

Sunder Rajan, Rajeshwari. (Ed.). 2000. Feminism and the Politics of Resistance. *Indian Journal of Gender Studies*. Special Issue Vol. 7. No. 2. July–December. New Delhi: Sage Publications.

Vohra, Harpreet. 2013. Symbolism of the Mountains: A Study of Selected Poems of Mamang Dai. *North-Eastern Hill University Journal.* Vol. XI. No. 1, pp. 49–51. Web: 28 October 2013.

Online Resources

Amte, Baba. *Anandwan: Forest of Joy.* <http://www.anandwan.in/about-anandwan/baba-amte.html>. Web: 23 September 2015.

Bhalla, Alok. 2010. Lost in a Forest of Symbols: Can Some Animal, Bird, Tree or Djinn Help Us Understand Myth and Folklore? *Indian Folklore Research Journal.* No. 10. 1–12. <http://indianfolklore.org/journals/index.php/IFRJ/issue/view/103/showToc>. Web: 7 May 2011.

Bhatnagar, Rashmi Dube and Reena Dube. *Female Infanticide in India.* <http://www.sunypress.edu/pdf/61058.pdf>. Web: 16 June 2011.

Caldecott, Moyra. 2008. *The Woman Who Was Turned into a Tree.* <http://www.spiritoftrees.org/folktales/country/folktales_country.html#africa>. Web: 10 April 2010.

Capra, Fritjof. 1996. *Extract from the Web of Life.* <http://www.schumachercollege.org.uk/learning-resources/extract-from-the-web-of-life>. Web: 20 May 2010.

Dai, Mamang. 2001. "Arunachal Pradesh – The Myth of Tranquillity". *Faultlines.* Vol. 5. <http://www.satp.org/satporgtp/publication/faultlines/volume5/Fault5-5mdhai.htm>. Web: 25 October 2013.

———. 2004. "Small Towns and the River". *Poetry International.* <http://www.poetryinternationalweb.net/pi/site/poem/item/17012/auto/0/SMALL-TOWNS-AND-THE-RIVER>. Web: 26 October 2013.

———. 2005. "The Voice of the Mountain". *India International Centre, Quarterly.* Vol. 2/3. <https://www.asu.edu/pipercwcenter/how2journal/archive/online_archive/v2_4_2006/current/indian/pdfs/Dai.pdf>. Web: 24 October 2013.

———. 2006. "An Obscure Place". *Muse India Archives.* No. 8. <http://www.museindia.com/viewarticle.asp?myr=2006&issid=8&id=354>. Web: 23 October 2013.

———. 2009. "Oral Narratives and Myth". *Glimpses from the North-East. National Knowledge Commission.* 25 October 2013. <http://knowledgecommissionarchive.nic.in/downloads/documents/nkc_northEast.pdf>. Web: 26 October 2013.

———. 2013. "The Nature of Faith among the Adis". *Understanding Tribal Religion.* Ed. Mibang. <http://www.nehu.ac.in/Journals/JournalJan13_Article4.pdf>. Web: 22 October 2013.

Delveaux, Martin. 2012. *Transcending Ecofeminism: Alice Walker, Spiritual Ecowomanism, and Environmental Ethics.* <http://www.lancs.ac.uk/staff/twine/ecofem/walkera.pdf>. Web: 6 February 2013.

Dorson, Richard M. 1963. *Current Folklore Theories. Current Anthropology.* University of Chicago Press. <http://www.jstor.org/stable/2739820>. Web: 7 September 2015.

Education for Justice. 2007. <https://educationforjustice.org/node/1356>. Web: 9 September 2015.

BIBLIOGRAPHY

Fredericks and Naomi. 2000. <http://www.gly.uga.edu/raisback/CS/CSFourCreations.html>. Web: 14 March 2013.
Goddess Gift. 2002. <http://www.goddessgift.com/goddessmyths/egyptian_goddess_isis.htm>. Web: 14 March 2013.
Harding, Stephen. 2008. *What Is Deep Ecology?* <http://www.schumachercollege.org.uk/learning-resources/what-is-deep-ecology>. Web: 20 May 2010.
Hawthorne, Susan. 2009. *Kolam.* <http://susanscowblog.blogspot.in/search?updated-min=2009-01-01T00:00:00-08:00&updated-max=2010-01-01T00:00:00-08:00&max-results=50>. Web: 12 March 2010.
Hill, Julia Butterfly. 2012. <http://www.juliabutterfly.com/en/about_julia/portraits>. Web: 3 April 2010.
The Hindu. 2010. *Let Every Child Watch a Sapling Grow to a Tree.* <http://www.thehindu.com/news/cities/Bangalore/article448619.ece>. Web: 11 July 2010.
Jayaprakah, Bellie. 2006. *Badagas of the Blue Mountains.* <http://badaga.co/doddarushloka-badaga-proverbs>. Web: 11 July 2015.
Kelin, Daniel. 2007. "The Drama of Folklore: Stories as Teachers". *Indian Folklore Research Journal.* No. 07: 64–76. <http://indianfolklore.org/journals/index.php/IFRJ/issue/view/2/showToc>. Web: 7 May 2011.
Lakota Sioux Prayer. *Mita Kuye Oyasin.* <http://nhpeacenik.livejournal.com/>. Web: 20 February 2011.
Lewis and Clark. 2005. *The Unheard Voices.* <http://archive.adl.org/education/curriculum_connections/na_quotes.html>. Web: 30 October 2015.
Maathai, Wangari. 2004. *Nobel Lecture.* Oslo. <http://www.nobelprize.org/nobel_prizes/peace/laureates/2004/maathai-lecture-text.html>. Web: 11 August 2011.
Masih, Archana. 1997. "Interview with Mahasweta Devi". *Independence Has Failed.* <http://www.rediff.com/news/dec/24devi.htm>. Web: 7 March 2010.
McTaggart, Lynne. 2009. *Remaking the World.* No. 256. <http://www.resurgence.org/magazine/article2895-remaking-the-world.html>. Web: 18 November 2009.
Nagpal, Sahil. 2008. *25 years of Appiko, a Green Movement to Save Trees in Karnataka.* <http://www.topnews.in/25-years-appiko-green-movement-save-trees-karnataka-289834>. Web: 22 September 2015.
Nirmala, Mary. 2009. *Sugathakumari, Excerpts from an Interview.* <http://samyukta.info/site/node/336>. Web: 12 January 2011.
Patsani, Bipin. 2012. Old Voices and New: Literature from Arunachal. *The Seven Sisters Post Literary Review.* <http://nelitreview.tumblr.com/post/24306757462/old-voices-and-new-literature-from-arunachal>. Web: 22 October 2013.
Pellowski, Anne. 2012. *Why Trees Whisper.* <http://www.spiritoftrees.org/folktales/pellowski/trees_whisper.html>. Web: 17 July 2012.
Proposal of Bolivia to Rio+20. 2009. *Universal Declaration of the Rights of Mother Earth.* <http://motherearthrights.org/universal-declaration/>. Web: 20 December 2010.
Roy, Arundhati. 1999. *The Greater Common Good.* <http://www.outlookindia.com/article.aspx?207509>. Web: 17 April 2010.
Sarah, Inam. 2012. <http://www.merinews.com/article/rendezvous-with-padmashree-mamang-dai/15864177.shtml>. Web: 26 October 2012.

Sasson, Remez. 2001. *The Tiger.* <http://www.successconsciousness.com/index_000021.htm>. Web: 4 December 2010.
Schwager, Don. 2014. *The Parables of Jesus.* <http://www.rc.net/wcc/readings/parables.htm>. Web: 20 September 2014.
Selvamony, Nirmal. 2001. *Oikopoetics and Tamil Poetry.* <http://www.angelfire.com/nd/nirmaldasan/oikos.html>. Web: 15 November 2010.
Sexton, Anne. 2001. <http://www.poemhunter.com/poem/red-riding-hood/>. Web: 12 July 2014.
Shiva, Vandana. 2010. "Interview by Wilma Massucco". *The Earth Is Female.* <http://www.scribd.com/doc/40066173/The-Earth-is-Female-Vandana-Shiva>. Web: 19 June 2011.
———. 2011a. *Forests and Freedom.* No. 266. <http://www.resurgence.org/magazine/article3390.html>. Web: 14 July 2011.
———. 2011b. *Who Will Feed the World?* <http://www.resurgence.org/magazine/article3297-who-will-feed-the-world.html>. Web: 20 February 2011.
———. 2012. *Navdanya – Environmental Activist Vandana Shiva.* <http://www.navdanya.org/news/232-environmental-activist-vandana-shiva>. Web: 11 April 2012.
Tagore, Rabindranath. 2011. <http://tagoreanworld.wordpress.com/?s=tapovan>. Web: 11 July 2014.
Tum, Rigoberta Menchu. 1992. *Nobel Lecture.* <http://www.nobelprize.org/nobel_prizes/peace/laureates/1992/tum-lecture.html>. Web: 11 August 2011.
Tutu, Desmond. *We, the World.* <http://www.wetheworld.org/mission.htm>. Web: 12 August 2011.
Velmans, Max. 2009. How to Define Consciousness and How Not to Define Consciousness. *Journal of Consciousness Studies.* Vol. 16. No. 5: 139–156. <http://cogprints.org/6453/1/How_to_define_consciousness.pdf>. Web: 20 September 2010.

Works Consulted

Anand, Mulk Raj. 1974. *Folk Tales of Punjab.* New Delhi: Sterling Publishers.
Bahadur, K. P. 1991. *Folk Tales of Uttar Pradesh.* New Delhi: Sterling Publishers.
Bailey, M. Kathleen and David Nunan. (Eds.). 1996. *Voices from the Language Classroom.* Cambridge: Cambridge University Press.
Bates and Hunter College Women's Studies Collective. 1995. *Women's Realities, Women's Choices.* New York: Oxford University Press.
Beauvoir, Simone De. 1988. *The Second Sex.* (Trans. H. M. Prashley). London: Pan Books Ltd.
Bernstein, Basil. 1971. *Theoretical Studies towards a Sociology of Language.* London: Routledge and Paul.
Borgohein, B. K. 1974. *Folk Tales of Meghalaya and Arunachal Pradesh.* New Delhi: Sterling Publishers.
Borgohein, B. K. and Roy Chaudhury. 1975. *Folk Tales of Nagaland, Manipur, Tripura and Mizoram.* New Delhi: Sterling Publishers.
Bose, Tara. 1971. *Folk Tales of Gujarat.* New Delhi: Sterling Publishers.

BIBLIOGRAPHY

Braidotti, Rosi, Eva Charkivicz, Sabine Hausler and Saskia Wieringa. 1994. *Women, the Environment and Sustainable Development: Towards a Theoretical Synthesis.* London: Zed Books.

Brown, Gillian and George Yule. 2001. *Discourse Analysis.* Cambridge: Cambridge University Press.

Cameron, Deborah. 1993. *Feminism and Linguistic Theory.* London: Macmillan.

Chakravarti, Uma and Preeti Gill. (Eds.). *Shadow Lives: Writings on Widowhood.* New Delhi: Kali for Women.

Chaudhury, Indhu Roy and Veena Srivastava. 1991. *Folk Tales of Haryana.* New Delhi: Sterling Publishers.

Chaudhury, Bani Roy. 1969. *Folk Tales of Kashmir.* New Delhi: Sterling Publishers.

Cheria, Anita and Edwin. 2004. *A Human Rights Approach to Development: Resource Book.* Bangalore: Books for Change.

Devi, Mahasweta. 1999. *Five Plays.* Calcutta: Seagull Books.

———. 2000. *Our Non-Veg Cow and Other Stories.* Calcutta: Seagull Books.

———. 2003. *Chotti Munda and His Arrow.* Calcutta: Seagull Books.

Dundes, Alan. 1990. *Essays in Folklore Theory and Method.* Madras: CreA.

Fernando, Priyanthi and Gina Porter. (Eds). 2002. *Balancing the Load: Women, Gender and Transport.* London: Zed Books.

Franco, Fernando, Jyotsna Macwan, and Suguna Ramanathan. (Eds.). 2000. *The Silken Swing: The Cultural Universe of Dalit Women.* Calcutta: Stree.

Fuss, Diana. 1989. *Essentially Speaking: Feminism, Nature and Difference.* New York: Routledge.

Gilbert, Sandra and Susan Gubar. 1984. *The Madwoman in the Attic: The Woman Writer and the Nineteenth-Century Literary Imagination.* New Haven: Yale University Press.

Hooks, Bell. 2000. *Feminist Theory: From Margin to Center.* London: Pluto Press.

Humphreys, Tony. 2002. *Self-Esteem: The Key to Your Child's Future.* Dublin: Gill and Macmillan Ltd.

Jacob, K. 1972. *Folk Tales of Kerala.* New Delhi: Sterling Publishers.

Jeyaseelan, Thomas B. 2002. *Women Rights and Law.* New Delhi: Indian Social Institute.

Jha, Rajesh Kumar. 2010. *Women and Human Rights.* New Delhi: Mohit Books International.

Karuppaian, V. and K. Parimurugan. 2001. *Tribal Ecology and Development.* Chennai: Department of Anthropology, University of Madras.

Kothari, Rita. 2006. *Speech and Silence: Literary Journeys by Gujarati Women.* New Delhi: Zubaan Books.

Lee Mckay, Sandra and Nancy H. Hornberger. (Ed.). 2006. *Sociolinguistics and Language Teaching.* New York: Cambridge University Press.

Lewis, John. 1984. *Anthropology Made Simple.* London: Heinemann.

Lourdu, T. 1997. *Nattar Valakkatriyal: Cila Atippataikal.* Palayamkottai: Folklore Resource and Research Centre.

Majumdar, Geeta. 1971. *Folk Tales of Bengal.* New Delhi: Sterling Publishers.

BIBLIOGRAPHY

Merchant, Carolyn. 1981. *The Death of Nature: Women, Ecology and the Scientific Revolution*. San Francisco: Harper and Row.

Miri, Sujata. 2006. *Stories and Legends of the Liangmai Nagas*. New Delhi: National Book Trust.

Mohanty, Chandra Talpade. 2003. *Feminism without Borders: Decolonizing Theory Practicing Solidarity*. New Delhi: Zubaan Books.

Monteith, Moira. (Ed.). 1986. *Women's Writing: A Challenge to Theory*. Sussex: The Harvester Press Ltd.

Mooney, Annabelle and Betty Evans. 2007. *Globalization: The Key Concepts*. New York: Routledge.

Narasimhan, Sakuntala. 1999. *Empowering Women: An Alternative Strategy from Rural India*. New Delhi: Sage Publications.

Pakrasi, Mira. 1969. *Folk Tales of Assam*. New Delhi: Sterling Publishers.

Parmar, S. 1973. *Folk Tales of Madhya Pradesh*. New Delhi: Sterling Publishers.

Raju, B. R. 1974. *Folk Tales of Andhra Pradesh*. New Delhi: Sterling Publishers.

Rosa Caldas-Coulthard, Carmen and Malcolm Coulthard. (Eds.). 1996. *Texts and Practices: Readings in Critical Discourse Analysis*. London: Routledge.

Sahi, Jyoti. 1994. *The Child and the Serpent: Reflections of Popular Indian Symbols*. Bangalore: Asian Trading Corporation.

Seethalakshmi, K. A. 1969. *Folk Tales of Tamilnadu*. New Delhi: Sterling Publishers.

———. 1972. *Folk Tales of Himachal Pradesh*. New Delhi: Sterling Publisher.

Sheorey, I. 1973. *Folk Tales of Maharashtra*. New Delhi: Sterling Publishers.

Stein, Jane. 1997. *Empowerment and Women's Health: Theory, Methods and Practice*. London: Zed Books Ltd.

Stibbe, Arran. (Ed) 2009. *The Handbook of Sustainability Literacy: Skills for a Changing World*. Devon: Green Books Ltd.

Stubbs, M. 1983. *Discourse Analysis: The Sociolinguistic Analysis of Natural Language*. Oxford: Basil Blackwell.

Wajnryb, Ruth. 2009. *Stories – Narrative Activities in the Language Classroom*. Cambridge: Cambridge University Press.

Zimmerman, Michael E., J. Baird Callicott, George Sessions, Karen J. Warren and John Clark. (Eds.). 1993. *Environmental Philosophy: From Animal Rights to Radical Ecology*. Englewood Cliffs, NJ: Prentice-Hall.

INDEX

Adams, Carol 144
Adhikary, Qiron 29, 134
Ahimsa Consciousness 48, 60, 90, 106, 107, 117, 128, 162, 163, 165, 167, 176
Amma-I-Appan tales 36, 57, 65–71
Amte, Baba 8
Andersen, Hans Christian 166
Andrews, Jane 114
'The Animal Manifesto' (Bekoff) 144
Animal Rights and Feminist Theory (Donovan) 158
Annamangai tales 36, 87–95
The Appeal of a Tree (Sailani) 114
Appiko Movement 5–7
Aqua-Stree tales 36, 37, 124, 131–43
Arjun (Devi) 117
Athena's Wit tales 36, 78–86
Aves-Eve tales 37, 145–57

The Barefoot Book of Earth Tales (Casey and Wilson) 23
Beck, Brenda 25
beehive cosmos 34–5
Bekoff, Marc 144
Bhalla, Alok 158
Bhil folktales 29, 59, 61–2, 64, 66, 70
Bhoomi Register 53–6, 103
Bhoomi Tales 29
biological mother 26
'Birthplace' (Dai) 139
The Brother Bird 155

Caldecott, Moyra 109
Cameron, Deborah 31

Carson, Rachel 145
Cheney, Jim 4
The Child Who Taught a Lesson to the King (Maariammal) 99, 100
The Child Who Was Poor and Good 98
Chipko Movement 5, 23, 48, 110, 118–19, 123, 125
Chipko women 5
Claus, Peter 25, 85
The Clay Mother-in-Law 90
The Clever Daughter-in-Law 89
conscientisation 1, 4, 43
consciousness, words of 1–2
creativity 5
critical consciousness 5
cultural ecofeminism 87

Dai, Mamang 137–9
Daly, Mary 98
Delveaux, Martin 107
Desai, Neera 95
Devi, Itwari 125
Devi, Mahasweta 13, 74, 117
Do Good unto Your Enemies (Dhanalakshmi) 165
Donovan, Josephine 144, 158, 159
Dorson, Richard M. 24

earth-based spirituality 12–13, 19, 37, 58, 61, 64, 103, 107, 117, 135, 142, 167
Earth Care: World Folktales to Talk About 63
Earth Democracy; Justice, Sustainability and Peace (2005) 6

INDEX

The Earth Only Endures-On Reconnecting with Nature and Our Place (Jules) 126
Earth tutelage 19–22
eco-critical theory 40
The Ecocriticism Reader 14
ecofeminism: conscientisation 4; cultural 4, 87, 130; defined 2; integration of 33; practicality 38; simplicity 38; tree of thought 3–5
Ecofeminism (1993) 6, 49
Ecofeminism and *Ecofeminist Natures* 5
ecofeminist discourse 30–3
ecofeminist-linguistic framework 25, 32, 34, 35, 36, 39, 41, 51–2, 56, 117, 141, 169–70, 173–6
Ecofeminist Literary Criticism 170
Ecofeminist Literary Criticism: Reading the Orange (Donovan) 144
Ecofeminist Natures (Sturgeon) 11
ecofeminist pedagogy 3, 20–2, 78, 144, 174
ecofeminist praxis 2–3, 22, 51–2, 76
ecofeminist school of thought 3
ecofeminist spirituality 37
Elephant and the Hunter (Kee Raa) 121
Estes, Clarissa Pinkola 166

Fauna-Fem tales 37, 157–68
female protagonist 26
Feminism as Experience: Thoughts and Narratives (Desai) 95
The Feminist Critique of Language (Cameron) 31
First There Was Woman 59, 60, 62, 63
First There Was Woman and Other Stories: Folktales of the Dungri Garasiya Bhils (2007) 29
Flora-Fem metaphors 106
A Flowering Tree 106–8, 111, 113, 117
Folklore and Discourse (1999) 24
Forests and Freedom (Shiva) 110
Freire, Paulo 3, 4

Gaard, Greta 10
gender discrimination 11
The Gift of Truth 114
The Girl Who Understood the Birds 147, 148
Glotfelty, Cheryll 14

The Goddess of the Mahi River 134
A Golden Sparrow 152
The Greedy Man (Anjalai) 127
Green Belt Movement 9
green crusaders 5–10

Her-Meta tales 36, 72–8
Heron Boy 151
holistic pedagogy 43
Holmstrom, Lakshmi 82
The Honest Woodcutter and the Fairy 119
Hossain, Rokeya Sakhawat 130, 131
How the Mahi River Married the Sea 133–4, 136

interconnectedness 44
interweaving woman 23
Isis Panthea tales 36, 57–65

Jesudasan, Usha 49
Jung, Anees 118, 119

Kircher, Cassandra 52
A Kitchen in the Corner of the House (Ambai) 92
The Kite's Daughter 149, 150
Krishnan, Rajam 13, 14
Kumar, Suresh 161

Labovian model 32
Labov, William 31
Lamb, Sarah 74
Leaders Are Sown (Dhanalakshmi) 128–9
A Life of Contentment (Saroja) 92
linguistic ability 5
Little Red Cap 165–7
Lovelock, James 15

Maathai, Wangari 9, 10, 44, 121
The Magic Bowls 119
maldevelopment 108
A Man Is . . . (Anjalaiammal) 164
The Man Who Loved Two Women 93
Maslow, Abraham 39
Maya and Laya 95–6
Metaphysics as a Guide to Morals (Murdoch) 162
Mies, Maria 4, 49, 152

INDEX

A Missed Shot (Paapu) 116
'The Missing Link' (Dai) 138
Mitchell, Juliet 103
The Monkey and the Woodcutter
  (Kee Raa) 164
Morphology of the Folktale (Propp) 25
Mother Earth 2–3
Mother Earth Discourse 1–2, 4, 23–56;
  beehive cosmos 34–5; Mother
  Earth Motifs 36, 170; Mother Earth
  Relationships 37, 59, 61, Mother
  Earth concerns 39–41; Mother Earth
  Consciousness 46–51; Mother Earth
  Lingua Franca 51–2; Mother Earth
  Worldviews 41
Murdoch, Iris 162
The Mustard Seed 115–16
Muthukumaraswamy, M. D. 24
My Mother, Her Crime (Ambai)
  102, 134

Naess, Arne 14–15, 135, 175
Narmada Bachao Andolan (NBA) 5,
  8, 45, 48, 132
narrative discourse 31
Nattupura Kathai Kalanjiyam
  (Rajanarayanan) 30
natural philosophers 16–19
'nature-culture' connection 2
nature-culture, reweaving 175–7
Nature Woman 102–3
'Navdanya' (2012) 130
New Woman/New Earth 3
Nonviolence 162

*Odhidhama Niddhana, Oddidhama
  Erandina* 54
'Oikofeminist' approach 40
oikos theory 121
*Older Women's Narratives in West
  Bengal* (Lamb) 74
oral tales 27
Orenstein, Gloria Feman 52

Patkar, Medha 132
Pedagogy of the Oppressed (Freire) 4
Pellowski, Anne 111
*The People Who Hugged the Trees: An
  Environmental Folk Tale* (Rose) 23
The Pigeon's Bride 156

pluralism 45
The Pomegranate Queen 113
The Porcupine Daughter 159–60
Prakrithi Samrakshana Samithi,
  organisation 8
Pretty, Jules 126
The Princess and the Parrots 154
Psychoanalysis and Feminism
  (Mitchell) 103
Purananuru 42, 46

The Rain God's Bride 140
Ramanujan, A. K. 27, 28, 72, 75, 85,
  110, 150
Rampal, Anita 162
Reading the Orange (Donovan) 159
'The Red Shoes' (Andersen) 166
Respect for Life (Kee Raa) 163
Rich, Adrienne 147
Romaine, Suzanne 30
Roy, Arundathi 9
Ruether, Rosemary 3

Sailani, Ghanshyam 114
Sanykisar, the Crow-Girl 150
Sapir–Whorf hypothesis 41
Sardar Sarovar Project (SSP) 8
Second Sight (1986) 110
seeds of silence 1–2
self-actualisation 39, 59, 61, 83, 92,
  109, 123, 130, 135
self-esteem 39, 51, 55, 61, 64, 83,
  135, 174
Selvamony, Nirmal 40
The Separation of Heaven and Earth 69
'Serpent God Worship Ritual in Kerala'
  (Kumar) 161–2
The Serpent Mother 160
Shakthi Consciousness 47–8, 60, 86,
  90, 106, 122, 128, 129, 154, 156,
  158, 163, 176
Shakthi Feminist Folktales from India
  (2003) 29
Shanthi Consciousness 50–1, 60, 80,
  90, 128, 163, 167, 176
Shiva, Vandana 46, 49, 93, 108, 119,
  127, 128, 130, 152
Silent Spring (Carson) 145
Silent Valley Movement 5, 7
sisterhood 95

INDEX

Sis-Tie tales 36, 95–104
Snow White and the Seven Dwarfs 100, 102
social ecofeminism 87
Soil Not Oil (Shiva) 6, 130
Sona and Rupa 96
Soni's Story (Rampal) 162
'The Sorrow of Women' (Dai) 138
South Asian Folklore: An Encyclopedia (Claus) 85
The Sower and the Seeds 115
Spagnoli, Cathy 63
The Spiral Dance (Starhawk) 87
spiritual ecowomanism 107
Sres, Marija 29
Stanadayini (Devi) 74
Staying Alive (Shiva) 6, 132
Stolen Harvest: The Hijacking of the Global Food Supply (1999) 6
Sukhu and Dukhu 97, 98
Sultana's Dream (Hossain) 130
sustainable development 6

Tapovan (Tagore) 120
Tellus-Ma tales 36, 124, 125–31
Teresa, Mother 88, 89
Terra Mater Lexis 52–3
Those Clever Crows 151
The Tiger 158
The Tiger Woman 163
Toward an Ecofeminist Standpoint Theory (Slicer) 21
The Tree and Its Fruits 115
'tree-hugging' Chipko Movement 6
Tylor, Edward B. 160

Unbowed (2006) 5, 9
Unbowed (Maathai) 121
Unpublished Manuscript (Ambai) 100
Unveiling India (Jung) 118

Vana-Devi motif 36
Vana-Devi tales 104, 118–23

The Vanishing Face of Gaia: A Final Warning (Lovelock) 15
voluntary simplicity 38

Walker, Alice 12–13, 27, 48–50, 107, 144
Warren, Karen J. 4, 12
The Weeds in the Grain 125
What the Cloud and the Stars Wished For (Loganayagi) 140–1
When the Kurinji Blooms (Krishnan) 13, 40, 53
Where Do the Sparrows Live? 153
Who Is Greater? (Saroja) 120
Why Trees Whisper (Pellowski) 111
Woman and Bird (Rich) 147
woman–nature proximity 1, 10, 22, 28–9, 38, 117, 122, 169
woman–nature relationships 2, 11–12, 18, 32, 59, 96–7, 133, 135
The Woman Who Was Turned into a Tree (Caldecott) 109
women: first creation 58; oral tales of 29; patriarchal domination of 12; speech and silence 30; storytelling sessions 26; thought process of 35
women–nature–culture 30, 87, 169, 175
The Women's History of the World (Miles) 58
'Women's Tales' (Ramanujan) 28
Women Who Run with the Wolves (Estes) 166
The Wood Maiden 122–3
Woody-Woman tales 36, 104, 105–18
Woolf, Virginia 102
wordsmiths 10–16
A Writer's Activism (Walker) 13

The Youngest Daughter-in-Law and Her Snake Brothers 161

Zvelebil, Kamil 25